Philosophy of Education

Philosophy of Education

Thinking and Learning Through History and Practice

John Ryder

ROWMAN & LITTLEFIELD
Lanham • Boulder • New York • London

Published by Rowman & Littlefield
An imprint of The Rowman & Littlefield Publishing Group, Inc.
4501 Forbes Boulevard, Suite 200, Lanham, Maryland 20706
www.rowman.com

86-90 Paul Street, London EC2A 4NE

British Library Cataloguing in Publication Information Available

Library of Congress Cataloging-in-Publication Data

Names: Ryder, John, 1951– author.
Title: Philosophy of education : thinking and learning through history and
    practice / John Ryder.
Description: Lanham, Maryland : Rowman & Littlefield, 2022. | Includes
    bibliographical references and index.
Identifiers: LCCN 2022018297 (print) | LCCN 2022018298 (ebook) | ISBN
    9781538166611 (cloth) | ISBN 9781538166628 (paperback) | ISBN
    9781538166635 (epub)
Subjects: LCSH: Education—Philosophy. | Education—Aims and objectives.
Classification: LCC LB14.7 .R94 2022 (print) | LCC LB14.7 (ebook) | DDC
    370.1—dc23/eng/20220713
LC record available at https://lccn.loc.gov/2022018297
LC ebook record available at https://lccn.loc.gov/2022018298

For teachers and educators everywhere

Contents

viii   *Contents*

CHAPTER 4. DOMINATION AND LIBERATION: FREIRE'S PEDAGOGY
OF THE OPPRESSED   111
    Liberation, Authenticity, and Love   113
    Banking, Problem-Posing, and Dialogue   124
    Revolutionary Pedagogy   136

PART II

CHAPTER 5. EDUCATION AND ITS PROBLEMS   145
    The Goals of Education   146
    Pedagogical Methods and Testing   152
    Educational Equality and Tracking   155
    Educational Content and State Education   160
    Education and Social Justice   165

CHAPTER 6. EDUCATION IN CONTEXT: NATURE, KNOWLEDGE,
AND EXPERIENCE   169
    Nature and Its Relations   171
    Experience and Knowledge   184
    Educational Principles   195

CHAPTER 7. EDUCATION IN CONTEXT: SOCIETY AND THE STATE   203
    Society and Social Relations   205
    Political Relations and the State   228
    Educational Principles   237

CONCLUSION   245
BIOGRAPHICAL SKETCHES   255
    Plato   255
    Jean-Jacques Rousseau   256
    John Dewey   257
    Paulo Freire   259
NOTES   261
INDEX   267
ABOUT THE AUTHOR   275

Acknowledgments

Much of this book is based on a master's course in the philosophy of education that I taught a number of times over the course of several years at what was then the Department of Education (now the School of Education) at the State University of New York at Cortland. I was a member of the Department of Philosophy at the time and was asked to develop and teach the course by Ron Butchart, who was then in a position of sufficient responsibility in the Department of Education to make such a request. It turned out to be one of the most pedagogically satisfying experiences of my career. I am indebted to Ron and his department for affording me the opportunity to teach the course and to all the graduate students who enrolled over its several iterations. These were, for the most part, primary and secondary school teachers who were working all day and pursuing a master's degree in the evenings for permanent certification by the State of New York. Many of them were nervous—being not, in their own opinions, prepared for serious philosophical study—and some were more than a little intimidated. They all, however, contributed substantially to the quality of the course in that they were remarkably adept at situating the abstract philosophical concerns with which we dealt in the context of their own practical experience. I like to think, too, that at least some of them genuinely benefited from the course. In any case, I am in their debt as well.

The initial draft of this book was written during the first few months of the COVID-19 pandemic. I found myself at home with time on my hands, and this seemed an appropriate use for that time. Fortunately, there were others who also had some available time and who were willing to spend some of it reading the chapters as I finished writing them. I would specifically like to thank John Marciano and John Bing for their close reading, comments, and advice. The book is better for their efforts. I would also like to thank the composer and conductor Michael Summers, who was gracious enough not only to read the manuscript but also to point out a basic mistake I had made in chapter 1 in my account of the relation of musical keys and the modes in Greek music. I hope that I have corrected the mistake, and I am grateful to Michael for pointing it out. What mistakes remain in the book are, of course, my own responsibility.

The editors at Rowman & Littlefield have been most helpful, as were the comments and suggestions made by several of the anonymous readers to whom the editors sent the initial proposal and sample chapters. This is a proper occasion for me to express my gratitude.

I am, as always, indebted to Lyubov Bugaeva, who has been for years and remains a constant source of inspiration and a powerful critic.

I have had the good fortune to work with first-rate teachers at all levels, in various capacities, and in a number of countries. If this book offers readers and students insights into the process of developing educational principles, it is due at least as much to what I have learned throughout my career from all those whom I have taught and with whom I have worked as to any contributions of my own.

John Ryder
May 2022
Tucson, Arizona and
St. Petersburg, Russia

Introduction

At one point during my administrative career, I found myself for the first time supervising a degree program in architecture. Actually, my supervision was indirect in that the program was housed in a Department of Architecture that had a chair, and the department was housed in a school that had a dean. Then came me, but even at that remove I had enough opportunity to engage with the design of the program and with the architects who taught in it to learn a great deal about the discipline. The most striking feature of the discipline of architecture—to me, at any rate—and of the degree program through which students were drawn into it, was that it was almost a university curriculum in microcosm. To complete a degree in architecture, and to be a successful architect, one had to have some degree of mastery of fields as varied as materials science, civil and electrical engineering, geometry, design, art history, drawing, politics and sociology, aesthetics, chemistry and physics, cultural history, economics, communication, and, of course, construction. It is small wonder that the typical undergraduate degree in architecture requires five years of intense study to complete.

This experience with the discipline of architecture taught me something I had not fully realized before, which is that some disciplines or fields of study are unusually capacious in that, to function successfully in them, one has to look in several directions at once, directions that might have appeared otherwise to be disparate and unrelated. Architecture is one such discipline; philosophy of education is another.

PHILOSOPHY AND EDUCATION

This work is an investigation into the philosophy of education, and into specific issues and questions that constitute the field, one that builds on

the idea that in the process of examining philosophical aspects of education, one must come to terms with other, seemingly unrelated, branches
of philosophy. Specifically, the study of philosophy of education requires
that one also address questions in metaphysics, epistemology, social and
political theory, philosophical anthropology, and ethics. This means that
our philosophical conceptions of matters directly associated with education
are related necessarily to how we understand reality in general, knowledge
and knowing, social relations and political aspirations, the general traits of
what it is to be a human being, and the principles according to which we
ought to behave. To engage philosophically questions of education while at
the same time exploring these issues, and the relations between them and
education, is what it means to undertake a systematic study of the philosophy of education.

In her book on the philosophy of education, first published in 1995,
Nel Noddings took a similar approach. She points out that contemporary
philosophers tend to ignore the larger, traditional philosophical issues and
focus instead on conceptual analysis of distinct topics related to education,
for example, the nature of knowledge, as if they were separable from other
concepts and from educational practice. Noddings makes the point that she
approaches the general topic differently: "Many of us believe that philosophy went too far in rejecting the eternal questions, and there are signs that
philosophers may once again invite their students to join in the immortal
conversations."[1] Noddings includes herself among those philosophers who
see value in thinking about basic questions of education within the context
of larger philosophical issues. The present volume is written very much in
the spirit that Noddings evokes.

It is a bit disingenuous to say that the experience with architecture taught
me that some disciplines cast a wide net, though architecture's net is much
wider than any I had encountered before. But my engagement with the
philosophy of education, in fact, had provided this insight long before. In
my years as a full-time professor of philosophy, the position that I held at
the State University of New York at Cortland, I had the opportunity to teach
a graduate course in the philosophy of education in what was then the
Department of Education. The course was intended for, and populated primarily by, working teachers who needed or wanted to complete a master's
degree. I had built into the design of that course the understanding of the
philosophy of education as a systematic enterprise in the sense described
above. And that same design has been appropriated for the current study.

We will return in a bit to the details of such a systematic study of the
philosophy of education. For the moment it will be wiser, I think, to consider the object about which this study presumes a richer understanding,
and that is education. It is customary for philosophers, and I frequently do
this myself, to begin a study with definitions. In this case, however, I would

prefer to approach the topic in a different way, largely because I do not want to beg any questions, or lose any readers, by insisting on a definition of education that others would not accept. Education is a massive topic, as we all know well, which encompasses matters from policy to institutional structures to ends to means, and a great deal more. This is simply too much for a philosopher, even one accustomed to generalizations, to capture sensibly in a single, workable definition.

Instead of trying to define education, it will be more useful to recognize that however we may disagree about particulars, we all have a general working conception of what education is, one that is sufficiently clear for most of us to recognize it when we see it. If that is so, then let us begin with that general (even if sometimes inchoate) sense of what education is; it will be sufficient. Without an explicit definition, we also will not be doing something else common in philosophical explorations, and that is positing assumptions from which one then draws inferences. Philosophers are predisposed to a need to prove things, usually on the model of a geometrical proof. In that case, one begins with a small number of stipulations and assumptions and then proceeds deductively to a conclusion. This is not a method that is available to us without a definition to work from and, indeed, without any assumptions unique to education from which to extrapolate conclusions. We should not regret this situation, though, because the philosopher's predisposition to prove things is rather misguided anyway. Philosophy is not mathematics, which is a good thing, because if it were something analogous to mathematics, we would have to acknowledge ourselves to be miserable failures. It ought not to be controversial to recognize that in the history of philosophy very little of any significance has been proven with anything like the closure afforded by a mathematical proof. It is always possible to disagree with, restate, reimagine, rethink, or continue to debate philosophical propositions—any of them. So we will not try to prove anything here; consequently, we do not need definitions or assumptions from which to begin the analysis. In the end, my hope is to offer an understanding of matters central to a philosophical approach to education that is coherent, plausible, and useful in ways that will have to be specified.

If that is where we will end, how, then, do we begin? I would like to propose that we begin with a series of questions that the rest of the book will attempt to address in various ways. At the risk of sounding like a gimmick, I propose that we approach the philosophy of education, again appealing to nothing but our rough and ready sense of what education is, by asking, though with a twist, the typical questions of a journalist. When a journalist approaches an event, she wants to know what happened, who did it and whom it affects, when did it happen, where did it happen, why did it happen, and how did it happen. This is a fairly comprehensive set of questions, and clear and sufficiently ramified answers to all of them will give any reader or listener a very good sense of the event.

I have said, though, that we will ask these questions of education but with a twist, and the twist is this: When the journalist asks who, what, when, where, why, and how, she is doing so descriptively; she wishes to describe an event so that we understand well what had happened. In our case, however, we will ask these questions not descriptively but prescriptively. This means that our interest here is not to understand what education is like so that we can answer the several journalistic questions. Our interest rather is asking what education ought to be like, or how we should think about it, and we are pursuing that normative goal by wondering the following: who should educate and who should be educated; what should be taught; why should people be educated and why should they be taught what they are; when should or can education take place; where should or can education take place; and how should people be educated.

These questions, understood normatively, provide the intellectual structure of this exercise in the philosophy of education. One of the first points that becomes clear when we begin to try to answer these questions normatively is that there must be appeals to broader philosophical issues. None of these questions, or so I would posit, can be answered with a sufficient degree of clarity and justification without venturing systematically into questions that have to do with reality in general, with what we understand knowledge to be and how we achieve it, with social ideals, with a conception of the general character of human beings, and with desirable principles of social interaction with one another. Answering the normatively construed journalist's question, then, requires that we engage in the study of systematic philosophy of education.

There are two ways this can be done, and the following pages take up both. One approach is historical, and the first four chapters of the book are examinations of how four prominent thinkers about education have dealt with the relevant questions. There are several advantages of such a historical approach to the subject. One of them is that, taken together, the historical analyses will provide illustrations of what it means to think systematically about philosophical issues in education. Another is that it serves as something of an ostensive argument in support of doing the philosophy of education systematically through a demonstration of the accomplishments of important thinkers in their own efforts. Plato, Rousseau, John Dewey, and Paulo Freire, the figures whose thoughts on education we will explore, all placed their ideas in relation to broader philosophical conceptions and, or so I will argue, to good effect. That does not mean that we are obliged to agree with them, and, in fact, as we will see, there is a great deal of disagreement among them. It does mean that they will help us see that to think carefully about education in a philosophical vein, it is necessary to do so systematically.

The second way that the normative questions may be pursued is through a direct philosophical analysis—undertaken systematically, of course. With the discussions of Plato, Rousseau, Dewey, and Freire as preparation, I will offer in the final three chapters my own understanding of both the background philosophical conceptions we have good reasons to endorse and answers to the normative questions that have been posed. In the end, the reader will be the judge of the adequacy of any of it.

It is worth saying more about why Plato, Rousseau, Dewey, and Freire have been chosen as the philosophers to study and as the figures to whom we can look as models for our own independent inquiries. The first point to note is that this is not an overview of the history of the philosophy of education.[2] If this were an effort to provide a history, then many other figures and conceptual structures would have to be surveyed as well. It would also be necessary to move beyond the European–American context if a proper historical survey were our goal. Indeed, even the present interest in treating the four selected figures as illustrative could have been filled with different choices. Plato, Rousseau, Dewey, and Freire are not necessarily the most important philosophers of education, though they are certainly among the most important.

They are also usefully illustrative in several ways. For one thing, they represent a wide temporal range, in that their study spans antiquity through very recent times, and a diversity of cultures from classical through modern and contemporary, and European through North and South American. Such a span helps us to realize that the educational concerns that constitute the field are not unique to our time and place and that therefore an analysis of them can have implications beyond one's own immediate social and historical context. Taken together, they are also useful because they represent a fairly wide range of philosophical ideas, both broadly and in relation to education specifically. For example, and in very broad strokes, Plato thought that the material world is a reflection of an ideal realm, while Dewey was a naturalist; Plato was hostile to democracy, while Dewey was its avid proponent; Rousseau regarded society as largely antithetical to the individual's nature, while Dewey regarded the individual as basically social; Plato thought that social structures were largely fixed by the nature of things, while Freire emphasized the necessity that individuals have the power to frame their lives and the relations among them according to their own lights. With respect to education, again through superficial contrasts simply to make the point, Plato thought that people should be educated, and differently, according to their natures and their proper place in the social order, and that girls and boys should receive the same education, while Rousseau argued that the individual should receive an education as independently as possible from social influence and that girls should be educated differently from boys and for different purposes; Dewey and Freire were closer to one another, but even in their cases the differences can be telling. Dewey understood one of the primary concerns in education to be to develop in children what he called the "method of intelligence," while Freire was more interested in structural designs in education that will enable individuals in solidarity with one another to develop sufficient power to resist and overcome social and economic exploitation.

A third point worth mentioning about the value of studying these specific figures is that they represent their times and places well. Though I do not wish to overstate the point, Plato represents important aspects of the classical European world's understanding of itself, both in what he exemplifies and in how he diverges, so that studying his work helps us to grasp not just his ideas about education and philosophy generally but also aspects of his world. The same may be said in both respects of the other figures. Rousseau, as we will see, both expresses and resists in interesting ways a number of the prevalent conceptions that characterize eighteenth-century Europe. Dewey was considered "America's philosopher," though some would take issue, perhaps because, despite his influence, his thinking also embraces the social nature of the individual to a degree not common in American culture. And Freire is an illustrative example of a thinker who applied in creative ways, among other intellectual sources, the influential Marxism and socialism of the late twentieth century, especially in Latin America, where it has played a significant social, political, and economic role, and in Brazil specifically in the 1960s, where it was a form of resistance to the military dictatorship then in power.

The point should be made, however, that this volume is not an effort to analyze these figures and their ideas in their own times and places. That would be an exercise far beyond our purview. For example, consider the case of Plato alone. A full understanding of his *Republic* would require a study of Plato's life, his travels, and the broader cultural milieu in which he lived and worked. This in turn would require a study of the historical and cultural influences on Plato and classical Greece in general, including their diverse sources. It seems clear, for example, that there were some similarities between some of Plato's ideas and those of classical India and that some intellectual and cultural exchange was likely, and a full picture would require that this relationship be explored. Along the same lines, it has also been argued that the classical Greek world was the recipient of important influences from Africa, Egypt in particular, and the Levant. Some of these are controversial matters, but getting a full sense of Plato and his *Republic* would demand their consideration. We obviously are not in a position to do that, because it would require volumes, some of which in any case have already been written.[3] Our approach, then, is to work with the ideas in the form in which they have reached us and to do the best we can with them. Their rich contexts and sources, though, should be kept in mind.

There are comparable problems and complexities with respect to the other figures we discuss. That we do not examine the complex sources and contexts of Rousseau's ideas and their time should not incline a reader to think that they do not exist, nor that there is no considerable literature about them. The same comment applies to Dewey and his American context and Freire and his. The reader should also keep in mind that how we understand such historical philosophical systems is itself a matter of contemporary controversy. We might make much, for example, of the fact that seventeenth- and eighteenth-century ideas about freedom and social contract were made in a society that relied heavily on slavery. That this seemed not to concern thinkers at the time does not mean that it should not concern us or that we do not need to reexamine their ideas in light of our own times and values. The same may be said of Dewey's time and place. He wrote extensively and passionately about freedom, human development, and democracy, but he had little to say about the racism and sexism that dominated his America and his intellectual world.[4] These facts of the matter are to be noted and taken into consideration, but, as in the case of the fuller picture of the ancient world, they are beyond our scope.

There are, of course, places and times missing in this overview. I might, for example, have included Confucius in our survey. He was certainly a critical figure in Chinese philosophy, and it is probably safe to say that he and his ideas had far greater impact on the development of Chinese society, culture, and education than did Plato and the others on theirs. Moreover, in the *Analects*, Confucius ranged over a number of more general philosophical ideas and their relation to education, as did many of his followers, so we would benefit from a study of Confucius as being another illustration of the systematic philosophy of education. One could no doubt make similar claims about such figures in other world traditions. Education in Indian philosophical contexts comes to mind, as would education in Islam or Christianity, for that matter, where Ibn Sina (Avicenna) and Augustine or Aquinas would be relevant figures. They were prominent systematic thinkers who had extensive influence on their cultures and societies and on education in their respective contexts. These figures and their times and places are not included in this study not because they do not belong or because they are not worthy of consideration. Quite the opposite is true. They are not included, rather, because I do not have the competence to consider them confidently and with the background knowledge they would deserve. I invite those who do have the confidence to take on the task of adding their voices to the conversation.

This is an appropriate point to mention that the figures on whom we will focus represent, for the most part, traditional Western approaches to philosophy and education that have been challenged by a number of philosophers in recent years, as we have mentioned above. As we become more sensitive to the ways our intellectual and cultural traditions have denigrated and excluded others, largely on racial, ethnic, and gender grounds, it has become necessary to look at our past with fresher eyes and more carefully applied analysis. For example, several feminist philosophers of education have argued that in order to understand knowledge, rationality, and inquiry in ways that do not suppress women's voices and insights, a new approach to epistemology is required. Wendy Kohli, for example, makes just this point in her essay "Educating for Emancipatory Rationality."[5] Along similar lines, Maxine Greene has taken a fresh and influential approach to the important social and political concept of freedom in her book *The Dialectic of Freedom*. We will have the occasion, especially in chapters 6 and 7, to explore how our general philosophical commitments apply to such concepts as reason and freedom, to their implications for social justice, and to the educational principles that the conceptual analysis implies. While we will not deal directly with current feminist and anti-racist efforts to liberate important concepts from their historical inadequacies, the general conceptions we develop of nature, knowledge, experience, and society will underwrite them, or so we shall argue.

SYSTEMATIC PHILOSOPHY OF EDUCATION

It would be wise at this point to introduce in more detail the idea of a systematic philosophical study of education before we launch into a consideration of historical examples. Perhaps the best way to do this is to offer an illustration of the idea.

Let us suppose, for example, that we have a more or less strict Calvinist conception of reality, knowledge, human nature, and social relations. We can imagine what some of the details of such a view might be, without, I should add, attributing them to any historical or current form of Calvinism or to any specific Calvinist communities. As Calvinists, we would believe that all aspects of reality are determined by an omnipotent God, one who is the creator of all that exists and who is responsible for its existence. Everything that exists depends on God for its creation and its continued existence; nature, then, is dependent on a nonmaterial, ideal entity. What we think we know about God and nature might be a complicated matter. First, we would believe that there is a revealed text that unerringly expresses God's will and what God regards as most important for us to understand. This revealed text is not metaphorical, not analogical, and not symbolic. It is the literally true expression of God's word and will. Depending on when we lived, we might have thought in various ways about nature. In premodern times, we might have developed our conceptions of nature by drawing inferences from our experience through forms of rational inquiry drawn from Aristotle, Augustine, and such prominent interpreters as Ramus. By the early eighteenth century, we would have been struggling to incorporate the latest results of modern science, especially Newton's, into our conception, as did the profound colonial American philosopher and theologian Jonathan Edwards. Regardless of how we did this, we would be confident that nature is secondary to God and that, whatever other methods we might also use, our understanding of reality rests on God's revealed word.

Our understanding of human beings, how we relate to one another, and the social structures we create would have to be consistent with our conception of God and our knowledge of him. As for human beings and the characteristics we can expect people to have, even if we think that God created us in his image (the pronoun is presumably not intended with a literally gendered meaning), we are still a weak and deeply flawed copy. One way we will think of this is that we are by nature sinful, and it is a constant struggle for us not to allow that sinful nature to prevail in our thoughts and actions. The sinfulness that we would detect in our natures amounts to a failure to embrace our subservience to God and a failure to act toward one another in ways that God expects. Our ethical principles, to put it in a different way, derive from God, and it is to God and to God's word that we would turn if we want to understand how we ought to act.

Our social structures would, one imagines, be organized to make it more likely that our lives are lived on Godly principles and expectations. We would be likely to arrange our communities around religious worship and institutions, most likely churches of some kind. Those communities could be subject to leadership of elders selected in one way or another, or, if we were suspicious of hierarchical power and interpretation, they could be a looser set of congregations. In either case, our laws and public institutions would be established consistent with what we understand to be the truth about heaven and earth, and about human being and its purposes. Since we are confident that we know the nature of God and God's will, we would not be likely to accept the presence of other ideas in our communities because they would pose a threat; basically, they would be the expressions of evil.

These details could be modified in various ways, but, in general, this is how we would think as committed Calvinists in a theocratic social structure. With respect to education in such an environment, we would also expect that our ideas of what education is for, how it is conducted, and what its content ought to be will be consistent with our general Calvinist ideas and ideals. For example, we would think, presumably, that the primary purpose of education is to enable for each of us, to the extent that is possible, a clear understanding of God and God's intentions, especially about how we are to live our lives. The primary source of instruction is likely to be God's word and any sets of commentaries on his word that over time likeminded people have come to accept and value. Our reality would be fixed and its principles eternal; ours would not be a world in which exploration and inquiry about knowledge of the fixed reality and its laws and regularities would be valued. We would be taught social habits that revolve around theocratic principles of various kinds, and we would teach our children how to control their natures, not how to develop them. We would be more likely to teach conformity with the truth than creative ventures into the unknown.

The point of this little exercise is to illustrate that we can expect our ideas about education to be consistent with our broader views of reality, knowledge, human nature, society, and how we should best interact with one another. This would be true for Calvinists of the sort I have described, as it is equally true for all of us. Most of us are not Calvinists of this sort, and we are consequently rather unlikely to endorse even the very general ideas about education that I have attributed to Calvinists. The reason, of course, is that each of us, or each set of us defined in some specific way, will develop or gravitate to ideas about education that are consistent with our ideas of reality, knowledge, human being, and society, and to the extent that our ideas about those matters differ for each of us, or for each set of us, our conceptions of education will differ. This is the reason that the study of the philosophy of education has to be done systematically. If we are doing anything more than offering personal opinions about education, our analyses and their conclusions have to relate educational matters to broader philosophical issues.

Two important points need to be made at this juncture. The first is a reminder that ours is a normative enterprise. Our interest is not simply in what we, in fact, do think about educational questions and their related and broader philosophical matters. The concern, rather, is to make an effort to determine what we ought to think about all of it—education, reality in general, knowledge and cognition, human nature, society and politics, and ethical interaction. When stated that way, the whole effort seems gargantuan and quite possibly so intimidating that it may feel pointless even to begin. In fact, though it is gargantuan, it need not be intimidating, and it is certainly not pointless. Each of us needs to have reasonable expectations of herself. We are not going to reach final, incontrovertible positions with respect to any of these questions; we do not expect to "prove" anything. We can, however, achieve ideas, opinions, and conclusions that are coherent, plausible, and valuable, even though they are always available for and subject to further critical engagement and ramification. The project is never finished, a fact that we should understand, but which we should not allow to paralyze us.

A second relevant fact of the matter is that because in the process of systematic philosophical inquiry into questions of education, we necessarily engage many difficult and important issues, it is likely that we will disagree with one another on many points. This is normal. Certainly, Plato, Rousseau, Dewey, and Freire disagree about many aspects of education and nearly everything else, and so will we. The question is what we should do about those disagreements. One temptation is to be relativists about them and say simply that one person's opinion is as acceptable as another's. Another approach, at the other end of the spectrum, is for each of us to insist that her view is right and that anyone who disagrees is wrong and, possibly, even evil.

Both of those approaches are unacceptable, and, in any case, neither is assumed in this study. The reason they are unacceptable, and consequently not put to work in this volume, is that in either case it is impossible to live with the results of our inquiries. If we think that everyone's view is right, even when they are inconsistent with one another, then there are no grounds on which to decide among them. If everyone is right about curriculum, for example, then any decision we make in favor of one approach over another is to do an injustice because it means failing to do what we ourselves grant is right, or at least as right as the choice we have made. That is incoherent. However, if each of us insists that only her view is right and that all others are not only wrong but possibly evil, then we also have no way to make a collective decision about social policy and practice, other than through sheer force. We might try to design a way to act provisionally, for example, through some mechanism of majority choice, but if we regard the others' ideas as thoroughly wrong and evil, then we are not likely to accept collective decisions that favor them, in which case majority decision-making is impossible. In neither case, then, can we function in anything like a smooth fashion in the process of making social decisions and policy, a point that applies to social and political life generally as well as to education.

If disagreement is to be expected, and if we cannot for practical reasons either dismiss everyone else's ideas or embrace all inconsistent ideas as equally true, the only reliable alternative is to accept simultaneously the cognitive value of our inquiries and our own fallibility. This means that, on the one hand, we accept as a given that careful philosophical inquiry can, in fact, result in ideas that we can justify; on the other hand, we also accept as a given that in our analyses we could at any point be mistaken. Another way to say this is that while not all ideas are equally justifiable, and therefore we can reasonably look for the most justifiable position to hold, any conception or conclusion we reach is susceptible to additional critical investigation and revision. If we accept both the cognitive reliability of our inquiry and our own fallibility, it is possible to reach actionable conclusions, adjudicate disagreements, and accept revision of our own ideas, even those we most cherish. This is the presumption that underlies the rest of this book and underwrites its analytical method.

THE RELEVANT EDUCATIONAL QUESTIONS

When we wonder about the goals of education, for example, several possibilities come to mind. We might, as Plato thought, think that we educate individuals in order to develop their natures. We may want to create good citizens, or we may aspire to prepare, or, as some people might say, to train, individuals for the social role they will be expected to play. Along similar lines, though with less of an emphasis on social functions and more on economics, we might think that the purpose of education is to provide individuals with a basis for earning a living or preparing for a career or, to use a common American expression, for "getting ahead." We might favor one of these goals, or many of them, though if we favor several of them, we would eventually be compelled to prioritize them. In that case, of course, the question becomes: Which is more important than which?

The question of the content of education also offers a number of possibilities. Should we teach anything or everything? Maybe we should teach whatever we believe to be basic skills, though even then we would have the question whether some topics should come later, and, if so, which ones? Some people seem to think that we should teach, and children and students should be expected to learn, only what is "useful," which, of course, simply puts the issue a step back because we then have to ask what counts as being useful and for what. Do we care only about what is useful for making a living or perhaps for a good life or for happiness? These responses do not help much either, because they also raise as many questions as they answer. We would likewise wonder whether anything should be excluded, and, if so, what and why? As we will see, Plato thought that education should not include anything that will reinforce undesirable habits or personality traits in people. In our time, to give a comparable example, some Americans do not think that history textbooks should include material that is critical of the American government's actions. Even if we do not want to endorse censorship of this kind (and that question can be left open for now), it is still the case that we would have to establish priorities among the content we endorse. Some topics and capabilities, presumably, are more important than others—but which, and why?

The situation is no simpler when we think about methods. For one thing, we have to come to terms with what we think learning amounts to. At a recent meeting of a university board of trustees, one of the members, himself a prominent figure in the private sector, opined that he did not really see the point of professors anymore, since students can find any information they need on the Internet. In that comment the trustee expressed an idea of learning as the acquisition of information, and he is not alone in thinking of learning in that way. Plato objected to this way of thinking about education, as we will see. Freire also will have a good deal to say about this, but that can wait. For now, whether one agrees with the trustee or not, the question of how learning is undertaken and enabled has to be faced. Do we ever lecture? If so, in which contexts is it appropriate and in which not? How important is testing in the teaching and learning process, and can it be too heavily emphasized, assuming that it is important at all? Do we use grades because they are pedagogically valuable or because they are convenient? Another question of some importance (certainly for both Dewey and Freire) is who should exercise the greater control over content—children and students, or teachers, or administrators, or school boards, or perhaps government officials?

The where, when, and who questions are no less important. Is education a process that should occur exclusively, or even primarily, in classrooms or, for that matter, even in schools? Rousseau thought not, but what, we might ask, are the alternatives, and when or why would they be any better? Unlike in Rousseau's day, or even just a few years ago, we now have available to us online learning and teaching, which raise another whole set of "where" as well as "how" questions. And is education something for children, and, if so, until when? In our age, we assume that primary and most secondary school is obligatory, and increasingly some people think that tertiary education should also be expected. Is that right, and, even if it is, does education stop there? I am not thinking of an alternative in the platitudinous sense that "we are always learning," but whether there may be some deeper sense in which education is not something we should leave to the schools, in the sense that art is not something we should leave to the museums or democratic government to the polling stations. Dewey, for example, says in one of his more famous passages, of which this is a paraphrase, that education is not a preparation for life but life itself.

Finally, the question who should be involved in the educational process applies largely to children and students, but it really encompasses all the stakeholders in education. As for children, even if we think that we should educate them all, we have to wonder whether they should all receive the same education or whether it should differ. And if it should differ, on what grounds? Does gender matter, or socioeconomic background, or differing abilities and interests? And then there are questions about who should teach. Should certain credentials be required, as they now typically are? What about people with special skills or experience, regardless of credentials? And in the end, there is the frequently debated place of parents, and local school boards, and political figures.

OVERVIEW

It would be helpful to offer a brief overview of each of the subsequent chapters. The book is divided into two parts. Part I consists of four chapters and has a historical emphasis, while in part II we will look directly and systematically at the philosophical issues related to education.

Chapter 1 focuses on Plato, especially his dialogue the *Republic*. This is not the only dialogue in which Plato explores education, teaching, and learning, but it is the one place where he develops a conception of the ideal education and does so in the context of an account of his metaphysical, epistemological, psychological, and sociopolitical ideas. By focusing on the *Republic*, it will be possible to clarify Plato's ideas about education and the ways they are integrated with his other conceptions. Here, as in the other historically oriented chapters, there is little critical reflection on Plato's general philosophical ideas or on his views on education. The point of the chapter is not to determine whether Plato had sufficiently good reason to think what he thought, or whether we should agree with him, but simply to indicate what he thought, why he thought it, and how the various components of his philosophical analyses are integrated. The critical questions will come in part II.

Chapter 2 focuses on Jean-Jacques Rousseau. Like Plato, Rousseau discusses social ideals, including education, in a number of works. Other of his writings (for example, on the social contract) will come up in our account, but the emphasis will be on an analysis of his book devoted to education and related matters, *Emile*. Here, again like Plato in the *Republic*, Rousseau gives an account of not only his preferred approach to education but also how and why his educational commitments are related to his ideas about nature and knowledge and, even more important in his case, how he understood human nature and the individual's relation to society.

In chapter 3, the concern turns closer to home, in place for the Americans among us and in time for all of us. John Dewey paid more attention to education and schooling than any other American philosopher, and he surely had a greater influence on educational theory and policy than any other. Dewey also wrote extensively and, over a long career, on matters of metaphysics (in his case, how we are to understand nature); on knowledge and inquiry; and on human being, ethics, and social and political theory. His studies of education span many volumes, but we will focus on *Democracy and Education* and look elsewhere when the need arises.

Chapter 4 turns to the work and ideas of Paulo Freire, the hugely influential Brazilian educator from the latter half of the twentieth century. Freire's analyses and ideas, developed primarily (though not exclusively) in his *Pedagogy of the Oppressed*, bring to bear on educational philosophy the socialist and revolutionary social and political theory that was common—indeed, prevalent—in those decades. Our look at Freire's ideas will clarify one version of the implications of socialist (in some respects Marxist) theory on education, and we will be able to see how those ideas rely on and apply certain conceptions of nature, knowledge, and human being.

The four historical chapters will provide examples of the necessity of systematic philosophy of education and four sets of systematically related ideas. No attempt, however, will have been made to adjudicate among them, and each of us will be in a position to decide for ourselves what we do and do not think acceptable among their ideas. Does one endorse the absolute idealism of Plato or the naturalism of Dewey, or neither? Is Plato right that gender is irrelevant to education, or does one prefer Rousseau's gender distinction? The sexism built into Rousseau's analysis is certainly not in favor in our time, though a great deal of sexism remains in our social policies and practices. Taking Rousseau seriously can force the issue for us. There are, of course, many other questions that come up. Do we support, as Plato argues, educating children differently for different roles in society and the economy, which amounts to a kind of tracking in schools, or do we support Freire's idea that education should be an exercise in enabling individuals to craft their development and futures according to their own lights? Do we accept Dewey's insistence on the importance of democracy or Plato's rejection of it? And what are the implications of our choices on how we approach education?

Part II does not attempt to answer those questions in relation to Plato, Rousseau, Dewey, and Freire. It does, however, take up the challenge of addressing the same sorts of questions with respect to education that were examined in the historical analyses. In chapter 5, we will pose the questions about education that, in our current circumstances, prompt philosophic consideration. The point will be to state clearly which are the most challenging educational issues that we currently face that raise philosophically pertinent questions. These then provide the basis on which to carry out the rest of the study.

Chapter 6 begins to provide answers to the general questions concerning education, though in the context of specific ideas about nature and knowledge, and of the character of human experience. I will provide an account, if only cursorily, of how it seems to me best to understand reality generally. The same will be done for an understanding of experience. As broad as this sounds, I do think that no serious approach to the issues more directly related to education can be undertaken without such an explicit consideration of metaphysics and epistemology. Once those ideas are articulated, their implications for philosophically relevant educational issues can be clarified.

Chapter 7 turns to an explicit discussion of relevant issues in social and political theory. Without an explicit idea of what we understand to be the desirable forms of social and political organization and processes, and of how we imagine our social and political structures can be most conducive of human life, it makes little sense to pose any normative questions about education. When at least general conceptions of social and political life are developed, education can be considered in their light.

With the analyses of nature, knowledge, experience, society, and politics behind us, it is possible to address the normative questions concerning the who, what, where, when, why, and how of education and schooling. The answers proposed and defended are, of course, my own, and as in the case of the historical figures, the reader is under no special obligation to accept them. The hope is, however, that by this point the reader will be in a much better position than she would have been previously to understand the ideas, and the relations among them, and to make critical judgments concerning them. Of course, one would also hope that the reader will be in a better position to undertake her own systematic analyses of the relevant issues in the philosophy of education than previously.

Finally, a word about the intended audience for this book: As I have indicated, it is based on a master's level course that I used to teach (at least part I is), so there is an obvious sense in which this is intended to be of value for students. The material can be a bit daunting for the uninitiated, which means that it is likely to be advanced undergraduate and graduate students who would benefit the most. Working schoolteachers at any level can also benefit from the book if they are interested in the topic. With these audiences in mind, I have tried to write as clearly as possible and to sound as little as possible like a professional philosopher. One has to achieve this result, though, without diluting the philosophical richness of the material and depth of the analysis. This means that, despite efforts to avoid unnecessary jargon and pretentious locutions, the ideas, concepts, and analyses remain difficult, and attention is required.

I would like to think that this book may also be interesting for philosophers and other scholars who have an interest in the subject. There are not, as far as I understand, any radically new interpretations here of Plato, Rousseau, Dewey, or Freire, so the discussions of them will be familiar to those who already know their writings. It may be that thinking their ideas through with an eye on their integration with questions concerning education proves to be a new angle for some readers and therefore perhaps useful.

Part II, which addresses relevant philosophical and educational issues directly, may well present some ideas that are unfamiliar for most readers. The discussions of metaphysics, epistemology, philosophical anthropology, and social and political theory rehearse positions I have articulated before and defend in other works. Nonetheless, the pragmatic naturalist philosophical tradition out of which my ideas and analyses grow may be something new even for philosophers, and I therefore go to some lengths to clarify and defend the ideas. One hopes that the philosophical treatment of education that is integrated with the more general ideas proves to be coherent and valuable for any reader who stays with the book to the end.

I would be remiss if I did not point out to the reader that whatever the value of the book's discussions of other philosophers, it is always advisable to turn to primary texts themselves. Whatever her role in the educational process may be, the reader would do well to turn to Plato, Rousseau, Dewey, and Freire directly, as well as to such more contemporary philosophers of education as Nel Noddings and Maxine Greene.

With that, we can turn now to education and its philosophical contexts.

PART I

CHAPTER 1

Reality, the Good, and the State

Plato's *Republic*

In Book IV of the *Republic*, Plato refers to education and upbringing as "the one great thing."[1] This is impressive considering some of the other topics that he discusses in the book, among which are the soul, the state, and knowledge, not to mention Truth, the Good, and Beauty, the latter sometimes translated into English with uppercase letters to indicate their profound importance. We would not be surprised to see Plato refer to any one of these themes as "the one great thing," but he does not; he reserves that accolade for education. While by itself this proves nothing, those of us who participate in the educational process can be forgiven if we take Plato's usage as license, even allowing for a bit of hyperbole, to consider ourselves involved in a process of great significance.

Plato obviously thought so, and he makes his ideas on education quite plain. He says, for example, that education should develop the several aspects of the individual harmoniously; that education is crucial for justice in society; that people whose natures suit them for differing functions within the state should be educated differently; that physical education is essential for the development of the soul; that some topics should be banned from the educational process (for example, some forms of music and poetry); that there should be no differences in the education provided to boys and girls; and that the leaders of the state should be educated in the most abstract forms of rational inquiry. What Plato means by these and other recommendations concerning education, what reasons he offers for thinking them, and how these ideas are related to and depend on other philosophical views that he has are the subject of this chapter.

Plato's specific ideas about education are his responses to the journalist's questions. The "who, what, when, where, why, and how" questions can be rephrased as questions about the people for whom education is conducted, the content of education, the phases of people's lives at which it is appropriate, the goals of education, and its methods.

THE CONTEXT OF THE *REPUBLIC*

Plato had something to say about many of these questions. In the opening pages of the *Republic*, he raises the issue that is at the heart of the whole book, that drives the discussion of education, and that has to do with the nature of justice. This text, as is typical for Plato's writings, takes the form of a dialogue between Socrates and one or more interlocutors. Socrates broaches the question of the nature of justice but is soon embroiled in a disagreement with the famous teacher Thrasymachus about whether justice or injustice is the most profitable value or principle on which people can act. Thrasymachus thinks that injustice is more profitable for a person because it allows one to take advantage of others, but Socrates disagrees. Without belaboring the details of the conversation or the argument, Socrates is able to demonstrate that injustice, contrary to being advantageous, is in fact the absence of harmony among the parts of something, or, as he puts it, things not being in proper relation to one another. This, it turns out, is as true of an individual as it is of a society. Justice, by contrast, is the condition in which something is functioning as it should, which is to say to its own advantage, because its various parts are acting harmoniously. Such a condition, however, does not happen automatically, or perhaps it is better to say that there are many factors that could impede such a condition. The smooth and successful functioning of anything, which is to say justice, requires help.

To see how justice in the sense of the harmony of parts works, and why it is more beneficial than injustice, Plato proposes that we consider a case on a larger scale than a single individual, on the grounds that the situation will be clearer in the larger case, just as large writing is easier to read than small writing. On that analogy, he suggests that we consider the case of a whole city and examine what justice is in a city and how to bring it about. When he refers to a city, of course, Plato means an entire society, which is understandable since in ancient Greece each city-state and its surroundings was a society unto itself, notwithstanding a common language and culture among them.

This, then, is how Plato moves from a discussion of whether a just person is happier than an unjust person to an analysis of a utopian society, or a republic. And it is in this context that the discussion of education comes into focus. Plato begins with the establishment of the society and asks about the people who should populate it. On the assumption that people should be expected to do what they do best, and that different people have different skills, the society will need a range of people to accomplish what the residents will require. They will need food, for example, and so there must be farmers and herders, as well as the merchants who will move the food to the city and retailers who will make it available to the public. They will also need shelter, cookware, and clothing, so there will need to be shoemakers and weavers, potters and cart-makers, builders and laborers, and thus the city will quickly become rather populated. Compelled by his friends, though against his better judgment, Socrates grants that the society could also introduce some luxuries, and so we would expect there also to be hunters, who will need weapons, and jewelers to create the decorative items for people. It will turn out that Plato thinks that for all these tradespeople and craftsmen it will be sufficient that they be trained in the skills necessary for their trades and crafts. The currently common idea that average working people do not need education beyond what they need to make a living is related to Plato's ideas about human nature and politics, some of the details of which we will consider later in the chapter.

However, we are not yet finished populating the city. To ensure that there is sufficient land available for the population's needs, including farms and land for hunting, the city will find it necessary to protect itself and possibly even to expand. For that reason, the city needs what Plato refers to as guardians or auxiliaries, which is basically the military class of the society. Unlike the trades- and craftspeople, who need to possess a single skill in order to function well, the guardians need to have two seemingly incompatible traits. They must, Socrates points out, at the same time be "spirited" toward the enemies of the society (with everything that trait implies) and gentle toward their compatriots, the people whom they must protect. Consequently, the guardians require an education far more complex and sophisticated than simply mastering a narrow set of skills.

We will return to the question of how the guardians are recognized at a young age, because Plato did not think that people's talents are necessarily hereditary, so for the moment we will simply assume that it is possible to do so. The question arises, then, regarding of what the education of children who will become guardians should consist. Plato thought, as we do, that young children are highly impressionable; consequently, he thought (also as we do) that we need to be careful which impressions we make on young children. Because they can be influenced to develop in a range of different directions, we want to be sure that they are guided in the right ways, however we define them. Here, then, is one of Plato's first concerns, which is that one of the initial goals of education is individual development.

THE EDUCATION OF THE GUARDIANS

We have seen two traits that the guardians will need to have. One is the necessary spirit to wage war successfully, which would include bravery and good judgment as well as the necessary physical capabilities, and the other is the emotional and moral capacity to protect and defend their compatriots. These two imply a third, which Plato refers to as a sensibility for philosophy, by which in this context he means that the guardians must value knowledge and its acquisition to the extent that they are able to do so. To serve one's countrymen, both abroad at war and in service at home, the guardians have to be thoughtful and sensitive. These are the directions in which their education should guide them.

Young Greek children apparently had developmental experiences similar to ours in that they were read stories and they spent what time they could in physical activity and play. This is natural and appropriate, Plato thought, but both sides of a child's life require some guidance, and Plato thought the most important place to begin is with the stories children are told. Guided physical development could wait a bit, he thought. The reason the stories are so important for him is that the stories we tell our children, which then and now are in the form of fables and tales, have a moral impact on children. He thought, and I would imagine that most of us are likely to agree, that the impact we want such tales to have is that the children listening to them develop desirable moral and character traits. In Plato's case, the traits he wanted the children to develop, and keep in mind that the children he is talking about are future guardians, are respect, courage, modesty, and all the personality characteristics that they will need as adults. It is critical that we avoid exposing them to models of greed, temerity, fear, cowardice, and similar traits.

The question Plato asks is how these personality traits can be inculcated, and his account focuses on the kinds of music and poetry we present to children. It may sound odd to us to be concerned at this point with music and poetry, but the reason is that in Plato's time and place, the literature available for children (and adults, for that matter) was primarily in the form of the legends of the Heroic Age, primarily the Homeric epics and Hesiod's discussion of the gods, and the poetry of some more recent writers such as Pindar and the plays crafted by playwrights Aeschylus, Sophocles, and Euripides. Also, though the Greek alphabet then in use had appeared some centuries before, it was still common practice for the poetry, tales, and plays of these kinds to be presented orally, often sung to some musical accompaniment, and in the case of plays, to include a "chorus." As a result, considering which literature to expose our children to means thinking about which music and poetry we should provide them.

Plato offers several specific requirements. First, the education of the guardians must not include any stories that place the gods in an undesirable light—for example, in which they might act in petty ways, or lie, or abuse one another or any mortals. The gods as they appear in Homer, for example, can be a morally questionable lot, and we should not allow the guardians to get the impression that such behavior is acceptable. Since at this point children are still too young to discuss in any useful way the gods' behavior, it is necessary that they simply not be exposed to it. Thus, Plato says, for example, "Indeed, if we want the guardians of our city to think that it's shameful to be easily provoked into hating one another, we mustn't allow *any* stories about gods warring, or plotting against one another, for they aren't true" (378b-c). The gods must always be presented as behaving in morally desirable ways and as the source always of good and never of evil. Any poet who speaks ill of the gods, no matter how prominent he may be, will not be permitted to speak or sing his verses to the children, and his work will not be performed by anyone else.

The young guardians should also not be exposed to stories in which gods (or people, for that matter) behave in excessively emotional ways. There should not be stories of lamentations, or money-grubbing and bribery, or drunkenness. Clearly, the behavioral ideal for the guardians, in addition to the traits of courage, "spiritedness," and gentleness, is moderation. It is a virtue for the guardians to be moderate in all their behavior and in their desires. Everyone knows and appreciates the desires for food, drink, and sex, Plato acknowledges, but it is important that the guardians not allow such desires to compel them into immoderate behavior. This can be a problem in relation to the Greek gods and their stories because they were rather prone to excess in their behavior, especially sexual. There are many stories of gods pursuing sex not only somewhat single-mindedly but also by lying and manipulating to manage it. Plato will have none of this in his education, because the guardians must not get the idea that this sort of behavior, and excessively strong desires of these kinds, are acceptable. It is also worth noticing that Plato thinks that such stories are undesirable not just for children and young people but for everyone. He would, it appears, ban them from the city entirely (391e-392). In fact, he makes a rather theatrical point that poets who tell such stories shall, as they approach the city, be greeted with honors but then promptly sent on their way and not allowed in (398a-b). The city must be purified of bad influences.

The content of stories is not the only problem for the education of the guardians because the style of presentation can be equally destructive to young people whose emotions are only forming and thus extremely impressionable. Some stories are presented in the form of laments, for example, which express a weakness that is not a virtuous model for guardians. Laments are to be avoided, as are any forms of imitation. This sounds a bit odd, but Plato thinks that when we take on an acting role, we can easily be influenced by the traits of the character that we imitate. If we portray weaknesses of various kinds, or moral deprivations, we run the risk of assuming those traits ourselves. Consequently, the only form of imitation that can be part of a young person's education is imitation of characters who embody the traits we want the guardians to develop.

Plato is so concerned about this sort of thing that he even takes pains to specify which musical modes are acceptable. To understand this point, a bit of musical background is called for. Modern Western music of all genres uses two of what the Greeks would have called modes. We call them modes too, and they are expressed through our major and minor keys. These modes generally, and the keys through which they are expressed, convey emotional states. Music in a major key is typically upbeat and happy, while music in a minor key conveys sadness, remorse, guilt, danger, and other similar conditions. The Greeks had several more than these two modes, seven in total, and thus their music, one might claim, had a wider range of emotional possibilities. Our two sets of keys express, respectively, two of the Greek modes: the Ionian mode is heard in our major key and the Aeolian mode in the minor. In light of the fact that Plato was concerned with the emotions to which the young guardians were exposed, and their intensity, one can see why he would be interested not only in content but also in the expressive traits of the various modes. As it happens, our major keys (the Ionian mode) and a couple others are rejected as being too soft and suitable largely for drinking parties. Similarly, our minor keys are suitable for dirges and laments, so that is also unacceptable. In the end, we are left only with the mode or modes "that would suitably imitate the tone and rhythm of a courageous person who is active in battle or doing other violent deeds, or who is failing and facing wounds, death, or some other misfortune, and who, in all these circumstances, is fighting off his fate steadily and with self-control" (399a-b). And, we should add, it is not only the modes but also the rhythm that concerns Plato, and for the same reason. Some rhythms in verse are more conducive than others to the kind of equanimity of character that the guardians should develop. Consequently, only those poetic rhythms conducive to virtue will be taught.

One of the terms that Plato uses frequently to describe the sort of person that education is intended to bring about is "harmony." A person has many different aspects, or parts—emotional, physical, ethical, appetitive, rational, among others—and the ideal person is one in whom the parts are harmoniously integrated. And not only should the parts be harmonious in relation to one another, but even within them there should be a kind of balance, so, for example, the desire for physical pleasure should not override the desire to behave properly. Another term he uses is "moderation." It is fine for the guardians to enjoy the pleasures of food and drink, for example, but only in moderation. Drunkenness, gluttony, and debauchery are unacceptable, and a future guardian ought not to be exposed to them or to any experiences that might incline him or her in those directions.

These are among the primary reasons that Plato is so careful about the guardians' education in music and poetry. For comparable reasons, the guardians are expected to achieve a balance or harmony between their body and "soul," and therefore physical training follows the initial exposure to what we would call "the arts." In the spirit of harmony and moderation, though, the young guardians will not be taught to be overly focused on physical training. The point is not to be obsessed with one's body and its condition but to achieve the kind of harmony required to be a good guardian. If an excessive emphasis is placed on physical training, Plato says, the result will be "savagery and toughness," while too little attention to it will result in "softness and overcultivation" in a person (410d). The latter leaves the guardian without the necessary strength, speed, and courage to engage the city's enemies, and the former makes him or her incapable of the empathy and gentleness necessary to assist and defend its citizens.

We will return below to Plato's philosophical anthropology, or his general understanding of human nature, but it should be made clear at this point that though he is interested, and genuinely so, in the harmony of soul, or mind, and body, he does in fact have a hierarchical conception of the nature of a person. For Plato, the soul is the ruler of the self, as he might put it. Soul and body are not of equal importance in that one of them controls the other, which means that the harmony between them must accommodate that unequal importance. Because the soul is the proper ruler of the self, then if the soul is properly formed, the person can be expected to make the right decisions, even with respect to the body and its development. Plato puts it this way: "It seems, then, that a god has given music and physical training to human beings not, except incidentally, for the body and the soul but for the spirited and wisdom-loving parts of the soul itself, in order that these might be in harmony with one another." And further, "the person who achieves the finest blend of physical training and impresses it on his soul in the most measured way is the one we'd most correctly call completely harmonious" (411e-412a).

It is important to remember, though, that all of this detail applies to the education of the guardians and that no one, including the guardians, inherits their nature. To make this point, Plato gives what is usually referred to as the "Myth of the Metals," which is an example of what he himself calls a "noble falsehood," false insofar as it is a myth, but noble in that it expresses a truth. The truth it expresses is that individuals are not to be constrained by ancestry, and consequently society cannot be organized along hereditary class lines. The myth is that human beings are formed by a god in the earth, and their natures are made from a mixture of metals. In the process, the god mixes iron and bronze in the natures of the farmers, craftsman, and laborers, silver in the characters of the guardians, and gold in the natures of the small number of guardians who are destined to be rulers of the city (425a-c). People are, then, importantly different from one another, and the most relevant differences differentiate these three groups. Moreover, individuals belong in one group not by virtue of birth but by the mixture of metals in the soul, or, as we might say, by one's nature. As one might imagine, correctly identifying an individual's nature, especially early in life, is of paramount importance. If a person who by nature is meant to be a guardian somehow ends up a farmer, then a great deal can go wrong. The farming will not be done well, and the individual will live a distorted life. Similarly, if a laborer is misidentified as a guardian, he or she will also live a distorted life, and the city will not be properly protected. Education, it turns out, especially for the guardians, is critical for them not only to be able to fulfill their tasks in the city but also to maintain the appropriate social relations among the citizens and ensure that each is in her proper place.

This issue raises the obvious question of who will make these determinations. It turns out that this feature of the city, that everybody is in his or her proper role, is precisely where we find justice in the city (434c). It is also, as it turns out, the trait that defines justice in each individual, or the just person. Just as the city has several groups or functions, such as producers and protectors, Plato argues, each individual soul has comparable parts, two of which Plato calls the appetitive and the spirited. In a just person each of the parts of the soul is performing its proper task. But something is still missing in the description of both the city and the soul. The answer to the question who will ensure that each individual is in the proper role is a small group of people that Plato calls "complete guardians," or rulers (428c-d). It is the rulers who have the knowledge necessary to make these and other necessary judgments about the health and development of the city. How they achieve that knowledge, or what constitutes the education of the rulers, is a central issue to which we will return in a moment. At this point, the comparison with the individual must be made complete, and we find Plato holding that in the soul there is also a third part, which is the rational, cognitive part, that rules the others. In other words, the key to justice in both the city and the individual is knowledge, which is another reason that education is "the one great thing."

We have spoken so far about the education of the soul and the body, but, of course, none of that takes place in a vacuum. The young guardians, like everyone else, live in some sort of social structure, and just as it is important to get the education right, social relations also must be properly ordered. It is here that we see Plato's thinking about both the economic features of the city and gender and familial relations, especially as they bear on the guardians' education. He does not want to overdetermine the details of these matters because, as he puts it, if the guardians are educated properly, then the right thing to do with respect to social and economic relations will be clear enough. Nevertheless, there are points that need to be made. He emphasizes as a priority that because moderation is so important, it is critical to avoid the extremes of poverty and wealth. Wealth, he says, "makes for luxury, idleness, and revolution," while poverty creates "slavishness, bad work, and revolution as well" (422a).

The way to avoid the extremes of wealth and poverty among the guardians is to eliminate private property entirely, in the sense of both productive property (such as farms or tools) and personal property. The guardians will have everything they need to live well, and they will have it in common. Plato understands that such an arrangement will necessarily have an impact on the family, so he argues that the just city is one in which children of the guardians will be raised in common by the whole group. There will be marriages, though they seem to be more for eugenic purposes than anything else. The rulers, as it happens, will subtly arrange marriages for individuals who are likely to produce the most desirable offspring.

A critical point to notice here is that such an arrangement is possible only if women and men are equal in all relevant respects. Plato argues that though there are of course important differences between women and men, none of them are relevant to the role that guardians must fill. Many women are physically stronger than many men, many women are more skilled in many respects than many men, and many women are more intelligent than many men, and vice versa. For these reasons, any woman whose soul is of the right sort, or has the right mixture of silver, will serve as a guardian just as any similarly described man would. By implication, then, and this is the relevant point for us, women receive the same education in music, poetry, and physical training as men, and for precisely the same reasons (456a-b).

Plato thinks he has painted a picture of the ideal city. In his view, if this is the ideal city, then not only does it have to be created properly, but it also has to be maintained without any "innovations." If the city really is the best possible, then any change will by definition be change for the worse. There is a great deal at stake in protecting the city from threats of this kind. Ensuring justice in both the city and its individuals is a responsibility that falls to the rulers and requires an extraordinary depth of wisdom and understanding. It is not difficult to imagine that such people will need a special and demanding education, and Plato gives this issue a great deal of attention.

THE EDUCATION OF THE RULERS

This is where things become complicated. In one sense the city is fairly simple, but it still requires a great deal of management, and some of the decisions that have to be made are serious indeed. Consider some of them. For each child born, a decision has to be made to which class of citizen it belongs—laborers, craftspeople and merchants, or guardians. Mistakes in such cases can have serious consequences because the whole balance of the city can be thrown off, so the rulers have to be very careful. Decisions about education have to be made, as conditions over time will change somewhat—for example, a poet may introduce something new, and the rulers will have to determine whether it is healthy for or detrimental to the society. In fact, the whole structure of personal relations among the guardians, and the raising of children, has to be managed. People will no doubt develop petty squabbles over time, or even serious disagreements. And aside from such matters, the communal living situation can easily be compromised without continual attention.

Other matters will also arise. Among the producing class, property or other sorts of disagreements may develop, and the rulers must be able to adjudicate such matters in ways that maintain the general balance and moderation in the society. Without this, justice in the city—not to mention justice within each individual—can be endangered. And then there are larger matters of state with which the rulers must contend. Relations with other cities, and with non-Greek foreigners, have to be maintained and matters of war and peace determined. There would also be economic questions, since in one way or another the goods produced have to be distributed, not only among the producers themselves but also to the guardians. Some sort of distribution mechanism, perhaps some form of taxation, would be necessary. Plato thinks that moderating wealth and private property will prevent the eruption of class conflicts, but one never knows, and the rulers must mitigate the effects of such conflicts were they to arise.

One of Socrates's interlocutors is suspicious of all this and asks Socrates to explain how it is possible to bring about such a city. Socrates's response is interesting, and it is a point we will see again in Rousseau. He does not claim, he says, that the city can be achieved. He has been describing an ideal situation, and it may be that it cannot be made actual. However, even if it cannot be actualized, that would not detract from its value as an ideal. Socrates is telling us what the ideal city would be, as he understands it, and the presumption is that even if we cannot actualize it, the closer we get to the ideal, the better our actual circumstances will be (472). In other words, the criterion of adequacy for an ideal is not whether it can be achieved but whether by approaching its actualization we create better circumstances. If that is the case, then the ideal ought to be accepted as an ideal toward which to strive.

In that case, the demand placed on the rulers is extraordinary, because they must not only make decisions to maintain the city and enable it to prosper but also be in a position to judge whether a particular action or policy is good. Deciding whether a given policy will work is one thing; determining whether it will work for the better, and is therefore good to put into effect, is another and far more difficult matter. The rulers must understand the structures and mechanisms of individual psychology as well as those of the state, so that they can be maintained, but they must also understand what is good for both the state and its citizens. To put the point crudely, the rulers have to know a great deal, and they not only have to know many particular things but also have a general understanding.

In order to judge whether a particular poem is good, for example, they have to know what counts as "good" with respect to poems. In addition to particular poems, then, they have to know the model or ideal of a poem, because that is the only way they will be able to judge whether a particular poem is a good one. In fact, all of us do this when we make judgments, Plato thought. When a carpenter makes a table, for example, she has to have some idea of the ideal table to serve as a model on which to base the new table. Or imagine a physician who will treat a patient. The physician can know when something is wrong, what is wrong, and what will count as a cure, because the physician already has in mind an idea of what a person's health should be, which is to say that the physician has a model in mind of the ideal healthy person.

The ruler is in a similar situation, except that the issues with which the ruler has to deal tend to be somewhat more abstract. The ruler has to know not just the ideal table or healthy body but also the good of the soul and of the state. Moreover, since presumably the good soul and the good state have something in common—goodness—the ruler has to know the good itself. To know what counts as good in general is to possess a great deal of understanding and wisdom, and when asked who could possibly meet the demands that are placed on the ruler, Socrates says that clearly a ruler has to be someone who loves learning and wisdom, which in Greek is, basically, a *philo sophia*—a philosopher. Plato says that the ideal city can only be properly ruled by philosophers.

If that sounds ridiculous to you, you should know that it also sounded ridiculous to Socrates's interlocutors, who nearly laughed him out of the room at this point. In Greece at this time the people who called themselves philosophers, and whom we have come to know as sophists, were itinerant teachers, some of whom had questionable reputations. It was difficult for Socrates's colleagues to imagine that the ideal city needed them to rule it. Socrates agreed, but he said that the reason it seems absurd is that they are not really lovers of wisdom, and much of what they teach is not knowledge of an important kind at all. The sophists tended to proffer opinions rather than knowledge, he claimed. They talked about what is the case and how to manage it, rather than what would be good in the way of belief and implementation. The difference between opinion and knowledge, Plato thought, makes all the difference in the world, and he goes to considerable lengths to clarify the point. All of this is critical to sort out because the ruler must be educated in such a way that she can achieve genuine knowledge, distinguish between knowledge and opinion, and apply that knowledge to bring about and maintain the good.

We have now introduced the two most abstract topics in the *Republic*: the models, or forms, of existing things and the nature of genuine knowledge. These are the issues of metaphysics and epistemology that have been mentioned earlier. Plato's ideas about the most important aspects of education, important because they are required for people and their society to be good, are directly related to his ideas about the reality of ideal types, the forms, and the nature of knowledge. To explain his thoughts on these matters, Plato uses some of the most famous analogies and metaphors in all of world literature, but before we turn to them, it will be helpful to state more directly what he thinks.

Plato thought that every particular thing of a specific kind—a horse, or a chair, or a person, or a book, or an idea—is the sort of thing that it is because it reflects more or less completely an ideal type of the thing. It is rather like the relation between a dress and a pattern. A dress is made on the basis of a certain pattern, and in fact many dresses may be made that exhibit the same pattern. In such a case, the pattern is the model of that kind of dress. The pattern tells us what shape the dress should have, what its dimensions should be, how its parts will function and be related to one another, what its material is, and other such matters. It is the ideal type of that dress, of which each individual dress is an imperfect copy. Plato thought that there exists an ideal type or model, rather like the dress pattern, for every kind of existing entity. Unlike the dress pattern, however, the models for all existing things are not themselves material objects, but rather ideal types. He referred to them as forms. Just as the dress pattern exists independently of the individual dresses, and independently of the dressmaker, the forms exist independently of their particular exemplars and independently of us, so that in addition to all the material horses that exist, there also exists the form of "horse," as odd as that sounds. Unlike the dress pattern, though, while the horses are all material entities, the form of horse is an ideal entity. And it is not an idea in our minds, so to speak, but it is an ideal (which is to say, nonmaterial) entity that exists independently of all material horses and independently of us.

All such forms are not only immaterial and perfect but also eternal and unchanging. Unlike the dress pattern, the ideal forms of existing entities do not come into existence and go out of existence. They are, rather, eternal. This may sound odd today, but it is worth realizing that until the middle of the nineteenth century it was assumed that all species were eternal forms of this kind. That is the reason that Darwin's evolutionary theory was so radical and disruptive, even in the title of his book. Talking about the origin of species was oxymoronic, most people would have thought, because species were presumed to be eternal and unchanging. Plato thought that this was true of everything. Furthermore, because the forms were the unchanging models of individual entities, they must be not only eternal but also complete and perfect. Individual things with their many imperfections come and go, but their ideal reality is eternal, perfect, and unchanging.

Now, take the next step, which is that different kinds of entities may share traits with other kinds; for example, tables are one form of furniture, but there are also many other types of furniture, such as chairs and cupboards and benches and similar objects. There is an ideal form for each of these kinds of thing, but there is also a more general form for furniture. So, there are forms of various levels of generality, each embodying the good or ideal of its specific kind. Without belaboring this point, we can imagine following this line of reasoning to a point at which we reach the highest possible level of generality and abstraction. This highest level, which is the model for what is good and ideal in everything, is what Plato called the form of the good. This is what the ruler has to know, and that fact presents two challenges. To understand what it means for the ruler to know the form of the good, we have to have an idea of what counts as knowledge at this level of abstraction, and how it can be achieved. Taken together, these questions address the goal, content, and method of the education of the rulers.

We can begin with the question what it can mean to have knowledge at this level of abstraction. The basic idea is that for Plato, knowledge is to be distinguished from opinion, which we have already seen in Plato's distinction between the sophists and genuine philosophers. We know that it is possible for us to have a variety of concepts of things, or opinions about this or that, and we often disagree in those opinions. This is all normal and to be expected, but we should realize, he thinks, that none of this is knowledge. Knowledge does not admit of varying opinions. For such knowledge to be possible, it has to be that the object of knowledge does not itself change. If the object of our inquiry were to change, then the best we could have would be shifting concepts of it, and they would be opinions. The certainty that genuine knowledge enables, he thought, can only be achieved about that which does not change. Since all individual things are contingent, which means that they come into existence and go out of existence, knowledge of them is impossible. The best we can achieve is opinion. What is not contingent is permanent, and permanence can be ascribed only to the eternal and unchanging forms. Therefore, genuine knowledge is not of individual things but of the forms. A good veterinarian, for example, can treat horses well not because she is familiar with any number of individual horses but because she has knowledge of the form of horse, of the ideal type.

To understand this point, it may be helpful to think about it in terms of geometrical objects—for example, a triangle. One of the reasons this sort of example helps is that Plato had such mathematical entities in mind himself. Remember that in the fourth century BCE the Greeks did not have anything we would recognize as science available to them. They did, however, have fairly sophisticated mathematical expertise, especially in geometry. Pythagoras, for example, had long been well known among Greek scholars, and the kind of knowledge of mathematical entities that he and his followers developed was regarded by many Greeks as models of genuine knowledge. The relevant point is that the Pythagorean Theorem, to continue with this example, which is that $a^2 + b^2 = c^2$, is a model of genuine understanding, which, as we will see below, is close to knowledge, for several reasons. First, it is an assertion about an ideal type. It is not a claim that applies only to this or that right triangle, but rather to the general form of right triangle. In fact, it is probably not even precisely true of any specific right triangle that we might draw, for the simple reason that a triangle we draw will be imperfect to some extent, so that the precise relations that the theorem expresses will not be accurately descriptive. It is, however, precisely true of the ideal type of right triangle, because the ideal type is perfect, and therefore the relations described by the theorem apply. Moreover, the theorem does not change—it is the same now as it was 2,500 years ago, because the ideal type of right triangle (which is what the theorem refers to) is not only perfect but also eternal and unchanging. This is not something about which one may have this or that opinion or even about which one may disagree. Knowledge and certainty are achieved in the theorem's expression of the nature of the ideal form of right triangle.

Plato thought that the forms were in many ways like the abstract entities of geometry. To put it a different way, the ideal type of right triangle is to right triangles in nature (if there are any), or those we draw, as ideal forms are to any particular expressions of the forms. Just as a right triangle we draw is an imperfect copy of the ideal, perfect, and eternal form of right triangle, so a table we make is an imperfect copy of the ideal, perfect, and eternal form of table, or any particular horse is an imperfect copy of the ideal, perfect, and eternal form of horse. Furthermore, just as the Pythagorean Theorem counts as something close to knowledge because it refers to the form of right triangle, so we have knowledge, or better understanding, of entities in the world only if our expressions of that information refer to the forms. Understanding and knowledge are not about particular things any more than the Pythagorean Theorem is about particular triangles.

The rulers then must have knowledge of the forms, including, and especially, the form of the good. How does one get such knowledge? Our inclination, perhaps in part because we live in a time in which the practice of natural science is influential, might be to think that to achieve knowledge of an ideal type of something, we would study many particular examples of it and extrapolate general traits from the many particulars. Along these lines, we might think that the way a veterinarian would acquire knowledge of horses is to study many horses and from doing so arrive at generalities about the type. Plato did not see it this way, simply because as far as he was concerned, you can never infer the nature of perfection from any number of imperfect copies. The best we could get that way is a general conception of imperfect entities. As evidence, he might point to the fact that when we want to understand the nature of the form of the right triangle, we do not study examples of imperfect triangles and generalize from them. On the contrary, we apply the methods of rigorous and rational analysis directly to the perfect form. We learn about the form of the right triangle by rationally analyzing the form itself and drawing the deductive inferences that follow from the rational analysis. The rulers, consequently, will be able to acquire knowledge of the forms through reason, not through empirical study. Their education, therefore, must be in the principles and practice of abstract reason. This is in part what he means by saying that the rulers must be philosophers.

There is, however, an important difference between the rational analysis of mathematics and the sort of reason needed to gain knowledge of the form of the good. Plato called the latter process dialectic. When we are studying geometry, we posit some number of assumptions in the form of theorems and corollaries, and we reason deductively from them to a conclusion about some aspect of the shape we are studying. This is all very well for mathematics, Plato thought, but it does not help us with such subjects as the form of the good, basically because there are no theorems or other assumptions with which to begin. In the rational analysis of the form of the good, we do not reason *from* principles (for example, theorems and other assumptions) but *to* principles, or the nature of the form itself. This requires a different rational skill, one that takes a great deal of study, and a long time, to master.

Mathematical entities like a triangle are ideal forms, but not all forms are mathematical, despite the fact that we can acquire knowledge of them only through reason. In fact, Plato had trouble speaking directly about the forms, and so he used analogy and metaphor to try to clarify things, and the analogies and metaphors are worth a closer look, especially the most famous of them. The first helpful one is the metaphor of the sun, or what Plato calls the "offspring of the good." If we look first at the material world, we realize that the senses are critical for our familiarity with things and that the sense that seems to dominate for us is sight. Most of us engage the world largely through seeing it, and this is possible because there are objects to see and there is in most of us the capacity for sight. But objects and the ability to see them are not all that is needed, because without light the objects would be opaque to us and our capacity for sight would be useless. Light is what makes objects available to us through the capacity for sight. But even light is not the cause of sight, because there is something else that causes light, and that is the sun. Moreover, the sun is the cause of not only light but also the existence of the objects themselves; without the sun, there would be no one and nothing to see (506d-508c).

The sun represents the form of the good, and light is knowledge. The capacity for sight is our capacity to know, which is to say our intelligence. Our capacity to engage the world cognitively, our intelligence, is enabled by knowledge. Knowledge cognitively illuminates our world, but it can do so only because it also has a cause, and that cause is the form of the good. And, like the sun, the form of the good is the cause of not only knowledge but also everything we know, of all reality. The two sides of the sun metaphor, the visible and the intelligible, have implications for what we can and cannot know. The visible world, remember, is contingent and changing, and therefore we can have only opinions about it. Knowledge, by contrast, is possible only of the intelligible world, represented by light and by the sun itself.

This all sounds quite mysterious, and it did to Plato too. That is why he says that it is difficult to describe, and why he appeals to metaphors and analogies. To clarify the point a bit, he offers the image of what is called the "divided line." Imagine a vertical line divided by a short horizontal line about two-thirds of the distance from the top, and then each of the two sections divided again two-thirds of the distance from the top of each. There are now four segments of unequal length, the smallest at the bottom of the line and the largest at the top. We now label the sections A–D from the top, so that the longest segment, at the top, is labeled A, the next longest below it is B, then C below that, and finally D, the shortest of the segments. Plato tells us that the bottom two segments, D and C from the bottom, represent the visible world, with C representing material objects and D images of them, such as reflections, shadows, and illusions. Of such entities, the best cognitive access we can have is opinion, he says, with belief possible for material objects and imagination providing our sense of reflections and illusions. The top two segments, longer than the bottom two as a way of representing their relatively greater importance, is the ideal realm, of which we can have genuine knowledge. Segment B represents mathematical objects, and segment A, the highest and longest, is the forms. The understanding we may have of the mathematical objects of segment B we achieve through deductive reasoning, while the knowledge we have of the forms is possible through dialectical reason.

This is a more graphical way of representing the same point as the sun metaphor, and in the case of the divided line, the larger share of the line that represents the ideal realm is meant to convey its greater cognitive and moral significance. The ideal realm of the forms is in all relevant respects more important than the material world and whatever we can glean about it. The greater importance, we also need to realize, is reflected with respect to both knowledge and reality. We can only have belief and opinion about the material world, segments C and D, which is a pale reflection of the understanding and knowledge we can have of the ideal realm of mathematical objects and the forms. Similarly, with respect to their "reality," just as the shadows and illusions of segment D are caused by the material objects of segment C, so the material world as a whole is caused by the ideal realm of the forms. Moreover, Plato and many people who have followed him would say that just as material objects have greater reality than their shadows and reflections, so do the forms have greater reality than the material objects that imperfectly reflect them (509d-510b).

If that point is not clear enough, Plato gives us one more illustration of it, this time in the famous allegory of the cave. He asks us to imagine a cave, deep inside which there are people chained to the ground and forced to face the back of the cave, while behind them there is a fire burning. Between them and the fire is a wall, along which objects like puppets are constantly moving back and forth, and whose shadows are cast onto the back wall of the cave. The people imprisoned here spend their entire lives seeing only the shadows on the wall because the wall is all they can see. Understandably, such people will mistakenly think that the shadows are reality. Imagine, then, that someone is released from his chains and turns around to face away from the back of the cave. First, he will realize that what appears on the back wall is not reality but merely shadows or reflections of something more substantial. As this person looks past the fires that are creating the shadows, he realizes that the fires themselves must be caused by something. He may determine to find the cause, or perhaps he is dragged unwillingly, but in either case he makes his way out of the cave. This is not easy because the floor of the cave is quite steep, and even treacherous. As he makes his arduous way toward the mouth of the cave, he begins to see a light far brighter than the fire inside, and he realizes that this light is what makes the fire, and ultimately the shadows on the wall, possible. As he reaches the mouth of the cave, though, he is nearly blinded by the brightness of the light, all the harsher because he has spent his life in the relative darkness of the cave. As he begins to adjust, though, it becomes clear to him that even this light has a cause, and he finally comes into direct contact with the sun itself, at which point he understands the difference between reality and the appearances he had thought were real.

If it is not obvious already, the prisoners in the cave are us—that is, normal people going through our normal lives. The shadows cast on the wall, which represent the objects we perceive around us, are mere reflections and vague images, but we think they are real and substantial. The person who realizes that these are mere shadows and not reality is the philosopher, who in his love of knowledge and wisdom approaches reality directly. The steep and dangerous climb out of the cave is the education he must complete if he is to succeed in achieving knowledge. Eventually this difficult path leads him to the light of knowledge and to the source of all reality, the form of the good. At this point, he achieves the knowledge necessary to rule the republic properly and justly, and though he would prefer to remain in the brilliance of the sun, he must then turn back into the cave and assist the prisoners.

We are now asked to understand what sort of person this ruler, the philosopher-king, must be, what his education must be like to enable such a life, the knowledge that it makes possible, and the responsibility that it imposes on him. The rulers—both young women and young men, Plato takes pains to remind us—are drawn from the guardian class, so they must possess in soul and body all the traits of a guardian. What distinguishes them, among other characteristics, is "high-mindedness" and "ease in learning" (490c). Even as children they will demonstrate an unusually strong desire for learning and commitment to truth. Plato is careful to point out, however, that even a young person with these and other important virtues can be (in fact, may likely be) corrupted and distorted without the proper upbringing. Plato understood, as most parents do today, that life has many ways of misdirecting children. In the case of the future rulers, their fabulous virtues can transform, if misdirected, into equally fabulous vices. An ill-meaning fool is bad enough, but an intelligent person with wicked intentions is far more dangerous. Nothing, therefore, can be more important for justice in the city than the rulers' education.

Plato makes an important point that we would do well to take seriously. Many people believe, he says, that education is a process of "putting knowledge into the souls that lack it" (518b-d). But this is not right, he says. Actually, Plato thinks that we all contain information and some degree of understanding innately, as he argued in his dialogue *Meno*, in which Socrates draws out from a slave boy mathematical knowledge that he could not have been given by anyone else. This idea of "drawing out" knowledge is actually related etymologically to the English word "education," which derives from the Latin *educare*, which is "to bring up," which is itself related to *educere* through the prefix *e*, which means "out of" or "from," and *ducere*, which means "to lead." So even our own word contains the idea that education and upbringing are not putting something into a person but drawing it out. In talking about the rulers, Plato uses a different but similar metaphor and says that the education of the rulers is a process of "turning the soul" in such a way that it is led to knowledge. The question, then, is how this turning of the soul can be effected.

The rulers, remember, share the education of the guardians, so they will learn music and poetry with the others, and they will undergo the necessary physical training. Unlike the other guardians, however, they are expected eventually to direct their studies to the forms, so their studies must orient them toward rational inquiry. As guardians, they will already have been introduced to mathematics, because it is useful in war, and mathematics is also the subject that begins to train the rulers in reason. The guardians need applied mathematics, while the rulers need its purer versions. Plato has in mind arithmetic, since numbers are abstract entities and therefore point the student toward the rational, as well as plane geometry, because it is also the study of ideal forms, as we have seen in the case of the Pythagorean Theorem. Reason has to investigate not just surfaces, though, but also depth, and so solid geometry is the third subject, and with depth under one's belt it is possible to study astronomy. The reason astronomy is important is that it is the study of not just surfaces and depth but also motion. One gets the impression that had calculus been available to him, Plato would have placed its study here. For Greeks at this time, the mathematical relations of moving objects in the sky were related to the mathematical relations among musical tones—hence the idea of the "harmony of the spheres." The rulers must understand the mathematics of harmony as well as of the movement of heavenly bodies.

As impressive and daunting as this list of subjects is, it is only the "prelude," as Plato calls it, to the study that the rulers ultimately need. All of this mathematics educates the rulers in critically important rational inquiry and judgment, but because it consists of reasoning from hypotheses and first principles, the most it can produce is understanding, as we know from the divided line. The rulers, however, require knowledge of the forms, and for this they need to learn to reason *to* first principles; they need dialectic. Dialectical reason is the capstone of all the ruler's study because it alone will enable her to achieve knowledge of the forms, most important the form of the good.

All of the subjects, except for dialectic, are to be taught to the future rulers while they are still children, by which Plato seems to mean in what we would call primary and secondary schooling. These, remember, are the exceptional students, and so the education in these subjects that they receive is oriented toward theory rather than exclusively applied versions, as all the other guardians receive. There is a great deal of "tracking" going on here. By the time they reach twenty years, it will be clear which of them are able to see the unity in the subjects they have been studying, which is important because, as we have noted, progressively greater generality means greater unity, until all of being, knowledge, and virtue are united in the form of the good. The young people who can glimpse the unity in their studies show promise for their future as rulers. By the time they reach thirty years, it will be clear which of them have the understanding, commitment, and skill to study dialectic, which they will do for five years. Plato does not go into detail as to what constitutes the study of dialectic, but one may assume that his own dialogues, including the *Republic* itself, are examples of dialectic at work.

After five years of the study of dialectic, the fully educated rulers must be directed back into the cave.

POLITICAL STRUCTURE

And so we return to earth from the dialectical stratosphere, as the rulers themselves must return from their rational contemplation of the good, the true, the beautiful, and the virtuous, to lead the daily affairs of the city. For fifteen years, while they continue to study philosophy, they will conduct war and direct other matters related to young people, and at fifty years of age they will be the lawgivers for the city. After some period of time, when they have prepared others to take their place, they can retire to the contemplative life that is suitable for people of their natures and inclinations.

Education has resulted in the sort of people, at all social levels, who are capable of maintaining the just city. It still needs to be specified, however, what counts as justice in both the city and the individual, because this rounds out the reasons for which we seek justice in the first place, and the goals we have in educating people for it. The device Plato uses for this analysis is to say that there are five types of "constitution," or types of society, and they correspond to five types of person. The best he calls aristocracy, the polity that has been described in the *Republic*, and its corresponding type of person is exemplified in the ruler. The other four, in descending order of degradation, are timocracy (rule of "honor-loving" people), oligarchy (rule of the wealthy), democracy (rule of the citizenry), and finally tyranny (rule of a tyrant). Each of these types of society is a degradation of the ideal in that each in its own way distorts the proper activities and relationships of its parts, and the same applies to the corresponding type of person.

We may consider democracy and the democratic person as an illustration of the general point. Democracy is a society in which there is maximum freedom, and people by and large may do as they please. Though this seems to be an ideal condition, Plato says, it is not. Such a society, he says, has no criteria for leadership and no clear grounds on which to decide how people will or will not be educated. Because nearly everything is tolerated, the conditions necessary for strong moral and intellectual development can and will be ignored, and no society can survive, never mind prosper, under such conditions. The democratic person can be similarly described. She has no firm sense of what is more important and therefore can be expected to give a preference to whichever desires and inclinations she chooses to pursue at any given time. This is a disordered society and an equally disordered soul, one that will only lead, Plato argues, to tyranny and slavery (555b-561e). One way to understand this is with the idea that the only way democracy could be feasible is if there were a kind of equal potential among members of a society such that if the conditions of their lives were properly arranged (for example, with the right sort of education), they would be able to make use of the freedoms and tolerance afforded by democracy to their own and the society's advantage. This, as we will see in chapter 3, is how Dewey understood the situation. The problem from Plato's point of view, however, is that, as we know from the Myth of the Metals and his account of the parts of the soul, people do not have such equal potential. In that case, and without clear principles of leadership and a hierarchy of values, only self-indulgence and ultimately individual and social demise can result.

In the end, Plato holds that the timocratic, oligarchic, democratic, and tyrannical types of person are all unsatisfactory because they lead to unhappiness. They lead to unhappiness because they are souls that are disordered, either because they have no clear sense of what is more or less important, as in the democratic person, or because their lives are led by the wrong parts of the soul. Such people are invariably unhappy, sooner or later. The same may be said of the corresponding societies and polities. They, too, lead to nothing good because they are disordered. The happiest person is the one whose soul is led by that part which is most capable of leading, and that is the rational part, what Plato call the "philosophical" part, because that is the part of the soul that is able to grasp, or come at least close to grasping, the nature of the good. And a society ruled by those who can know the good directly, the philosophers, is happiest. The only place we can find genuine happiness is in the individuals and society that are structured in a way consistent with justice as it follows from the form of the good and as it is expressed in the correspondingly ordered soul. In other words, it is only the just person who can be happy and only in the just society that a happy life can be lived. Thus, Plato demonstrates what he set out to do at the beginning of the *Republic*.

EDUCATIONAL PRINCIPLES

We may close the discussion of the *Republic* with a summary of how such ideas about reality, knowledge, society, and the nature of human individuals are related to and condition Plato's specific ideas about education.

Plato's understanding of the goals and purposes of education can be considered in general and more specific respects. At the more general level, the purposes of education are to enable justice in the city and in individual people. The first, justice in the city, follows from his social and political theory, which clearly stipulates how the society should be organized. If the structure and functions with the city fail to operate properly, the city cannot function, and justice is undermined. Consequently, education properly conducted is a necessary condition of the success of the society. The second goal, which is justice in the individual, or the just life, is related in a similar way to Plato's philosophical anthropology. Plato believed that a person, or what he calls a soul, is constituted by several parts, specifically the appetitive, spirited, and rational parts. As important as the appetites (or desires) and emotions are, they have to be under the control of the rational part of the soul if the person is to live well and be happy. The reason is simply that we all have conflicting desires and potentially strong drives and emotions, and if they are allowed free rein, then our lives will be chaotic and, in the long run, unhappy. The way we learn to control and moderate our desires is through proper upbringing and education.

Plato's social theory and his philosophical anthropology also imply two other goals of education. One of them is that it prepares all people to occupy their proper place in the social order, and this is as true for the craftsman, farmer, and merchant as it is for the guardian and ruler. That we should be thought to have identifiable and differing roles in society is itself a component of how Plato understood the nature of individuals as well as the requirements of society. The second additional goal that warrants mention here is Plato's idea that education is necessary to avoid the extremes of wealth and poverty. Left unchecked, he thought, an unequal division of wealth would be inevitable. However, this situation would damage the individuals themselves as well as the society as a whole. In the case of individuals, both extreme wealth and extreme poverty would impede the moderating control of the rational part of the soul. In society generally, the impetus that wealth would give to individuals will strengthen appetites and emotions, which in turn will impede the smooth functioning of the social order and its relations among people and classes. The case is similar for those individuals in impoverished positions, whose material condition will render them unable to meet the expectations society has of them.

As important as all this is, however, the one goal of education without which the rest, including justice itself, is impossible is that the rulers must achieve knowledge of the good so that they can lead society properly. That Plato takes this view, and that it is as important as it is for his utopian construct, is due to his metaphysical ideas. A good society will remain good only if it is led by people who know what it means to be good. And for Plato, goodness is not a matter of opinion but an objective fact about reality. The kind of fact it is for him is described by his theory of forms and by the view, expressed obliquely through the analogies, metaphors, and allegories, that the pinnacle of reality, that from which all of existence and knowledge flows, is the form of the good. Without knowledge of the form of the good, the rulers cannot lead the society, and it will fail. The rulers achieve such necessary knowledge only through systematic and rigorous education. There is, Plato thought, no other way.

This description of the goals already begins to imply the relation of other components of Plato's educational theory to his more general philosophical conceptions. If we consider the "who" question, it is clear that, given his social theory and his conception of human beings, Plato thinks that all children require education, but it is very different from one set of children to another, depending on their natures and their places in society. Plato was, in other words, a strong proponent of what we would call tracking in education. Because of their social roles, the children of craftspeople, farmers, and merchants require only the training necessary for them to fulfill their functions. They need nothing else, and, in any case, because of their natures, which he described in the Myth of the Metals as bronze rather than silver or gold, they would not be able to comprehend or make use of any other sort of education. The guardians and rulers, as we know, have different natures and are educated differently. It is important also to keep in mind why Plato had the view he did about gender and education, in part because it seems somewhat progressive to us. He knew of course that there are many differences between boys and girls, and between men and women, but he was convinced that they were irrelevant to whether and how children should be educated and the goals of the education they receive. Throughout the society, from workers to guardians to rulers, and from childhood through adulthood, boys and girls, and women and men, had the same or comparable roles to fill and therefore required the same education.

These comments describe pupils and students, but we ought to give a moment's thought to the role Plato did or did not give to adults in the educational process. He has little or nothing to say about teachers, other than that those who have gained a command of their own roles and knowledge are the people who are expected to pass it on. There is nothing resembling an education of teachers, nor any credentialing process. Those who know something, or know how to do it, are those who are expected to pass the knowledge and skills on to the young. Additionally, Plato gives no role to parents, except of course for the children of the working class. In those cases, parents and other older members of the community will be the individuals who train children in their respective skills. Also in those cases, children presumably live with and are raised by their parents. Not so for the guardians and rulers, however. The children of the guardians are raised communally, and they are taught that all older women are their mothers and all older men their fathers. The communal attitude was especially important for the guardians because the nature of their social tasks requires that they collaborate closely and consider all their comrades to be family. There is no nuclear family and, therefore, no educational role for parents to play. The community raises the children and provides their education.

If the question of who is involved in education is tied to Plato's ideas about society and human being, his approach to the "what" question, the content of education, appeals to all four of the philosophic areas. It would be clearest to consider each in turn, beginning with the relevant metaphysical ideas. Recall that reality issues from, or "flows" from, as later Neo-Platonists would say, the form of the good and that the form of the good is an ideal, perfect, and eternal entity. Recall also that a well-developed person and a well-ordered society must exemplify the ideal standards established by the form of the good. These points have several specific educational implications. First, once education is properly structured and organized, it will produce the ideal people and the ideal society, and those responsible for conducting the educational process must be careful to avoid innovation. If it is already perfect, then any innovation is a deterioration in that it would push education away from its ideal condition. Second, because of this conception of the nature of reality, those responsible for education must achieve the knowledge of the forms in general and the form of the good specifically.

Further detail of the content of the education of the rulers follows from Plato's epistemology, his understanding of what knowledge is. In order for the rulers to know the forms, they must be educated in the most abstract form of rational inquiry. Plato called this kind of inquiry dialectic, by which he meant reasoning to first principles. Because ideal and perfect reality is unchanging and eternal, Plato thought that knowledge of it is possible. The material world, however, is an imperfect copy of the ideal world, as he points out in the divided line, and is constantly changing. Knowledge, however, is not possible of an object that is always changing; the best we can have is opinion about it. Thus, for the rulers to know the forms, the inquiry into them must be rational. To learn how to conduct dialectical inquiry, the rulers must first master slightly less abstract forms of rational inquiry, and they do so through the study of mathematics, specifically arithmetic, plane and solid geometry, astronomy, and harmony. Moreover, the study of mathematics that the rulers undertake is theoretical rather than applied.

Because of their knowledge of the forms, which is to say their knowledge of virtue and the good, it is rulers who make all the decisions about the content of education (and of almost everything else as well). In applying their understanding of the ideal social structures and relations of the state, and their insight into human nature, the rulers can judge what is and is not appropriate for everyone in the society. As a result, for example, given Plato's social and political theory, he reaches conclusions about what content should be included in the education of the guardians, and he advocates fairly rigid censorship to ensure that children's souls are turned in the right direction. Stories that set bad examples, and music that is conducive to questionable moral development, are banned from the educational process—in fact, from the city. Only that content remains that educates the guardians to be both spirited and sensitive, as their social roles to defeat the state's enemies and protect its people require of them. Both of these general goals require that the guardians undertake some advanced study, even in mathematics, but that its focus be applied rather than theoretical. The guardians do not need to know the forms; they need only know how to use mathematics to improve their skills in war and related activities.

As for workers, they need to be taught only what their crafts require of them. They must master that material because they are expected to exercise their crafts well, but they do not need to know anything more than that. This feature of workers' education follows from both the relevant social theory and Plato's philosophical anthropology. Workers have the simplest souls, bronze, as the Myth of the Metals tells us, and so their social and educational expectations are modest. The guardians, by contrast, being silver and gold souls, have more complex requirements. Their social roles, as we have seen, require that they be both spirited and sensitive, and, as a matter of personality, the guardians need to be harmonious and moderate. This is one of the reasons that censorship is so important. Guardians should be exposed only to those models of behavior that are conducive to desired moral development. Guardians also receive physical training, for applied reasons related to their military functions, but more important because such training is conducive to the proper development of the soul. In addition to what the guardians undertake, the gold souls, the rulers, are of course encouraged to deepen their innate love of knowledge and truth, and they are taught those subjects that will do so. Such differences in education by class and social function aside, all citizens will receive an education that is conducive to a properly ordered soul. This means that moderation and harmony is aspired to for all citizens, as is the control of the individual's appetites and emotions by the rational capacity each has, even if in different measure.

Plato has very little to say about pedagogical methods, or the "how" of education. He thinks, it appears, that as long as the rulers have genuine knowledge of the forms, they will be able to determine how best to reach educational goals. The rather obvious idea, presumably, is that the methods that best achieve the goal (for example, learning the process of geometrical reasoning) will be the methods that should be used. In any case, given the epistemology and social theory, it is clear that decisions about methods are to be made by the rulers. One of the detailed points he makes is that because of the nature of individual development, the guardians will receive their education in poetry and music before physical training.

Nonetheless, in light of his ideas about human being, Plato does make important observations concerning how we should educate. The first, and perhaps the most generally important, is his point that we educate not by filling students with information but, as he put it, by turning the soul toward its own proper development and fulfillment. This is informative less for what it asserts than for what it counsels us to avoid. Education is less about memorizing and retaining information than it is about developing one's capacities, and even personalities, or properly ordering one's soul. This point is related to another that Plato insists on, which is that education must be undertaken freely. No one learns or develops under duress, he says. We should note that, whatever other differences they may have, Plato shares this commitment to free and developmental education with Rousseau, Dewey, and Freire.

To continue the focus on methods for just a bit longer, we should make the point that Plato emphasizes the value of apprenticeship in the education process. This is clearly true for the craftspeople, farmers, and merchants, since it is basically the only way they will learn their trades. He also proposes it for the guardians, even with respect to warfare. At an appropriate age, he says, guardians should begin to take their charges and protégés into the field with them. One does not want to put them in danger, he remarks, and the guardians can be trusted to keep them safe while simultaneously introducing them by practice to the realities of the tasks that await them. Apprenticeship is also appropriate for the rulers, Plato implies, because that is how newly assigned rulers grow into their roles. Once younger rulers have mastered their expectations, their older colleagues can retire to a life of study and contemplation free, finally, of the quotidian demands of leadership.

There is even less in the *Republic* about where it is appropriate to undertake education, which may be explained in part by the fact that in classical Greece there was nothing that would pass for organized schools of the kind we are familiar with. More attention will be paid to this question by others who are closer to us in time. For Plato, we may assume that lessons would be conducted in a reasonably quiet place, that physical training would be done in open fields and competition grounds, and that apprenticeships will be conducted wherever is appropriate to the craft in question. One thing we do know is that, except possibly for the workers, the family home is not a site for the educational process because for the guardians there are no nuclear or even extended families. In this case, it really does take a village.

Plato is a bit more forthcoming on the topic of when during one's life education is appropriate, and here again the full range of philosophic ideas is in play. First, children are assigned to their social class from birth, as determined by the rulers. In this respect, tracking begins early. Second, Plato's entire approach to reality, knowledge, the city, and its people points toward the view that education is something that never ends. Workers will always be expected to improve their activities and guardians to refine their skills, and of course rulers, given their passion for knowledge and inquiry, will never stop exploring the forms. This fact, which we might now think of as "life-long learning," is somewhat more naturally conceivable in Plato's case than ours in that in his day, and in his utopia, there are no fixed academic calendars or a specific sense of a required number of years "in school." He does indicate certain points in their lives at which individuals take on specific subjects—for example, that rulers will study theoretical mathematics through their twenties and dialectic for five years beginning at age thirty. And, presumably, instruction for children in the working class will begin whenever they are old enough to learn, and similarly with the guardians. Nevertheless, the difference between learning and doing is rather less sharply drawn for Plato than it tends to be for us. Having said that, we may note that Dewey made a similar point for his own time when he said, as we cited earlier, that education is not preparation for life but life itself.

There will be occasions to think back to Plato's educational conceptions as our exploration continues. In some ways, many of Plato's ideas have little resonance for us, which may not be surprising given his distance in time and culture. But having said that, it is worth noticing that we may not be able to dismiss his thinking as irrelevant to us. On the one hand, those of us in modern liberal societies are not likely to give much credence to his arguments for censorship, although censorship plays a much larger role in our thinking than we may realize. We do, in fact, make judgments about what our children are exposed to, and often for reasons similar to Plato's. There are also societies around the world today in which a broad censorship, for various reasons, remains a feature. Along similar lines, Plato's idea that individuals are suited to very different tasks by their natures, and therefore should be steered in their education and social expectations accordingly, is quite different from our more commonly held view that individuals should be presented with options so that they might then choose lives for themselves. Nevertheless, we continue to track students in schools, and we continue to tolerate, even exacerbate, the differences in opportunities that are offered to our children as a consequence of the economic circumstances into which they were born. In some ways, we are willing to accept Plato's class distinctions and the educational tracking they imply more readily than we may wish to acknowledge.

These sorts of thoughts and possibilities for critical engagement will continue to come up as we look at other philosophic approaches to educational questions. And now that we have seen in some detail one example of the ramifications for educational thinking of general philosophical conceptions, we can go on to explore how educational ideas may change (or remain the same, for that matter) in the context of quite different systematic approaches to reality, knowledge, society, and the person.

CHAPTER 2

Nature and the Individual

Rousseau's *Emile*

For Plato, in order to achieve individual happiness and a corresponding social strength and security, it is necessary to orient education of all individuals to the place they will have in society. His approach to education, then, is structural, in the sense that we reach an understanding of education's challenges through the structure of the society to which one aspires. Jean-Jacques Rousseau's approach is quite different. If Plato's approach is structural, Rousseau's is temporal. The way to achieve individual happiness and social strength, on Rousseau's view, is to educate individuals in accord with their natural character and capacities. Consequently, the nature of the society properly educated people will produce is not the point of departure, as it is for Plato, but the end result. To show how that result is reached, Rousseau takes us through the education of a single individual, from infancy through adulthood.

Late in *Emile*, which is his extraordinary exploration of education (and much else as well), Rousseau offers the following description of his young charge Emile toward the end of his explicit education:

> Consider my Emile—now past twenty, well formed, well constituted in mind and body, strong, healthy, fit, skillful, robust, full of sense, reason, goodness, and humanity, a man with morals and taste, loving the beautiful, doing the good, free from the empire of cruel passions, exempt from the yoke of opinion, but subject to the law of wisdom and submissive to the voice of friendship, possessing all the useful talents and some of the agreeable ones, caring little for riches, with his means of support in his arms, and not afraid of lacking bread whatever happens. (418–19)[1]

This is how Rousseau imagines the result of the education he has spent the previous twenty years providing to Emile. As a description of a person's character, I would imagine that most of us would be pleased to claim such a young man as the product of our educational endeavors. *Emile* is Rousseau's fictional account of why he thinks that such a person as Emile at twenty ought to be the goal we seek in education and how we may achieve it. As we should expect by now, in developing his answers to those two themes of educational theory, as well as to the others, Rousseau has recourse to his ideas about the nature of reality, knowledge, social and political structures, and human nature.

As a point of departure, we may note that in his short description of Emile at twenty, Rousseau points to the full range of Emile's character traits, both those we might normally attribute to education and those we could plausibly consider the result more of upbringing. This is a distinction Rousseau does not make, largely because he thinks that the educator's role is to enable the full development of a student, and that includes moral, emotional, physical, and social as well as intellectual maturity. For that reason, *Emile* covers the upbringing and education of Emile from birth to the point at which he is able to take his place in the world as a well-formed individual and citizen.

This end, as it turns out, is much more difficult to achieve than one might expect because, in Rousseau's opinion, there is a deep tension between a person as an individual and a person as a strong citizen. The problem is captured from the famous first sentence of the book: "Everything is good as it leaves the hands of the Author of things; everything degenerates in the hands of man" (37). In the natural state of things, including the natural condition of a human being, things are at their best. For this reason, as we will see, Rousseau wants to raise Emile as a "natural man." But Emile cannot be simply a man of nature, fit only for the field or forest; he has to be a social and political man as well, a citizen. This is a difficult matter, though, if "everything degenerates in the hands of man." The challenge is to raise a natural man who is also a virtuous citizen. In Rousseau's treatment, as it turns out, a proper citizen can only be one who has been raised as a natural man because only a natural man can enter social relations without the good in him being distorted and "degenerated." Rousseau's philosophic challenge is to account for the possibility of a natural man as citizen, and his educational challenge is to describe how such a person can be raised.

THE CHILD

Before we begin to consider these difficult matters, a word is in order about the gendered language that has already been used, because it has been used purposefully. Rousseau was (if one may say this without unseemly anachronism) not a feminist. At the appropriate time in his life Emile's attentions will turn to the opposite sex, at which point Rousseau will introduce him to

Sophie. In *Emile*, this happens in Book V, the final chapter of the book, in which Rousseau also describes the education of Sophie. It is, to put it mildly, quite different from the education of Emile. Sophie is to be raised and educated to be a companion for Emile. Of course, he must be a companion to her as well, but the general weight of the experience of each is not equal. As a young man, Emile's experience is primary, and Sophie's is a supporting role. In some respects, Rousseau stood out as an exception in his own time and can speak to us now, but as far as gender roles are concerned, he was very much a product of his times. For that reason, I will use the masculine pronoun when discussing Rousseau's ideas about education more than I might in other cases. We might plausibly imagine, though, that except when he is speaking explicitly about gender roles, Rousseau's view of education and an educated man could in principle apply equally to a woman.

The resolution of the conflict between the natural man and the citizen is the culmination of Rousseau's analysis, and we will work our way to it. To do that, we need to begin with the natural man. If, as Rousseau has said, everything is "good as it leaves the hands of the Author of things," then from his birth Emile embodies the good. Clearly, Rousseau had no use for the idea of original sin, or even the idea that by nature people are morally compromised. If Emile is "good" in his natural condition, then the most desirable path for his development is to allow his natural characteristics and what we might now call instincts to develop. For this reason, Rousseau introduces one of his basic educational ideas, which is his commitment to "negative education." The teacher and even earlier the caregiver need more than anything else to get out of the way. Emile should be permitted to develop more or less unfettered. For this reason, Rousseau argues against swaddling for the infant because it restricts his movements. This principle extends to nearly all of Emile's activities, especially during his early childhood. Of course, he needs to be provided with an environment that is not dangerous for him, so that he can exercise his natural tendencies without hurting himself. The teacher will also be expected to guide Emile's experience so that his natural goodness has an opportunity to develop. At the same time, we have to be careful how we interact with the child. Children will naturally express their needs, at first by crying. In responding to those needs, we are automatically entering into social relations, and thus into dangerous territory. As we engage a crying child, we are either submitting to his will (or perhaps to his whims) or forcing him to submit to our expectations of him. Thus, Rousseau says, the child "must give orders or receive them," and his "first ideas are those of domination or servitude" (48). This is an innocent, but potentially fraught, step toward a socialization that will undermine what is naturally good in Emile. He should not be raised with the desire to please others, nor should he expect others to do as he pleases. One has to be careful.

"Civil man is born, lives, and dies in slavery" (42). For this reason, one of Rousseau's initial concerns has to do with where Emile will spend his time and receive his education, and Rousseau is unequivocal in his answer: "Cities are the abyss of the human species" (59). Perhaps the single most important action we can take in Emile's early education is to remove him from the city as soon as possible. As a material matter, cities are unhealthy, and given the level of sanitation at the time, this point may have been truer then than it is now. But aside from questions of health, if he grows up in a city, Emile will be affected by social conventions and expectations, and these will not be to his benefit. It is better, Rousseau says, for nature to be his teacher, not a governor (61).

As children do, Emile will explore his surroundings, more so as he is able to move on his own. In this way, he gathers impressions that are the basis of the knowledge he will develop. In this regard, Rousseau was something of an empiricist, as was fairly common among educated people in early eighteenth-century Europe. At around the turn of the century, the English philosopher and political figure John Locke had argued that people are born a "tabula rasa," or blank slate, and that everything they learn comes from their experience, by which he meant the sensory engagement with one's environment. This view of how we learn was immensely influential throughout the century, and it differed somewhat from an earlier idea that we are born with at least some innate knowledge. A century earlier, the French philosopher and mathematician René Descartes had argued that people have some ideas innately, including the idea of God. By the eighteenth century, both conceptions were available, and some people came down firmly in one camp or the other. Some others, however, accepted a combined view, and Rousseau was among them. In this respect, his ideas were influential later in the century, not least on Scottish Common Sense figures and, through them and also directly, on such people as Thomas Jefferson. Specifically, while believing that Emile needed to explore his surroundings because that is how he will learn, Rousseau also believed that all people have from birth an innate moral sense, and by their nature express an understanding of what is or is not fair or just.

The moral sense is important because it is in part what will enable sociability later in life. For now, though, in early childhood, the innate sense of justice is a valuable tool in Emile's development. If too much of his experience is with other people, he will develop tendencies to pursue his own wishes, assuming this to be fair and just, even in the face of others' wishes. In this way, even the naturally arising and valuable moral sense can be distorted into habits of imperiousness and domination. It is best, Rousseau thought, to help Emile avoid encounters with others and limit his engagements, as much as possible, to encounters with things, a practice made easier if Emile is moved out of the city. Rousseau's point here is that children will grow angry and resentful if their wills are impeded by other people, but not if they encounter resistance from things. Emile's moral sense, and what he learns, will serve him better if guided properly: "It is important to accustom him early not to give orders either to men, for he is not their master, nor to things, for they do not hear him" (66). Guided properly, this is what Emile will learn and grow to incorporate into his character.

Another advantage of a natural, negative education is that as a consequence of it, Emile will develop both expectations suitable to his human condition and abilities appropriate to his individual talents and gifts. These in turn will make happiness possible for him, both as a child and as an adult. We sometimes think that happiness derives from having whatever we want and that a free person is one who may desire as his whim directs him. Rousseau, however, and somewhat reminiscent of Plato, thought that such a condition is conducive to neither happiness nor freedom. As natural beings, we have some traits and capacities and not others. If after watching birds flap their wings I decide that I also want to fly by flapping my limbs, I will be disappointed. If I believe that my happiness depends on being able to do whatever it occurs to me to do, then unhappiness is likely to be my lot. To avoid such a condition, it is not necessary to diminish our desires, but happiness does require "diminishing the excess of the desires over the faculties and putting power and will in perfect equality" (80). Freedom has a similar requirement: "The truly free man wants only what he can do and does what he pleases. This is my fundamental maxim. It need only be applied to childhood for all the rules of education to flow from it" (84). It is worth noting that through the use of tools and technology generally, it is possible for us to expand our power, and even learn to fly, but the general principle that our desires should accord with our abilities remains applicable.

A natural education is critical to place a child on a path toward an emotional, moral, and intellectual development suited to a fully mature person. A second principle that Rousseau applies throughout his education of Emile is that to the extent possible, Emile should not be told what to think or believe. Rather, he should be guided into circumstances in which he will learn from direct experience whatever it is he needs to know. This applies to everything, from knowledge of the natural world around him to the moral principles he will need in his interactions with others. Some people think, and Rousseau here has in mind no less an authority than John Locke himself, that whenever possible we should reason with children so that they understand what is happening around them and what is expected of them. Rousseau thinks that this is ridiculous, on the grounds that children cannot understand reasoning because their rational capacities are not yet developed. To reason with them is to get their education backward. Children learn from their interaction with their environments. If their environment is limited as much as possible to natural objects rather than social relations, they will learn which of the things around them they can affect and which resist them; they will in that way learn to fit their needs, desires, and abilities within the natural framework of which they are a part. Nothing is to be gained by pretending that we can reason with them: "Of all the faculties of man, reason . . . is the one that develops with the most difficulty and latest. . . . The masterpiece of a good education is to make a reasonable man, and they claim to raise a child by reason!" (89). The time for reason and explanation will come later; for now, a child's best teacher is the world around him.

Because "everything is good as it leaves the hands of the Author of things," Emile learns best from his natural environment, and he may equally well rely on his own natural inclinations. For Rousseau, the most fundamental such inclination in all people is self-regard or self-love. Here he introduces an extremely important distinction between two kinds of self-love, and it is customary and most conducive to understanding in referring to them to use the original French. The two kinds of self-love are what Rousseau calls *amour de soi* and *amour propre*. The first, *amour de soi*, is love of oneself in one's natural condition or circumstances, and it is a most important and valuable instinct or inclination. We might think of it as including what we would call self-preservation, but it is more than that. We do not want simply to survive but to prosper, and we want to prosper because we regard ourselves and our own prospects as important and worthy of prospering. This is self-love as *amour de soi*. It concerns ourselves and our own circumstances. It is not concerned with our prosperity in relation to others. That is *amour propre*, and it is a much more dangerous inclination because desiring our own prosperity relative to others is the source of pride, arrogance, and a host of socially driven tendencies that undermine our natural development. *Amour de soi* is what allows us to grow, develop, expand our capacities, and in the end to achieve the happiness and satisfaction that we all want from a fulfilled life. *Amour propre*, by contrast, and if not handled carefully, can undermine all of that. In Emile's education by "things," so to speak, *amour de soi* arises naturally and is to be recognized and supported. If the educational process is being handled well, *amour propre* will not arise—or at least not in a young child. It will make its appearance later in life, when Emile is introduced into more complex social circumstances. By that time, though, if he is properly developed, his own mature character will blunt its sharp and destructive edge.

Amour de soi is by definition self-oriented, as are young children's lives generally. They early on develop a sense of what is or is not theirs, and Rousseau is concerned that they grasp what makes something theirs so that this sense is not extended beyond its proper range. Emile, he thinks, must begin to grasp what it means for something to be his property. To understand why Rousseau approaches this lesson as he does, a bit of background is needed.

A century before Rousseau, most prominently in the hands of the English political philosopher Thomas Hobbes, Europeans began to use the idea of what was called the "state of nature" as a way of understanding and justifying features of their lives, especially of their political lives. The idea, basically, is that a human being is not by nature social. We have already seen how basic this sense of a person is to Rousseau, and it was an idea common in his time. If human individuals are not by nature social, then society and all its features such as economic and political relations are in some sense artificial. Society is, we might say, a constructed overlay on people's natural condition. The political theorists of the time, including Hobbes, Locke, and Rousseau, used another intellectual device to account for how societies developed out of an asocial natural condition, and that device is what they called the social contract. Each of them had slightly different ideas about this, but they shared the view that in one way or another, people have constructed social relations by implicit or explicit agreement, presumably because people thought society to be in their interests. Whether any of the philosophers actually thought that such an initial agreement ever happened in history is a separate question. They were all convinced, though, that society is a constructed overlay on the natural human condition, and that the legitimacy of social and political structures rests on some sort of agreement among the members of the society or polity. In the American revolutionary context, this idea was expressed when in the Declaration of Independence it is said that government derives its legitimacy "from the consent of the governed," a phrase that the drafters of that document had taken from Locke, who first applied it in his theory of the social contract.

If the natural human condition is asocial, then one has to account for the basis of important social relations, and for many of these thinkers the most important social relation derived from the presence and legitimacy of privately held property. Here, again, John Locke was a critical figure because he developed the conception of the origin and legitimacy of private property that informed much of the social, economic, and political developments of eighteenth-century Europe. Locke acknowledged that in the state of nature, which, keep in mind, is a pre-social condition, and therefore without positive law of any kind, there can be no claim on anyone's part to a privately held possession. How, Locke asked, is an object in the state of nature (for example, a piece of land) transformed into private property? His answer was through human labor. A piece of land simply sitting there, outside of the remit of any legal structure, belongs to no one. But if I come along and "mix my labor with it," to use Locke's language, I thereby transform it from an object in the state of nature into my private property. A piece of virgin land in the state of nature belongs to no one; once I plant a tree on it and the tree bears fruit, then the fruit, the tree, and the land that nourishes it are mine. This is the theoretical basis of private property and private possessions.

Rousseau takes this quite seriously, and he treats it not only as a matter of social and political theory but also as a quite practical matter. In fact, he uses the principle to help Emile grasp what it means for something to be his property. He does not explain any of this to Emile, or reason with him about it, but, in good empiricist fashion, works with Emile to plant a row of beans. Since he is living in the countryside, it will be expected for Emile to be familiar with fields and crops, and even to want to produce something himself. This creates a "teachable moment," we might say today, in which we encourage Emile to plant, and we even help him to work the garden on a piece of land that he identifies. He learns to water the plants, to weed the field, and generally to tend to the garden. But Rousseau makes the lesson more complex than we expect, because in his telling, at one point he and Emile go to the garden only to find it torn up and the beans destroyed. They locate the gardener, who, it turns out, has been cultivating the larger plot of which Emile's garden was a small piece, and we learn that it was the gardener who tore out the beans. He did so, Rousseau and Emile learn, because he had planted melons in that patch, which were destroyed by Emile's beans. What Emile comes to understand from this is that it was the gardener, and not he, who had initially "mixed his labor" with the land, and so the garden was rightfully his, not Emile's. Emile and Rousseau then ask the gardener whether he might let them have a small corner on which to cultivate their beans, and he agrees, on the condition that they do not in the process disturb his plants and his property. They agree, and Emile learns not only what it means for something to belong to him but also, and as important, what it means for something to belong to someone else. In fact, the latter lesson precedes the former in importance (98-99).

Throughout his childhood, Emile's education looks much like this. A great deal of what we are accustomed to teaching children Rousseau thinks is pointless because they are not ready for it. He will not teach Emile principles of morality, for example, because it will, as we might say, go in one ear and out the other. Emile will learn what he should know from his own activities if they are properly guided. It is equally pointless, Rousseau thinks, to teach foreign languages, history, or geography to a child, even at the age of eight, nine, or ten years. As for languages, Rousseau thinks that developing his own language, and the way of engaging the world that it carries with it, is a process not even remotely well along at this point in Emile's development. Pretending to add another language is simply delusional. With respect to something like geography, Rousseau thinks that nothing useful can yet come of it because, as he puts it, "I set down as a fact that after two years of globe and cosmography there is not a single child of ten who, following the rule he has been given, knows how to get from Paris to Saint-Denis" (109–110). Better at this point to help Emile learn his way around his immediate environs. The rudimentary geographical understanding he acquires that way he will be able to expand and generalize when he has the ability and inclination to do so.

And in what may be the greatest surprise, Rousseau even objects to teaching reading to children of this age. Emile, he thinks, is likely to develop an interest in reading when he sees something of value in it, and of course at that point he can and should be helped. But forcing the issue would be precisely the wrong approach: "I am almost certain that Emile will know how to read and write before the age of ten, precisely because it makes very little difference to me that he knows how before fifteen. But I would rather that he never knew how to read if this science has to be bought at the price of all that can make it useful" (117). We teach children how to read, but often what they learn is to avoid it for the rest of their lives.

Rousseau will not teach the young Emile arithmetic or geometry either, and for roughly the same reasons. In his natural efforts to make what he wants out of the elements he finds available to him, he will learn what he needs at this point. In fact, as Rousseau puts it, "I do not intend to teach geometry to Emile; it is he who will teach it to me" (145). In his guided interaction with his environment, his world, Emile learns what he needs to know and develops his strengths and capacities in the most useful way possible. He also has extensive opportunity to develop physically, which is as important for Emile's overall education as anything else.

In these ways, Emile develops "up to the boundaries of childish reason" (158). As far as Rousseau is concerned,

> I see him bubbling, lively, animated, without gnawing cares, without long and painful foresight, whole in his present being, and enjoying a fullness of life that seems to want to extend itself beyond him. . . . His ideas are limited but distinct. If he knows nothing by heart, he knows much by experience. If he reads less well in our books than another child, he reads better in the book of nature. His mind is not in his tongue but in his head. . . . He knows how to speak only one language, but he understands what he says. (159–160)

In this condition, Emile moves to a new stage in his development and in his education.

THE ADOLESCENT

As Emile grows older, the pedagogical principles on which his education is based remain the same, but because his passions, his intellectual abilities, and his moral sensibilities are expanding, so, too, does the content of his education. There are, though, still fields of study for which he is not ready (at least not early in adolescence), so the teacher must remain careful in deciding what to teach and how to teach it. The principle on which the choice of content is to be made, Rousseau tells us, is that at this point in his life it is important for Emile to know not what there is to be known but what for him is useful to know. For example, he is not yet ready to understand social relations or matters of ethics, never mind metaphysics and epistemology. In learning what is useful for him, though, he will gradually build to those most important matters. For now, Emile will seek out what is interesting and useful for him, and Rousseau will make his curricular and pedagogical decision on that basis.

For example, in his wanderings Emile will begin to be curious about what he is seeing not just on the ground, which he has been engaging with all along, but also above him. Rousseau thinks that astronomy will be among the first more advanced topics that will be of interest to Emile, and, of course, it will also be useful to him as it helps him to orient himself in his meanderings. At the same time, Emile can be expected to pay more attention to how he gets from one place to another, and, in this way, he will have his rudimentary lessons in geography. In both cases, it will be useful for Emile to learn by trial and error, because his own mistakes may be the best teachers. One does not want to be too forceful at this point and feed Emile more than he can digest. It is enough, Rousseau thinks, to help him develop a taste for knowing such matters as astronomy and geography. If he develops the desire to understand the world as he encounters and engages it, then he will come of his own accord to an interest in such "sciences." For example, Emile will have noticed how stones of various materials act toward each other, and Rousseau will use Emile's observations in this regard to begin to teach him about magnetic objects and magnetism in general. At that point he is already on the path to rudimentary physics and other natural sciences. One can imagine that in similar ways he can develop a knowledge of basic botany, zoology, and even geology.

Once Emile is ready, Rousseau will give him the one book that he wants Emile to read, and that, interestingly enough, is *Robinson Crusoe* (184–185). This book captured the imagination of early eighteenth-century Europe precisely because it represents a man in relation to nature, without complex social relations, Friday notwithstanding. Rousseau could recognize a kindred spirit, and he thought that Emile would, too. Moreover, Emile would, presumably, want to some extent to imitate Crusoe, since their conditions were quite similar, and in doing so he would learn a great deal about the natural world and what its contents are good for. He will also learn more about what he no doubt would already have encountered, and that is agriculture. Rousseau wants Emile to know how to work the fields and to grow his food. Its utility is obvious, but it also represents an appreciation of a person's intimate and symbiotic relation with nature. We might also point out, though Rousseau does not make a point of it himself, that in eighteenth-century France, the most influential theory of economics and the basis of wealth was what is called physiocracy, which grounded a nation's wealth and economic health in agriculture. Again, in this regard, Rousseau was a child of his time and place. As for Emile, the countryside will teach him more than just growing things, because he will also engage in the processes of toolmaking, which involves him in blacksmithing and woodworking, which in turn bring him to metallurgy and carpentry.

At this point, Rousseau turns his attention to the passions, as with puberty Emile's emotional life begins to exert itself. He has a firm background, based in experience and usefulness, in the knowledge and understanding of his natural environment. He has developed this understanding in the most reliable way, through direct experience, and independently of pressure from his teacher or from any social expectations. He is as natural a young man as he can be, and this puts him in especially good stead as attention turns, as it must, to social relations. The passion that serves him best at this point, and it is one that has been allowed to flourish all along, is *amour de soi*, which is, so Rousseau claims, the source of the other passions. Recall that given the assumption with which the book begins, that whatever is natural is good, and the second conviction, that *amour de soi* is the source of not only self-development but also virtue, it ought not to be surprising that Rousseau regards people as having a natural benevolence. This is a decidedly different conception of human being from one that became prevalent in later times, including our own, that people are by nature self-serving, often at others' expense if need be. Rousseau recognizes that people can and often do act in this way, but he thinks that in behaving in such ways people are expressing not their inherent natures but a distortion of their natures, largely as a result of the corrupting influence of society. The problem is not self-interest and *amour de soi* but a love of self in relation to another, *amour propre*.

The challenge in education, then, is not to curb a mistakenly assumed natural tendency to prevail over others but to cultivate a natural benevolence, which becomes all the more necessary and difficult as Emile enters the broader society (214). If allowed to develop, the urge to advance oneself at the expense of others or even to evaluate oneself in relation to others (both born of *amour propre*) gives rise to jealousy and pride. If these problems take root in early adolescence, they are extremely difficult to expel. This danger is related to sex and Emile's education about sex. Rousseau is quite concerned about this, not because of modesty but because at this point in Emile's life, things can go quite wrong. With respect to talking with Emile about sex, he advises honesty and truthfulness but also saying as little as possible. The reason is that in these early teen years Emile is simultaneously driven to an interest in sex and less able than before or after to incorporate it into his emotional life. As Rousseau puts it, "if you are not sure of keeping him ignorant of the difference between the sexes until he is sixteen, take care that he learn it before he is ten" (217). Before ten or twelve, Emile can learn and somewhat understand biological facts of the matter without their meaning and import being swamped by passion and, as we might say today, hormones. By sixteen, he can be expected to be sufficiently mature to manage his passions well enough to develop a healthy and beneficial understanding of sex. The years in between are a much more fraught time in this regard. This is one of the more important of the areas in which a distortion of the passions in early development can have lifelong detrimental consequences, both for Emile and for anyone with whom he has sexually inflected relations.

The developmental, and pedagogical, key is to introduce Emile gradually into social relations of various kinds, while always attempting to have his sense of himself not depend on others. We do not want him to be insensitive to others or to ignore them; quite the opposite. Ideally, we will be able to help Emile develop a sense of sympathy for others, or pity as he sees them in their suffering. From his own experience, Emile will already know suffering, so he will recognize it in others. If Emile sees that others react to suffering as he does (and we can expect that he will be able to do so), then his natural benevolence will cause him to feel care and concern, rather than *schadenfreude* or self-satisfaction in not suffering whatever he encounters around him: "It is by these roads and other similar ones . . . that it is fitting to penetrate the heart of a young adolescent in order to arouse the first emotions of nature and to develop his heart and to extend it to his fellow" (226).

We are now broaching the area of moral development and education. The more Emile engages with others in social relations, the more he can be expected to compare himself with the people he encounters. *Amour propre* cannot be avoided entirely, only managed and guided. One of the features of social reality that we can expect Emile to notice quickly is inequality. This may be a surprise for Emile, because in the natural condition in which he has been raised there is no warning of it. As Rousseau puts it, "In the state of nature there is a de facto equality that is real and indestructible. . . . In the civil state there is a de jure equality that is chimerical and vain" (236). In fact, the social situation is so deceptive, because of de jure equality and de facto inequality, that Rousseau says it is necessary to break one of his own rules and to approach the issue not from direct experience but from the study of others. Emile at this point is introduced to the study of history. This is itself a dangerous road to travel because the study of history can be perilous. First, it is not obvious from which vantage point it is best to view the events of the past, and it is tempting to read the past with an arrogant presumption of one's own superiority. To read history this way is to defeat the purpose. Another problem is that in the study of history we are looking at past people and their doings through the eyes of historians, since most of us do not study historical times, events, and people through primary documents. This means that the events (and, more important, their meanings) have been digested by someone else, so that we are getting an understanding secondhand. This can be a problem even with the best of historians. Consequently, Rousseau wants Emile to be as positivistic as possible in his approach to history: "The worst historians for a young man are those who make judgments. Facts! Facts! And let him make his own judgments. It is thus that he learns to know men" (239).

As Emile becomes more and more familiar with people and society, past and present, there are pitfalls that should be anticipated and avoided. *Amour propre*, ever present, may incline him to wish himself to be in the circumstances of someone else. Such envy and comparative self-evaluation are not good for Emile, even if, as Rousseau says, he would prefer to be Socrates or Cato. It is of course fine for Emile to want to improve himself, and there may be many models in his study of history whom he would like to emulate. The emphasis, though, should be on his life and on how he wishes to live it, not on envy of another. Conversely, Emile must also be steered clear of developing a sense of superiority. The study of history—or current affairs, for that matter—can easily lead us to think that our fellow creatures are mad, or at least seriously mentally underdeveloped. That may be true in any given case, but it is not an attitude we want Emile to take toward others. He is at bottom no better than anyone else, nor they than he, and we want him to feel and understand that. Emile's natural benevolence, and his developed sense of empathy and equality with others, can be expected to incline him to calmness and equanimity in his dealings with people. He has received, we might say, an education for peace: "Emile dislikes both turmoil and quarrels. . . . This spirit of peace is an effect of his education which, not having fomented *amour propre* and a high opinion of himself, has diverted him from seeking his pleasures in domination and in another's unhappiness" (250–251).

One issue that Rousseau has not yet raised with Emile is religion, which, because it is so prominent a feature of social life and the lives of the people with whom Emile is coming into contact, is now a topic that needs to be addressed. Rousseau was himself a religious man, after his own lights, but he thought that it is a mistake to introduce children to religion. As with other important and complex topics or fields of study, it is not appropriate, he thought, to introduce students to something they cannot understand, and children cannot understand religion. It is a fair guess that most adults do not understand it either. If children develop habits with respect to ideas they cannot understand, the only possible result is distortion and confusion.

Religion is too important for that, he thought. The only thing a child can do with religious ideas and propositions is to repeat words. But surely the point of learning religion is not simply to repeat meaningless words. If that were the case, a trained parrot could be a bishop. It is far better to wait until Emile is mature enough to make some sense of religious ideas, and he will then be free to make whatever use of them he sees fit.

The even minimal introduction of religious matters brings Rousseau and Emile to the study of speculative matters, which include metaphysics and epistemology. Like Plato, Rousseau realizes that much of what he thinks about education flows from these general ideas, and so he is at pains to clarify them for us. Moreover, he believes that for Emile to have control over his own life, his intellectual maturity is no less important that the emotional and social. To discuss his ideas about nature, knowledge, and religion, Rousseau uses the literary device of a story told to him by a certain peripatetic vicar, whose personality traits to some extent resemble those Rousseau would like Emile to have. He is a kind of Stoic, of the sort that Rousseau admires. This vicar tells us what he believes in a set piece called "The Creed of the Savoyard Priest" (266–313).

Like many intellectuals in Europe and the Americas at this time, Rousseau was suspicious of religious authority and tradition. His suspicion of prevailing religious institutions brought down on him the wrath of the Catholic leadership in France and the Calvinist leadership in Geneva, but, to our edification, it impelled him to articulate what he thinks are the good reasons for accepting certain religious ideas and commitments. If we do not blindly accept tradition, then we need other sources for knowledge, and this rule applies to religious knowledge no less than to knowledge of nature, people, and morals. Here we find Rousseau advocating the blend of empiricism and rationalism to which we alluded earlier. He begins by noting as an obvious point that he exists, as René Descartes had done a century earlier, though while Descartes asserts that it is the fact that he thinks (*cogito*) that indicates his own existence, Rousseau ascribes his confidence to the fact that he senses.[2] In this way, unlike Descartes, Rousseau readily concedes his own empiricism and commitment to experience as the source of knowledge. He also has no use for skepticism, which holds that we cannot know about the world around us, or even whether there is a world around us. For Rousseau, such a view is a self-indulgent intellectual dead end and not worthy of serious people. We are to assume that someone as well educated as Emile will never be attracted to such nonsense.

We are, then, able to know the world around us through experience. About that world, there are several points we can make. Rousseau accepted the recent discoveries of Isaac Newton, like most of his contemporaries, and the general view of the material world that they expressed. Among the prevalent Newtonian ideas about nature is that matter is passive, which Newton had expressed in the First Law of Motion, to the effect that an object at rest stays at rest until acted on by another in motion. Newton in this regard was accepting the passivity of matter, an assumption about matter that had prevailed unchallenged at least since Aristotle, and Rousseau accepted it as well. There were challenges to this view at the time—for example, by the American colonial intellectual and political figure Cadwallader Colden—but they were a minority voice.[3] In this respect, Rousseau sided with the majority, and he also accepted the other common, general view of nature as a machine. The entire physical universe was a mechanical system that could be understood, as Newton had shown, on mechanical principles.

This view had two important implications for Rousseau. The first is that though nature is a machine and matter is passive, it is clear that there is also a principle of activity that can be noticed in experience, in our sense of ourselves. It is clear that we can act on the basis of our own wills and determination. Unlike physical objects, we do not stay at rest until acted on by an outside force. We are capable of moving ourselves, which for Rousseau implies that though we are obviously material bodies, we cannot be described in wholly material and mechanical terms. The human self, or the soul, is a different sort of thing, an active thing, and therefore not material. Unlike many other philosophers of the time, Rousseau is reluctant to adopt the terminology that was in common use to describe this dualism. Descartes, for example, had referred to material and mental substances, but Rousseau refers simply to active and passive "principles." Whatever the terminology, though, Rousseau clearly endorses a dualistic conception of human being.

The second significant implication of the view of nature as passive and mechanical is that it leads Rousseau, as it had led and continues to lead many others, to arguments for the existence of God that he is careful to make clear. The first is a version of what is commonly called the cosmological argument for the existence of God, which in Rousseau's hands goes roughly as follows: If matter is passive, as Newton has shown that it is, then the first cause of motion in matter cannot be matter itself. The universe in its continuous and regular motion does not explain itself. There are causes of this or that motion, and there are causes of those causes. This regress, however, cannot go on infinitely. Therefore, there must be something other than the material world, something outside nature, that is the cause of its motion. We have seen that through our own individual wills we are able to initiate motion within nature, and we can generalize this observation to say that motion of the universe as a whole is similarly due to the exercise of will. Clearly, however, it cannot be our finite will that is responsible for the motion of nature generally. There must exist, therefore, a will that is supernatural, in the sense of being outside of nature, and that is the first cause or first mover of the natural world and all that is in it. That first mover is what we call God.

The second argument for the existence of God that Rousseau believes to be implied by nature's passivity is what is commonly called the argument from design, or the teleological argument, and it was also widely accepted in the eighteenth century. When we observe the world, we notice that there is order and design in it. Objects do not move about haphazardly, and the order that we see in the smallest components and the largest reaches of nature suggest an intelligence responsible for it. If we were not to posit such an intelligence, then we would have to say that the order is random, and there is no good reason to think that the design in nature is spontaneous. Imagine, he says, appealing to an analogy that was common at the time, that we are wandering about in a field or on the beach, and we encounter a watch on the ground. Even if we do not know what the object is, as we study the complexity of its structure and the meticulous design required for it to continue to operate, our natural inference will be that some intelligence was responsible for the watch's order and design. No other inference would be even remotely plausible. But if we are to make such an inference to account for the complexity and design of a watch, we surely would be justified in making a comparable inference to account for the complexity and design of the universe. If a watch has an intelligent designer, then so does nature as a whole.

These two arguments assume the ancient idea that matter is passive, and the modern notion of nature as mechanical. If we were to hold a different set of assumptions about the traits of nature, then these two arguments would be much less plausible. But that is a discussion for another time. For Rousseau, they give him what he calls "articles of faith" that allow him to fill out other aspects of his general philosophic conception. He has described God with the attributes of intelligence, power, and will, and he explicitly adds another, which is goodness. God is not only an intelligence that is sufficiently powerful to animate the world and to give it order but also the source of nature's inherent goodness. The only justification Rousseau offers for attributing goodness to God is that it is, he says, a necessary consequence of the intelligence and power that is able to create the world in the first place. Whether that is a sufficient rationale is an open question; what is clear is that the goodness Rousseau attributes to God is the reason he can say with such confidence that "everything is good as it leaves the hands of the author of things."

A second implication of the goodness of God and nature is Rousseau's attribution to people of a natural benevolence, itself an aspect of each individual's innate moral sense. This view in turn gives Rousseau his distinctive philosophical anthropology. Though our knowledge of the world is largely due to our experience, our understanding of what we learn, and of ourselves, is due to the impetus we take from our moral sense to reach the highest truth and beauty concerning the world. It is also the impetus that, if not distorted, drives how we live our lives. Since we are driven by our own natures to pursue the good, Rousseau proposes, the most coherent way to understand our own freedom is as the freedom to will the good and to pursue justice. This has a Platonic sound to it, though for Plato justice is achieved when the individual soul and society are properly ordered through the wisdom of the rulers, whereas for Rousseau, justice in the individual is achieved when our natural propensities are permitted to develop without social distortion.

The rest of the priest's profession of faith is taken up by his rejection of religion based on revelation or tradition and his insistence that the most reasonable and defensible faith is the natural, rather than revealed, religion he has described. These are the conceptions of nature, knowledge, human being, and religion to which Emile is exposed. Because they reflect the principles of Emile's own upbringing, and therefore of his experience, we can expect him to be curious about them and to reflect on them to the extent that he is able. He does not need to grasp them at once, since they will be with him his whole life. And what he does with them in the long run will be up to him. Rousseau clearly thinks, though, that because they are so reasonable and clear, Emile can be expected to find them congenial ways to understand himself, his world, and his God.

There remain two most important aspects of Emile's development and his education, both bringing him into complex social relations. At this point in his life, Emile's attention will be taken by matters of the heart, and his life will advance necessarily as a member of a specific society.

THE CITIZEN

We should recall the description of Emile at the age of twenty years with which the chapter began. This is the young man who will now take on a romantic partner. As one might imagine, not everyone can be suitable for such a person. Emile's life partner—Rousseau calls her Sophie—must herself be educated in such a way that she and Emile can forge a bond that will be beneficial for them both. Here, though, Rousseau takes a position that is difficult for us to accept because it clashes so thoroughly with how in our time we think about women's place in society, the equality of women and men, and the education of women. The most it is reasonable to do at this point is to note his position, wonder how it is possible for a thinker as interesting as Rousseau to be quite so retrograde in his approach to women, and move on. In general, I will simply assume that it is possible to bracket his account of women's education as a peculiarity of him, his place, and his time and assume that, for our purposes, it is possible to generalize the principles of Emile's education so that whatever we may think is valuable in it may equally well be applied to Sophie.

Rousseau makes clear his disagreement with Plato with respect to women's role in society and their education. Recall that in the *Republic*, Plato argued that the differences between men and women were irrelevant with respect to social roles, status, and education. Rousseau refers to Plato's "civil promiscuity which throughout confounds the two sexes in the same employments and in the same labors and which cannot fail to engender the most intolerable abuses" (363). In Rousseau's opinion, men and women should complement, not reflect, one another. They will of course share some personality traits and abilities. They will be, as we might say today, comfortable in their own skin, not vain and not envious, generous and empathetic. But they will have very different strengths. Girls, and Sophie is no exception, are docile and subject to proprieties, Rousseau says. They are by their natures not able to examine difficult matters rationally, religion among the more important of them. Unlike Emile, therefore, Sophie will have the religious ideas of her mother and later those of her husband (377). Since they are not able to engage abstract ideas, as they get older, their education is not oriented to understanding the world but "directed to the study of men or to the pleasing kinds of knowledge that have only taste as their aim" (386).

All of Sophie's education is based on the assumption that her function in life will be to support Emile. They will have a satisfying domestic life, but each in different ways and for different reasons. She will enable him to be an active, contributing member of his society, without being one herself. Rousseau is clear about this point: "In the union of the sexes each contributes equally to the common aim, but not in the same way. From this diversity arises the first assignable difference in the moral relations of the two sexes. One ought to be active and strong, the other passive and weak. One must necessarily will and be able; it suffices that the other put up little resistance" (358).

There is little point to developing the details of this perspective. All of Sophie's education, by contrast with Emile's, is structured for this supporting role. When they have both reached the point that independently they cannot develop further, they will be introduced. At first, each is a curiosity to the other, and there is a rather elaborate dance that Rousseau puts them both through before they recognize that they love and need each other. Here, though, Rousseau reveals to Emile that he is in fact not quite ready to settle down with Sophie. He is entering adulthood, and though a satisfying domestic arrangement is certainly one aspect of a successful adult life, it will not work unless Emile is also prepared to enter society as a full-fledged citizen, and that is not yet the case. To reach that point, Rousseau tells Emile that he must leave Sophie for two years of travel, after which he may return and settle down with her.

To be a social individual, Rousseau says, it is necessary to know the nature of men, and Emile's knowledge in this respect is not yet sufficient. His own character is fully formed at this point, and as a product of a negative education and the encouragement of his natural proclivities, Emile is as mature—intellectually, morally, and emotionally—as one could reasonably expect. But his experience is more with nature than with people, and even his study of history, as valuable as that is, has its limits. He needs a broader experience if he is to know people as social creatures, and he needs to see them in various social and political contexts. The purpose of his travel, then, is not frivolous or a matter of entertainment. On the contrary, it is a critical piece of his education as a social being.

Emile's challenge in his travels is to explore relations with fellow citizens, so he now must undertake the study of government. We are now confronting the conflict with which we began the discussion of Emile's education, which is the tension between his place as a natural man and the necessity that he live as a citizen in a society and a polity. Rousseau would appear to agree with Aristotle in this regard, that the human being is a political animal. Another way to pose the problem is to ask the question: How is it possible for a properly developed and educated person (Emile in our case) to live as a citizen, given that society is a threat to his natural character? To answer this question and resolve the conflict, Rousseau introduces the concept of the "general will." This is a difficult concept, the meaning of which is at best obscure. Let us first see what Rousseau has to say about it and why he thinks it is crucial, and then an interpretation will be possible.[4]

Rousseau has said that Emile must travel in order to study several governments and evaluate them as to their adequacy. In order to do that, though, one first has to have a sense of the "principles of government," by which Rousseau means an adequate theory of government that will provide the criteria to evaluate existing governing arrangements and state institutions. Political theory is necessary, and for this Rousseau is reluctant to rely on anyone's authority. He is well aware of the work of Hobbes, Locke, Montesquieu, and others, but he finds them all inadequate to the task.

To devise an adequate theory of government, we must begin at the beginning, and the beginning for Rousseau is the state of nature, a condition which in principle is prior to society, law, and government. Even in the state of nature, he notes, there are families, and individuals grow up subject to some degree of authority. Beyond families, however, the only basis on which to expand social relations is the agreement of people to do so, which is the social contract. The nature of that agreement is what forms the basis of legitimate government. Rousseau provides a succinct statement of what he takes the social contract to imply: "Each of us puts his goods, his person, his life, and all his power in common under the supreme direction of the general will, and we as a body accept each member as a part indivisible from the whole" (460). This is the first mention of the general will, and it is the key to the creation of the *body politic*, which is to say the community as a single polity. A citizen, as a member of the body politic, is thus obligated in two directions—as a member of the polity to the whole, and as an embodiment of the whole to the other individuals who constitute the polity. It is the general will that orients these relations.

In creating the polity through the contract, the people have established only one authority, and that is themselves collectively. This authority is the sovereign, and the sovereign is itself nothing more than the general will. Since each "signatory" to the contract has subjected himself to the whole, or to the general will, then the freedom that the contract enables is one's subjection to oneself through the general will. The source of positive law in this case is the expression of the general will. The most defensible political arrangement is one that enables the general will, in the normative form of law, to express itself such that individual wills accord with it. The consistency of individual wills with the general will is the condition of freedom, and that form of government is best which is conducive to freedom so understood. Moreover, when particular wills accord with the general will, little government is needed (465).

Clearly, the idea of the general will is critical for Rousseau's understanding of political life and of the character of a citizen, and by implication what it is to educate for citizenship. Unfortunately, its meaning is not at all clear, and it begs for interpretation. One of the reasons for the difficulty is that Rousseau is struggling here with a fundamental problem of philosophy, which is the relation of the one and the many. In social and political respects, the problem of the one and the many amounts to the problem of how a "one," or a unity, can be forged out of the many. The motto of the United States— *e pluribus unum*—simply states the fact; Rousseau is trying to explain how such a fact is possible. To put the point more plainly, the question amounts to how a populace, a "many," constitutes a community or state, a "one."

There are many possible answers to this question, and political philosophers have been grappling with it for a very long time. Plato's answer, as we know, is that the state, or the one, is the context in which individuals have their place and their meaning. This is the reason that for Plato, individuals are raised and educated in order to play a certain role in the community, which in this case is to meet the needs of the state and, if handled properly, their own natures. Some have understood this approach as somewhat conducive to fascism, in that the health of the state is more important than the health or happiness of any of its individuals. If one were to say in an unqualified way that individuals should be raised and educated to meet the needs of the state, and that the interests of the state take precedence over the interests of the individual, then one would be expressing something like fascism.

Plato, of course, would not have put it in quite this way, largely because he believed that the happiness of individuals and the health of the state are not in conflict and that, if organized properly, each implies and guarantees the other. This is the reason the topic of the *Republic* is so important, and it is the reason, as far as Plato is concerned, that education is critical to individual and social prosperity. One problem with this sort of pleading on Plato's behalf, though, is that fascist thinkers also argue that the best interests of individuals are served through the state. In the case of fascism, however, there is typically an enemy, often an internal enemy, that threatens the purity and health of the state and against which the citizens must be vigilant. This view is not in Plato. Even the guardians have as a function not to purge the state of impurities, as fascists will often say, but to protect the state, and thereby its people, against enemies. Whether in the end it is possible to maintain a Platonic conception of the relation of the individual and the state without collapsing into fascism remains an open question.

Another approach to the problem of crafting a political unity out of a popular multiplicity is traditional liberalism, which in one way or another provides the basic conceptual underpinnings of the modern state. Modern liberalism developed sufficiently through the eighteenth century to inform the most significant political developments of the time, the American and French revolutions, and it has developed greater maturity through the nineteenth and twentieth centuries, as it continues to develop today. Liberalism places its primary focus on the individual. It is the individual who has rights and who can claim the recognition of those rights on the part of other individuals and of the state. Sometimes these rights are considered "natural," or, as the American Declaration of Independence describes it, some of people's rights are "endowed by their creator." Other fundamental statements of liberal principles (for example, John Stuart Mill's *On Liberty* from 1859) explicitly reject the idea of "natural" rights, arguing that the rights that individuals should have derive from their social condition. In either case, liberalism's central concern is with the individual and the individual's rights. This leaves liberalism with the challenge of how to ground the state. From its earliest days, the liberal justification of the state is to protect individuals' rights and entitlements. One of the earliest statements of the rights the state must protect comes from John Locke's *Two Treatises on Government* (1689), in which he argues that the basic role of the state is to protect the rights of life, liberty, and property. The Declaration of Independence altered that formulation slightly to "life, liberty, and the pursuit of happiness." Whatever the details, the "one" of liberal theory derives its purpose and justification from the rights of the many.

Given Rousseau's emphasis on the natural, nonsocial individual, one would expect him to endorse a more or less liberal position on the nature of the state, its justification, and its relation to the citizen. His thinking, however, is more complex than that, and he has problems with both the Platonic and the liberal alternatives. The Platonic, "statist" approach tends to be tyrannical, in the sense that the individual is made subject to the interests of the state. If upbringing and education are organized that way, he thought, then the individual is being distorted and his natural, virtuous development is impeded. This is what Rousseau means when he says early in *Emile* that we have to choose between raising a man and raising a citizen, because we cannot do both—or at least not at the beginning. If we raise a citizen, he says, we are preventing the development of the man.

But liberalism, he thought, makes the opposite mistake. With its emphasis on the individual, it can conceive only of a many, but not a "one." Some liberals have happily noticed this, as, for example, did Margaret Thatcher when she famously claimed that there is no such thing as society. Carl Schmitt, the influential German critic of liberalism through the first half of the twentieth century, makes a similar objection.[5] In liberal theory, Rousseau might say, there is no unity of the many, only a plurality. Various illustrations are possible. In the economy, for example, the "free market," which is a central component of liberal theory, provides no sort of community of individuals; it is merely a collection of interacting individuals each pursuing his or her own interests, as Adam Smith initially described it in 1776 in *The Wealth of Nations*. In politics, to offer another example, liberal democracy again provides no community but is merely an arena for competing interests to pursue the power necessary to reach their ends. To understand Rousseau's objections, it is important to see how and why a collection or multiplicity of individuals differs from a "unity" or a community. This is itself another difficult and complex question, but one way to understand it is to say that a community requires shared interests among its members. It is not simply a collection of people but a group of people with something in common. This common or shared element can in principle be anything. The American philosopher Josiah Royce, for example, spoke about a community of memory, wherein people share a past, and a community of hope, in which the shared element is common aspirations.[6] In the next chapter, we will see that John Dewey uses the idea of common interests extensively in his thinking. We will take up more directly this question of the relation of the individual to the community in chapter 7.

For now, the point is to understand why Rousseau rejects liberalism's emphasis on the individual, and the reason seems to be that something must be shared, or held in common, by people in order to engender a unity or community, and whatever this is provides meaning and purpose for individuals. He does not use this example, but we might think about a musical note in relation to a musical phrase of which it is a part. A single note in isolation (for example, middle C on a piano keyboard) has some characteristics, but it has no significance or meaning. However, when it is part of a musical phrase, it may take on a great deal of significance. In the key of C major, the note can take on the meaning of completion or resolution, a relaxing of tension and a return home. All of this complex meaning can be carried by middle C, but only because it shares with other notes the context of a specific musical phrase. Something like this, presumably, is what Rousseau has in mind when he says that a multiplicity is not a community, and therefore the individualism of liberalism fails to enable the creation of a unity out of a meaningful many. So statism of the Platonic sort does not value the individual enough, and liberalism does not value the community enough. A third alternative is required.

The alternative as Rousseau develops it is in his concept of the general will. In a society composed of natural men, which is to say of people brought up and educated as Emile has been, all of the individuals will share the traits and implications of natural, undistorted reason and of natural virtue, or the moral sense. Rousseau, we should emphasize, is not a relativist of any kind. He believed that objective truth and "the good" will not differ from individual to individual. Our common natural condition, we might say, reveal to us both the world and our responsibilities in it in roughly similar ways. It is this shared understanding, rationality, and moral sense that constitute the general will. In a society of natural men, then, the individual will, which is to say each person's interests, good, virtue, and so forth, will accord with the general will. This is what it means for us to be free. We are not compelled by the sovereign (for example, the state) to think, feel, or act in this way or that. On the contrary, it is our very natures, which we have in common, that constitute and express the community, such that our individual wills and the general will by nature coincide.

Rousseau did not want to commit himself to any specific form of political arrangement. Specific forms of state organization (for example, monarchy, republic, oligarchy, or some other) are various ways that the general will is expressed and executed in a society. Not only do different societies embrace differing political structures of these kinds, but Rousseau also believed that no one of them is necessarily better than the others. Local conditions of specific times and places, he thought, could render one or another form appropriate. In some cases, monarchy may be called for, in other cases a republic, and so forth. However it is in any specific case, freedom and justice require not the authority of the majority of individual wills, as liberal democracy might suggest, nor the subservience of individual wills to the state, as a Platonic statism implies. Freedom and justice, rather, require the compatibility of the individual will with the general will, a condition possible only in a society composed of free, natural men and women. These are people educated as Emile has been (and as Sophie has been, if we are prepared to grant Rousseau the sexism embedded in the distinction between them as he draws it).

With this understanding of the relation of the citizen to the state, and with his experience of several different forms of government and the societies and polities that embody them, Emile returns home from his travels. He will have developed considerably in maturity not only from broader social experience but also from having in his travels learned one or two additional languages, along with a great deal in natural history and the arts. He has also learned that his wealth is not in property or in the things he may accumulate but in himself and the natural propensities he embodies. He has learned, in a spirit that is reminiscent of Buddhism, to value what he has without being attached to it, which is to say without giving it the power to define or dominate him. As for his place as citizen, "Whatever country it is, he owes it what is most precious to man—the morality of his actions and the love of virtue. . . . The public good, which serves others only as a pretext, is a real motive for him alone. He learns to struggle with himself, to conquer himself, to sacrifice his interests to the common interest . . . [laws] give him the courage to be just even among wicked men . . . [they] have taught him to reign over himself" (473).

Thus educated, Emile the man and citizen takes up his life with Sophie and his place in society.

EDUCATION

Like Plato, Rousseau holds that the general role or purpose of education in a society is to enable the development of the virtuous individual and a sound, equally virtuous, polity. Rather unlike Plato, though, Rousseau thinks that the best route to these ends is to educate the natural person, and here we can begin to speak about the person rather than the man. If we simply leave aside Rousseau's sexist assumptions about what girls and women are or are not capable of, there is nothing in his account of the goals and methods of the education of Emile that could not apply equally to Sophie. With only minimal apologies to Rousseau, then (and on this point he deserves a good talking-to rather than an apology), we will summarize his views as if they are intended for any person. This is the only possible way they might be useful for us.

Rousseau's emphasis on the natural person is somewhat unusual for his time. Roughly a century before him, to give the most well-known example, the English political philosopher Thomas Hobbes, who had written one of the first analyses of the concept of the social contract, referred in his *Leviathan* (1651) to life in the state of nature as "solitary, poor, nasty, brutish, and short." Nature, which for Hobbes and Rousseau is the condition outside of the structures of society and an organized polity, is, Hobbes thought, decidedly unpleasant. Rousseau thinks differently, in that nature for him is entirely and absolutely good, as he states in no uncertain terms in the opening words of *Emile*. This general, metaphysical conception, together with his view of society as tending to corrupt its members, is what leads Rousseau to believe that education must focus on what is natural in the child and provide the conditions that allow natural goodness to develop. A second general goal, which is the virtuous state, follows from the same principle. The third goal of education, related to the first two, is also a consequence of Rousseau's social and political theory, and that is the creation of the citizen. It is only for the natural person that the individual will can conform to the general will, which is the condition of freedom, citizenship, and a properly ordered state.

We know that Rousseau disagreed with Plato about the abilities of women and the reasons for their education. He thought that boys and girls (and young men and women) should receive very different educations, as a consequence of both his idea that they are different by nature and the notion that they have different social functions. It is in man's nature to be a citizen, he believed, and it is in woman's nature to assist him. He also disagreed with Plato, interestingly enough, in refusing to make the kind of class distinctions that Plato made. Aside from the distinctions based on gender, Rousseau thought that all people are by nature equal, and it is therefore in all their interests, as well as in the interest of society, that they be educated in the ways that will enable the natural character of all to emerge. In fact, Rousseau's sense of class equality renders his gender differentiations more striking.

Rousseau pays a great deal of attention to the content of education, more so than does Plato. The reason has to do with his understanding of a person's inherent traits, of how a person's abilities develop over time, as well as his conceptions of how learning happens and knowledge is achieved. Rousseau's empiricism, which is to say his view that knowledge comes from experience, is the direct source of his recommendation that whenever possible, a child's learning should come from his or her own direct experience. Such experience, to be of pedagogical value, cannot be haphazard, but that is a point to which we will return below when we discuss methods of instruction. For now, the important point is to be clear about the impact of Rousseau's empiricism. We have also seen, though, that his belief in experience as the source of knowledge was not absolute, a point that distinguished him from some other prominent thinkers of his time, most notably Locke and the Scottish Enlightenment philosopher David Hume. Rousseau believed that even though we are born to a considerable extent with a mind that can be described as a blank slate, which is then filled in, to continue the metaphor, by experience, we are also born with an innate moral sense. The moral sense, if the teacher can prevent it from being distorted or obscured, serves the child as an instinctive guide in drawing lessons from experience.

And eventually, when the right time comes in a child's development, the innate moral sense generates the content of moral instruction, especially as it guides the young adult through the challenges and difficulties of social life.

It is clear, however, that Rousseau's philosophical anthropology has the strongest impact on his sense of the content of education. The two most basic aspects of the nature of human being, Rousseau held, are our innate goodness and benevolence, and our passion for our own successful trajectory in life that he calls *amour de soi*. The teacher must be alert to a child's emotional development, but because of the relation between *amour de soi* and *amour propre*, it is critical that the former not be permitted to transform into the latter, especially early in a child's life. The moral content of a child's education is to focus on his interest in himself and on what interests him. In that case he will learn because it matters to him. What has to be avoided is the temptation a child will eventually have to compare himself to others and to evaluate himself in relation to them. Because of *amour de soi*, a child's education must be self-centered. This is also the reason that a child must be carefully taught what property is, which includes what it means for something to be his and, at least as important, what it means for something to belong to someone else.

Another important feature of Rousseau's understanding of human being is that he was one of the first influential thinkers to advance the idea that childhood is a distinct phase in a person's development. This is the reason that he was so careful to emphasize the introduction of educational content with an eye on a child's level of development. Early on, as one would expect, a child's activity is largely physical, which Rousseau thinks should be cultivated more systematically as the child grows, because in the end, physical development is as important to a person as intellectual and moral growth. A child's early experience in the countryside will also likely give him a familiarity with plants and animals, an attraction that can be deepened into a knowledge of horticulture and husbandry as the child grows.

Academic skills and fields of study are also subject to the levels of a child's development and are not to be forced. In this regard, we find Rousseau advocating against trying to reason with children, on the grounds that early in life, children are not sufficiently developed to engage in rational inquiry or even understanding. Such abilities are the consequences of a good education, not the starting points. Similarly, and equally surprisingly, Rousseau advocates against teaching a child to read. First, it will be much more successful to teach a child to read when she expresses an interest in doing so. More important, though, Rousseau believes that if we introduce topics and skills before a child is able to handle them, we are likely to end up with no skill, or no appreciation, or some sort of distortion. In the case of reading, he is concerned that a child forced to learn to read too early will grow to dislike reading. He offers a similar analysis, and for similar reasons, of the introduction too early of instruction in religion. In that case, the problem is that a child is simply too undeveloped intellectually to understand the difficult and abstract concepts that constitute religious belief and is therefore liable either to understand nothing or to take on absurd or even monstrous conceptions.

Other subjects are to be introduced as a child develops. The sciences are likely to come first because of the child's continuous interaction with nature, and mathematics will also be possible as a result. As she matures, the more abstract subjects of religion and philosophy become appropriate. Rousseau's approach to the human and social topics is noteworthy. History is to be introduced, and the reason is that at some point a child needs to begin to understand how and why people behave as they do. Because we ought not to allow a child to spend much time in social circumstances, other than normal play with village children, a child cannot begin the process of understanding people through experience. The threat of *amour propre* is ever-present. History is the best alternative. And of course, the study of politics and government comes last. It is in some sense the most important and in another sense the most dangerous of educational topics. It is of the utmost importance because a young person needs to understand political theory in order to guide her own life as a citizen; it poses the greatest danger because without careful understanding, social life and politics can destroy the natural person.

Rousseau pays as much attention to methods of instruction as he does to content, and for similar reasons. Because of his general philosophical anthropology, he advocates an educational method that is fundamentally negative. By a negative education, he means that the best pedagogical actions we can take are to get out of the child's way and allow her natural propensities and goodness to flower. At the same time, because of his general empiricism, he advises us that we should not feed a child information but allow her to engage the world. That is how she will learn. Of course, that engagement has to be guided by the teacher. A child will learn something from unstructured activity and play, and so it has its place, but too much of what she learns will be haphazard and far less useful to her than it might be. The point is not that a teacher has no role, but rather that the teacher's role is not to feed but to guide. This means, then, that we ought not to tell a child what to think or even what is true, even or perhaps especially in matters of the greatest importance, like religion. Knowledge and ideas are valuable for a young person to the degree that she can make sense of them, incorporate them into what she already knows and thinks, and, most important, see the use of them. For a child or young person's education to have such effects, it is necessary, Rousseau thought, that the child be given what reliable information there is with respect to a topic, and then allow the child or student to make of it what she will.

Rousseau is also convinced, and this has to do with his sense of the goodness of nature and the threats posed by society, that it is far better for a child to learn through experience with things than experience with people. A child's engagement with things, both natural and artificial, will help her to understand her limits and abilities. A child understands her place in nature, even if inarticulately, and for that reason will not become either imperious or subservient to things. She will learn from them. Other people are a different and more dangerous matter. Engaging with other people, in the context of social expectations, when a child is not ready is, as we have seen several times, conducive not to learning and development but to the deleterious effects of *amour propre*. Experience with people outside one's family and in broad social circumstances, especially early in life, is more likely to produce the ethical distortions of arrogance and pride as it is to teach anything of value.

In other aspects of instructional method, Rousseau draws his ideas from his sense of the developmental character of children. So, for example, we ought not to reason with children since they cannot learn anything from such an approach. A child's early self-centeredness implies that we should teach, and guide a child to, only what is useful, or what she is likely to see as useful. As the child develops, a broader range of methods is possible, including reading, learning through indirect experience as one does in the study of history, rational inquiry, and of course travel as a method for the study of societies, polities, peoples, languages, and cultures.

Rousseau does not have much to say about where education is to take place, but what he does have to say, he is adamant about. Because nature is inherently good, and because society tends to be corrupt and a corrupting influence, it is almost necessary that a child be removed from social circumstance as early as possible. The best place for the pedagogical process and for a child to grow and learn is in nature as opposed to cities. There is too much value in nature, and too much danger in cities, to forego an education in natural circumstances. Even if one could avoid the corrupting influences of the city, an education without the many benefits that nature offers is impoverished at best. Toward the end of a student's education, however, the situation is quite different. At that point, with a sufficiently developed intellectual and moral capacity, a student needs exposure to cities and societies and peoples and cultures if she is to complete her education.

The question of timing is, for Rousseau, related entirely to his understanding of the process of a child's development. Even as an infant, we ought to attend to an understanding of a person's nature, and so, as he advises, we ought not to swaddle a child because such constriction impedes her natural freedom. As we have seen, topics and subjects are introduced when the child is developmentally ready for them. We should not reason with a child because a child is not capable of reason; we should not force reading on a child until the child is ready for it and sees its value; we should introduce books only when the topics to be taught are complex enough that immediate experience is not sufficient; we should avoid social engagements for a child until the necessary emotional capacities are sufficiently developed; and the examples could be multiplied.

Rousseau was a broad, deep, and idiosyncratic thinker. Like the *Republic*, *Emile* ranges over nearly the full range of philosophical and educational topics. This should not surprise us, though, for two reasons. The first is that the whole point of our study is to illustrate how that range of philosophical topics is critical for a serious and systematic study of educational theory. The second reason it should not surprise us is that the resemblance to Plato was purposeful on Rousseau's part. In writing *Emile*, he had undertaken to respond to Plato, and *Emile* is intended in part to supersede the *Republic*. Rousseau thought he had a better idea, and he went to great lengths to show us what it was and why he thought it was better. The reader will judge for him- or herself whether he was right.

But there is a slightly different evaluative question we should ask at this point. There is no doubt much of what Rousseau thinks that any one or more of us disagree with, but there is also quite a bit of good sense here, or so it seems to me. The question we might ask, and we could ask it with respect to Plato as well, is that given how different our circumstances are from Rousseau's, is it even possible to incorporate into our teaching and learning environments anything that he recommends? For example, even if he is right about the virtues of educating in nature, the vast majority of schools, teachers, and students are not in a position to do that. In that case, then, what use are such ideas to us? The answer to this question, and again, it also applies to Plato, and for that matter to anyone's ideas and recommendations, is that we are best advised to regard them as pointers rather than as literal prescriptions. If, for example, we think Rousseau has a point when he emphasizes experience with things as a pedagogical device, we may not be able to limit our children or students to the farms and fields, but we can devise ways even in modern classrooms to put the general ideas to use. The same can be said for many of the other ideas, even the more idiosyncratic ones, that he recommends to us.

It is to some extent possible to read John Dewey's educational philosophy as an effort to do just that. We can now turn to his treatment of many of these questions.

CHAPTER 3

Experience and Democracy

Dewey's *Democracy and Education*

Plato referred to education as "the one great thing" because he thought it was the critical factor in enabling the development of a happy individual and a just state. Rousseau, too, thought that education was necessary for the full development of a natural person and for a society and polity in which the individual will and the general will coincide. John Dewey agreed with Plato and Rousseau in believing that education was the key to a fulfilled life and a just society. Like them, he also thought that the society in which he found himself—in Dewey's case, the United States in the early decades of the twentieth century—was inadequate to the task of conducting education in the manner required in order to meet its proper goals.

He disagreed with them, though, regarding how to achieve these ends, especially given that prevailing social conditions were not adequate to the task. We cannot, he thought, create a new society from scratch, so that Plato's approach (even if the ideas are to some extent interesting as ideals) is not a guide to anything constructive. Dewey was in this respect not a revolutionary. As for Rousseau, Dewey thought again that though some of the ideas are interesting enough to be taken seriously, we are not anymore (if we ever were) in a position to educate children individually or entirely outside of social relations. If Plato's solution was to create and maintain a new society, and Rousseau's was to bracket society to enable individual development, Dewey's solution was to reform the schools to make them the social institutions essential for a democratic society. Our examination of Dewey's philosophical and educational ideas will clarify the details of his thinking and his reasons for it.

Dewey wrote a great deal about education. While he was at the University of Chicago in the late 1890s, he founded the Laboratory School and was its director and inspirational leader until he left Chicago for Columbia University in New York City in 1904. The ideas that guided the Laboratory

School, and what he learned from his experience there, are the content of some of his earlier writings on education, specifically *School and Society* and *The Child and the Curriculum*. His most extensive study of education and its philosophical atmosphere was *Democracy and Education*, published in in 1916. He briefly summarized his ideas some years later in *Experience and Education*. Our focus is on *Democracy and Education*, with an occasional appeal to *Experience and Education*. It was in *Democracy and Education* that Dewey worked out most systematically his educational and pedagogical ideas and related them carefully to his broader philosophical commitments.[1]

Dewey was without question the most influential educational theorist in the United States in the first half of the twentieth century. Not everyone agreed with him, of course, but if you were thinking or writing about educational theory, you had to deal with his ideas. If you agreed, generally, then you would travel with him, so to speak; if you disagreed, you had to go through him. There was no way around him. This alone makes Dewey an appropriate figure for us to consider. However, he also saw himself as in the general conversation about education in which Plato and Rousseau were engaged, so his thinking is to a considerable extent a response to theirs.

In addition to being a most significant figure in educational theory, Dewey was sometimes called "the philosopher of experience" and, as already mentioned, "the philosopher of democracy."[*]Experience and democracy were perhaps the two most important and central concepts and themes of Dewey's mature philosophical thinking, and, not surprisingly, they were also central to his ideas about education. In fact, they provide an ideal conceptual scaffold on which to consider his educational ideas, so they will structure our examination of his thinking.

EDUCATION AND EXPERIENCE

Among the ideas that Dewey shared with Plato and Rousseau is the rejection of the understanding of education as providing information to people. Unfortunately, this view is all too common today, as it evidently also was in Plato, Rousseau, and Dewey's times. Plato's preferred metaphor was that education "turns the soul," or points a person in the right direction, which is to say, toward the truth. Rousseau preferred to think of education as providing the opportunity for the natural traits of a person to unfold—hence his "negative" education. Dewey did not like either of these conceptions, for reasons we will develop. He preferred to think of education as a process of enriching experience.

Experience is the key to understanding Dewey's philosophy. It is the hub from which emerge his philosophical anthropology, metaphysics, epistemology, and social theory. Since it is also the concept in terms of which he understands education, we can make a first pass at his conception of experience with an overview of how he uses it in characterizing the goals, methods, and content of education. That will allow us to look at the idea of experience directly and in some detail. Once we have a fuller understanding of what Dewey means by experience, we can return to the ways he employs it to develop his philosophy of education.

Dewey may have agreed with Plato and Rousseau that education is not a matter of filling people with information, though he goes to some lengths to criticize their alternatives. Plato, you will recall, thought that once the ideal society was created, the rulers would have to guard against any innovations, on the grounds that if the social situation were ideal, any change would have to be change for the worse. In that case, education becomes to a considerable degree a process by which the prevailing social structures and principles are passed on to the young, and the young prepared to take their predetermined places in that social order. Dewey thought that this was mistaken: "The business of education is rather to liberate the young from reviving and retraversing the past than to lead them to a recapitulation of it" (DE 79). He also had little use for Rousseau's idea of education as unfolding what is already there in a child's nature. His concern with that view is that "The goal is conceived of as completion, perfection. Life at any stage short of attainment of this goal is merely an unfolding toward it" (DE 61). The problem with the first is that in simply preserving the past we foreclose any future into which we may grow, individually and socially; the problem with the second is that we are forever preparing, rather than living the experience of the present as a fullness and completion in its own right. He has similar objections to other common ways of thinking about education, including education as preparation for life rather than, as he famously put it, "life itself," and the common conflation of education with training, a distinction to which we will return.

Dewey is clear about what he rejects, and he is equally explicit about what he proposes. Education is reconstruction, he says—specifically, the reconstruction of experience: "the ideal of growth results in the conception that education is a constant reorganizing or reconstructing of experience. It has all the time an immediate end . . . the direct transformation of the quality of experience" (DE 82). This passage seems on the face of it to be clear enough, in that it consists of normal English words. In fact, however, in order to be understood properly, it requires a good deal of conceptual unpacking. To understand his short description of education, we have to come in close quarters with the ways he uses his terms, and we will do so soon.

Before doing that, though, it will be useful to afford Dewey the opportunity to make a few more observations about the relation between education and experience. He is quick to tell us, for example, that while education is a matter of experience, not every experience is educative: "A genuinely educative experience, then, one in which instruction is conveyed and ability increased, is contradistinguished from routine activity on the one hand, and a capricious activity on the other" (DE 83). In this short passage, Dewey makes a conceptual move that is typical of him. He identifies a commonly stated dichotomy and then rejects both of its terms. In this case, he refers first to education that fosters routine activity (for example, rote memorization of material to be given back on command) and then to its often-cited alternative, capricious activity (for example, unstructured and unrestricted activity of children in a classroom). Both of these are a kind of experience, but neither of them, he thinks, is educative, because neither is the kind of reconstructed experience that can reliably lead to growth.

There are two additional points that Dewey would make at this juncture. One is that "[t]he essential contrast of the idea of education as continuous reconstruction with the other one-sided conceptions which have been criticized . . . is that it identifies the end (the result) with the process" (DE 84). It is common in philosophy (and, more important, in the course of our normal lives) to make a distinction between what we want to achieve, our "end," and what process or activities we use to reach that end, the "means." In one sense, this is a perfectly reasonable distinction: if I want two boards to be attached, I will place them as I wish them to be, position a nail, strike the nail with the hammer as often as necessary, and try not to hit my fingers in the process. In itself, there is no problem there. The problem arises when, often unthinkingly, we draw too sharp a distinction between means and ends, thereby disassociating them from one another. We might think, for example, that there is no implicit relation between means and end in the case of the boards. We want them fastened together, and it does not matter much whether we use this or that hammer, or maybe a nail gun. In this case, we would have created a dichotomy between means and ends.

But of course, the relation is not arbitrary. Some means are more suitable to some ends, in that the achievement of the end is a function of the means. If we use glue instead of a nail, the boards may not fasten reliably. Or perhaps a screw would serve better than a nail. The means help to determine the end, and the end conditions to some extent the means. Moreover, the end is itself also a means, because there is a reason we want the boards fastened, so that the efficiency and reliability with which they are fastened itself has ramifications for a further end. In fact, Dewey wants to say, every means is in some respect an end, and every end is in some respect a means. To divide them sharply is to fail to appreciate this point. In the case of education, such a failure can have undesired consequences. What we do in classrooms is never just a means; it always and somehow is itself an end, just as every end is, as Dewey would say, not absolute but an "end-in-view" and itself a means in some other respect. Education as the reconstruction of experience understands the "identity," to use the term Dewey does, of the means with the end.

The integrated relation of means to ends has a bearing on teacher education as well, which, interestingly, is something Plato does not address, and Rousseau deals with only in the form of his advice to Emile's tutor. Dewey, by contrast, was very much interested in teacher education, a fact reflected in his creation of the Laboratory School at the University of Chicago and his association with Teachers College at Columbia University. The connection of the means–end question with teacher education arises in the fact that often enough, teachers will allow the means at their disposal to guide their selection of ends. A teacher who is more comfortable dictating to students what she thinks they should know is someone who is unlikely to embrace an end that is not implicit in that means (for example, the end of engendering creativity and self-control on the student's part). The point is not that "telling students" something (or, for example, lecturing) is never appropriate, because it would be misguided to think that. The point, rather, is that a teacher needs to understand the relation between her means and the ends she chooses. If one's means are unduly circumscribed, then so are one's ends. This is the point of the cliché that if one's only tool is a hammer, one will automatically try to whack everything. Ideally, in teacher education we will want to help future teachers understand the relation between means and ends and to develop a repertoire of means that are suitable to and will enable careful selection of educational purposes.

Another significant point that Dewey makes about the sense of education he proposes is that "the reconstruction of experience may be social as well as personal." This is so because in education so conceived, we realize "the potential efficacy of education as a constructive agency of improving society . . . [and] that it represents not only a development of children and youth but also of the future society of which they will be the constituents" (DE 84–85). Thus, we have seen three significant points: first, education as reconstructing experience differs significantly from commonly applied conceptions as well as prominent theories of education; second, by understanding education as the reconstruction of experience, we can avoid the pedagogically and philosophically inappropriate tendency to overlook the close relationship of means to ends, a particularly important point when applied to classroom methods; and third, education as the reconstruction of experience speaks to both of the main goals of education—that is, personal growth and social health.

To understand all this more meaningfully, we have to turn to Dewey's understanding of experience. To avoid (or at least minimize) confusion, we should note from the beginning that Dewey speaks of both experience in general and of a particular experience. In the first sense, experience is a mass term, and it refers to an aspect of the human condition. In the second sense, experience is an individuated term, and it refers to this or that individual experience. In its individuated sense, an experience, as he says, may be educative, but it may also not be. Similarly, an experience may be guided or it may be haphazard. In fact, in his 1934 book on aesthetics, titled *Art as Experience*, Dewey talks about *an* experience as implying a completion, or fulfillment of an activity, in which sense an experience has an evaluative connotation; it is a culmination, with a completed, qualitative character. In its individuated sense, an experience is significant in Dewey's thinking about education primarily in his discussions of curriculum and pedagogical methods, to which we will turn in due course.

Experience in general, however, which is to say its meaning as a central trait of human life, is the lynchpin in Dewey's philosophical thinking, and it provides the link between abstract philosophy and educational theory. When he says that education is to be understood as the reconstruction of experience, he is using the term in its mass, general sense, and the reference is to the impact of education on our lives as we all live them.

In the discussion of Rousseau, it was pointed out that he was to some extent an empiricist, as were many intellectuals of that time. An empiricist in its eighteenth-century sense was someone who thought that experience is the central fact of human life, and it is the source of all or nearly all knowledge. Such empiricism embodied a conception of experience as the largely passive reception of sense data by an individual, who then, by applying various mental faculties and processes, generated knowledge and understanding of the world. This way of thinking about experience is still very much with us—for example, if we were to say something like "I do not want just to read about the world but to experience it." In that case, we mean by "experience" seeing, and hearing, and touching, and direct sensory input generally.

Dewey would certainly recognize such a conception of experience, but he would insist that it is far too narrow to describe the whole of our ongoing engagement with our environments. For one thing, on the empiricist conception, experience is a passive affair, in that it imagines us passively receiving information through the senses, and the active part of the process is then "in the mind," so to speak. Dewey would point out that as a matter of fact, our engagement with our world is not only or even primarily passive in this way. We act on the world as much as undergo it, a feature of experience that we miss if we look at it the way the empiricists did. There must be more going on, and Dewey's approach to experience generally is an effort to describe what more is going on. In doing so, by the way, he influenced a whole school of philosophers and others, especially in the United States among philosophers who endorse what is sometimes called pragmatic naturalism, and his influence continues to be felt, as will become clearer in part II of this study.

In Dewey's hands, experience is not the passive reception of sensory information; rather, it is the ongoing interaction between the individual and her world, a process that is both active and passive. In fact, the passive reception of sensory data, assuming the questionable claim that there is such a process that is purely passive, would be only one of the ways that our environments act on us. For one thing, our environments are not limited to the physical features of our surroundings. They are just as much social as physical, historical as contemporary, ideational as sensory. I am impacted by my social circumstances no less than by the color of the trees outside my window (for example, by why today may be important to someone who is dear to me and what that inclines me to do). My own personal history, not to mention the history of my family, or my country, can have a far greater effect on me at any specific point than what I am seeing, hearing, or touching. Furthermore, the same is true for the ideas or ideals I accept. If I were a religious person, for example, any number of events would have an influence on me that they would not have otherwise. The point is that even if we think only of the (presumably) passive relation we have to our environments, there is much more happening than the reception of sense data.

The same, of course, is true for the active role we play in our worlds. We impact the physical environment in which we move in countless ways, even when we are asleep. What we do and say might have an emotional impact on people with whom we interact, and sometimes people, especially teachers, can affect the ways others think about and understand themselves and their worlds, possibly to a significant extent. We affect the world in as many ways and to as significant an extent as it affects us. All of this ongoing passive and active engagement with our world is experience, and it is the human condition.

Dewey referred to this process of engagement as an interaction, and sometimes as a transaction. Experience is the interactive give and take of the individual and her surroundings, physical and otherwise. To push the analysis a bit further, Dewey would want us to understand that in this interaction, each term, which is to say the person and her environs, does not merely affect the other, but *each constitutes the other*. To say that they constitute one another is to say that each is what it is, in more or less significant ways from case to case, because of the other. We do not often put it this way because we are usually not thinking at this level of generality and abstraction, but the basic idea should not be alien to anyone. Each of us knows that she is the person she is to some unspecifiable extent as a consequence of her environments. Our families have conditioned our natures, through both personal interactions and the transmissions of ideational commitments, belief systems, and patterns of behavior such as religion. The places we grow up, the schools we attend, and the children we play with all contribute to each of us being the person he or she is. And the process never stops. Our spouses, and careers, and children and grandchildren, all continuously condition who we are. In some ways, we are aware of these constitutive relations and can even to some degree manage them; in other ways, they are so many and so varied that we do not notice them.

A minute's thought will also make clear that there are as many and diverse ways in which our environs are constituted by their interaction with us. On the largest possible scale, the human impact on our physical environment is as clear an illustration as one could want. With respect to climate, the planet is now behaving as it is, and presumably will continue to so behave for some time, in part because of us. If the climate specialists who study this are right, then the climate now is not simply behaving differently from the past but also *in its nature* different from what it was. The relation between human beings and our planet is a constitutive one, in both directions.

Our environs are constituted by their relations with us in far less grand ways as well. Our family members, especially those to whom we are close, are who they are, for better or worse, to a considerable extent because of their relations with us. We each may similarly impact the fields in which we work or the places we live. We play an active role in the construction of our environments, just as our surroundings play an active role in our formation. The relations are mutually constitutive. This fact of the human condition is what Dewey refers to when he talks about experience and its interactive and transactional character.

Dewey used a specific term to describe the mutually constitutive condition in which an individual finds herself with respect to her environments, and that term is *situation*. He develops the meaning of the term in general philosophical contexts and in relation to education. He speaks, for example, about the relatively equal importance of what a child brings to the classroom and the effect the classroom has on the child. More traditional forms of education tend to ignore one side, what he calls the "internal conditions," in favor of the "objective," or, as we have been describing it, the individual and her world. Dewey puts it this way: "The word 'interaction' . . . assigns equal rights to both factors in experience—objective and internal conditions. Any normal experience is an interplay of these two sets of conditions. Taken together, or in their interaction, they form what we call a *situation*" (EE 24). A classroom, or even a school as a whole, is a "situation" in this sense of the term, because it encompasses a complex set of constitutive relations among its elements. Pedagogy has to take this into account, and we will return to this consideration a bit further on in the discussion of methods.

For the moment, it is important to realize that for Dewey, a situation in this sense of the term is a way of describing nature generally, and in this respect his view is quite different from Plato and Rousseau's. Plato did not speak much about nature, but he had quite a bit to say about reality generally. For him, reality was an ontological and moral hierarchy, with the natural, physical world of particular objects at the bottom, and the abstract, ideal world of the forms at the top, crowned by the form of the good. This is the general view of reality that Christianity adopted early on, and it still informs Christian theology in many ways. Rousseau, by contrast, did address nature directly, and for him there were two important features of it. First, it was inherently good, and second, following the physics and astronomy of the time, it was to be understood as a great machine, wherein the many parts interact mechanically to enable the natural world to exist and hang together.

Dewey had a different idea of nature, and it is captured by his concept of a *situation*. A situation, recall, is a set of entities in mutually constitutive relations with one another. When such a set includes a person, then the description of that person's experience must take into account the ways she engages with the other elements of the situation. It may help to think of a situation as an ecosystem, wherein the elements of the system interact and condition one another. As it happens, I look out my window at the desert environment of the American Southwest. Like any environment, its many elements interact with one another. Much of the plant life indigenous to the area survives on relatively little water, and in fact has developed as it has in response to the low levels of precipitation. If I overwater the oleander in the garden, it reacts negatively with respect to its health. The climatic conditions do not simply affect the plant and animal life; rather, climate is one of the elements of the ecosystem that make them what they are. There are reciprocal relations among the plant and animal life in this, as in every other, ecosystem. The climate, the soil, the animals, and the plant life all interact such that each is in various ways what it is by virtue of the interactions. If the level of humidity were to rise significantly, there would be consequences for the animal and plant life, just as there would be on elements of the system if new plants or animals were to be introduced. It may be that we used to believe that the climate was not something much affected by other elements of the system, but we now realize that it is a mistake, perhaps a monumentally fatal mistake, to continue to think that.

To say that Dewey regards nature as innumerable situations of this kind is to be taken literally. The model of an ecosystem does not apply only to biological nature, though it surely does apply there. It is the reason natural selection can work as it does. But Dewey means it to apply to all aspects of nature, and by "nature" he intends to point to everything, whatever it may be. This is not to say that all of nature is related to people, because clearly there are natural objects (for example, in distant space or deep in the earth) that are unrelated to any people, other than in a minimally relevant spatial sense. It does mean, though, that Dewey understood nature not as a hierarchical system, as Plato did, nor as a machine, as did Rousseau. He took it, rather, as an enormously complex set of interacting elements, as multiple *situations* or ecosystems in infinitely varied relations with one another. He did not think that everything is related to everything, as some Hindus and Buddhists hold, but he did think that everything is related to something, and constitutively so. Everything is constituted by the relations in which it finds itself, whatever those may be.

When Dewey says that experience is an interaction, and that it is to be understood on the model of a situation, in his sense of the term, he is placing experience fully within nature and defining it as a natural process and condition. Experience, in that it is a situation in Dewey's technical meaning, is an ecosystem no less than any other situation. In this view, we could say that a person is the net effects of the innumerable relations that constitutes her experience. Of course, we can say the same about all the elements of a person's experience, which becomes a technical way of saying that, to some degree, a person's environing conditions are what they are because of their relations with her, and she is who she is by virtue of her environing conditions. Our ongoing interaction with our environing conditions, which is to say our experience, makes us who we are. If that is right (and Dewey thought it is), then it becomes easier to see why he thought that the environment we create in schools, and in a classroom, is at the heart of the pedagogical process. We will return to this point, but it is worth realizing even now that Dewey thought that in some, in fact many, respects our experiential milieu, the situation, is not something we can control. But often it is something we can control, and education, or more precisely schooling, is one of those aspects of experience that can be controlled and directed, largely though not exclusively by teachers and school administrators. It becomes a critical pedagogical question, then, how a child's experience is structured, and to which ends it is directed.

Before we can explore this aspect of Dewey's educational theory more carefully, it is first necessary to consider one other aspect of the general conception of experience at work here. Experience as an interaction implies not only a general idea of nature but also a way of approaching knowledge; it has epistemological implications, and they in turn lead us to Dewey's philosophical pragmatism. Traditional empiricists had a clear idea about the relation between knowledge and experience, which was that all knowledge derives from experience. This is what John Locke's idea of the tabula rasa suggests. In the empiricists' thinking, we receive sensory impressions from our surroundings, we then process them in the mind, and the result is knowledge. Their accounts were far more complex and subtle than I have described, but this is the basic idea. To put it in a bit more developed way, in this traditional conception, knowledge describes reality, and it is able to describe reality accurately because it is grounded in input from the world. As long as the sensory input is reliable, and typically we can check our sensory impressions to be sure they are accurate so to avoid illusions, then the ideas we form on the basis of them will accurately reflect the world around us. If our ideas accurately reflect the world around us, then we can be confident that we have acquired or achieved knowledge of the world.

This is the traditional, empiricist way of understanding the nature and role of ideas, knowledge, and the relation of knowledge and experience. Dewey thought that all of this is wrong. In this respect, he was influenced by two other important American philosophers of the late nineteenth century, Charles Sanders Peirce and William James. Dewey was much younger than they were, but he knew them both. Peirce was a lecturer in logic at Johns Hopkins University when Dewey pursued his PhD in philosophy there in the 1880s. Peirce and James were also part of the faculty at Harvard University, where in the latter decades of the nineteenth century they had, each in his own way, developed what is still referred to as philosophical pragmatism, to which Dewey in turn added his voice.

The basic idea of pragmatism is that we do not form ideas as images of reality. Rather, we both develop ideas and maintain them to the extent that they settle or solve problems for us. The problems can be of many different kinds—individual or social, intellectual or practical, serious or playful. Whatever the case, the pragmatists believed, we accept the ideas that we do because they achieve something we want to achieve, or to put it a different way, they resolve a problem of some kind. Ideas are not descriptions that reflect reality but tools with which we influence it. Indeed, the pragmatists had the idea that thinking only occurs in response to a problem encountered. You might think about this in terms of an analogy with watching television. If we are sitting in our favorite chair watching something we want to be watching, and the TV is working as it should, we generally enjoy the moment without reflecting on it. If something suddenly goes wrong—for example, the picture becomes distorted, or the sound disappears, or the program inexplicably shifts to something else—then there is a problem. At that point reflection is engaged, and we begin to think about how to solve the problem. Once we hit on an idea or set of ideas that successfully solves the problem and allows us to return to peacefully watching the television, the thinking ends. This is of course a simplified illustration, and there can be any number of complexities. For example, maybe this has happened before, and we now realize that there is a larger problem. The idea that we acted on settled things for now, but we have reason to think that the larger problem is not solved. In that case, thinking continues until it is.

There are many other aspects of the standard pragmatist conception of knowledge—for example, one would have to come to terms with the question of the meaning of truth, as Peirce, James, and Dewey all did, and a number of other issues which do not have to concern us. The point we need to grasp is that Dewey regarded knowledge, and its relation to experience, quite differently from the way traditional empiricists did. The most fundamental point for Dewey and all other pragmatists is that ideas are not reflections of reality but tools we use to solve problems. In that case, knowledge is to be understood not as an accurate picture of reality but instead as one of the ways we get on in the world, one of the ways we live our lives. If we return to the conception of experience, Dewey realized that it is not enough to say that experience is the mutually constitutive interaction of persons and their environments. The reason why it is not sufficient to leave it at that is that problems arise frequently in the course of our day-to-day lives and they require to be resolved. Experience, in other words, is not just situations but quite often what Dewey called *problematic situations*. A problematic situation is one in which for whatever reason or reasons, things are not hanging together; the ecosystem that is the situation, we might say, is not harmoniously coordinated. This is an elaborate and somewhat artificial way of saying something that we all know, which is that our experience includes countless and seemingly never-ending problems. Dewey's point, in what is sometimes called his *instrumentalism*, is that depending on the nature of the problem before us at any point, we will reach for whatever tool, or instrument, will solve it. Sometimes that tool is an idea, or set of ideas, if they are what is needed to settle the problematic situation. Knowledge arises not *from* experience, as the empiricists thought, but *in* experience, and the ideas that constitute knowledge are not reflections of reality but tools we use in experience to solve problems.

This way of thinking about ideas and knowledge has a great many implications, among the most important of which are for education. For one thing, because ideas are tools to accomplish something rather than images or reflections that depict something, to help a child learn to think is not a matter of instilling ideas in order to have an accurate picture of reality but of helping her to develop and use ideas to solve problems. For another, if life's interactions consist in some measure of problematic situations in which we find ourselves, or that we bring on ourselves, then experience (which is the general interaction with our environments) becomes all the more important as a pedagogical matter. To educate children such that they develop the knowledge, skills, and habits of mind that will enable them to live rich and successful lives, we need to come to terms with the experience of our students and with the general experience, as well as the individuated experiences, in which we place them in the educational setting.

We are now able to see more carefully the distinctive features of Dewey's association of education with experience and how his view differs from those before him. He has Rousseau in mind, for example, when he criticizes natural development as an aim of education. Rousseau's approach, he says, does not take into account the fact that nature provides the materials of experience and development, but not their purposes or aims. And he has Plato in mind when he rejects social efficiency as a goal of education. While, of course, the ability to function in a society is important for all of us, he says, there is nevertheless the danger of accepting the society as given, as one finds it. In a society where some are dominated by others (for example, in the kind of class structured society that Dewey thought is the case in America), a social efficiency that simply reproduces the domination is contrary to the ends of individual and social development. Indeed, it is contrary, as we will see, to the purpose of developing and sustaining a genuinely democratic society (DE 126).

If nature does not supply the aims of education, and simply reproducing social structures as we find them cannot be the goal of education, then what is? Dewey's answer, as we have seen, is that the process of education is the reconstruction of experience, the "transformation of its quality" in a way that tends toward richer and more satisfactory experience. First, since experience is constitutive of the self, as Dewey thought it is, and if in much of our experience we find ourselves dealing with problems, or problematic situations, then we need to develop the ideas and habits, intellectual and applied, that help us to work our way through the problems with which we must always deal. Moreover, if nature does not supply the aims of experience or education, and social efficiency does not supply them either, the implication is that in the process of our own experience, in our lives, it is we who supply our own aims and purposes. It is, in fact, we who supply the meaning in our own lives. To manage this, or to learn to manage it, children need more than just experience; they must learn to undertake their own experience in ways that have fruitful results for them. They need, Dewey would say, experience that is educative, which requires the intelligence necessary to guide their own experience. Such intelligence, and intelligent guidance of experience, is what enables growth and increasingly enriched experience. This is the purpose of the reconstruction of experience in the educational process, and it is the responsibility of schools, school administrators, and teachers to so organize education and pedagogy that it becomes a reality for school children.

This is the challenge for both educational content and methods, and it has to do with what Dewey calls their "value." In the end, the value of the content of education and of pedagogical methods is a function of their relations to life activities and processes, and to the specific purposes of those activities. "Since education is not a means to living," he says, "but is identical with the operation of living a life which is fruitful and inherently significant, the only ultimate value that can be set up is just the process of living itself. And this is not an end to which studies and activities are subordinate means; it is the whole of which they are ingredients" (DE 248). Education is not a preparation for life but a constituent of it. This fact of the matter makes the classroom something of a microcosm of life generally. It is also, by the way, the reason that to think of education at any level as solely or primarily a way to prepare students to make a living is narrow and ultimately stultifying. Education must aim far higher than that, if only because children deserve much more.

They deserve, Dewey might say, a life rich in intelligently guided experience. He also makes the point that such a life is an integrated one, if only because experience itself is an integration. This is one of the implications of understanding experience on the model of an ecosystem. If we think of life as just a collection of distinct experiences and interests, and of education as meeting separate needs and interests, we end up with a paralyzing conception of education characterized by too much pressure and over-specialization. But our experience should not be individuated in this way, as if the many things we do and the many aspirations we have are unrelated to one another. The issue of educational values, Dewey says, rests on the fact of the integration of experience (DE 257).

It was mentioned earlier that Dewey addressed many topics by identifying traditional alternative approaches to them, criticizing the standard alternatives as frozen conceptual dichotomies and proposing an alternative. His approach to the issues of educational goals, contents, and methods is no different. He thought that the way we have understood education, with respect to its goals, content, and methods, has been characterized by a debilitating and unnecessary set of dichotomies. We will be able to consider them more sensibly once we look closely at Dewey's social and political philosophy, but it is worthwhile at least to mention them now.

One of the classical dichotomies in our thinking about the aims of education is between labor and leisure. This distinction is grounded in ancient class divisions, as Aristotle made clear millennia ago. The other dichotomies he discusses are between theory and practice, physical and humane studies, and between self and the world. Interestingly, Dewey thought that all of these traditional, rigid distinctions culminate in the ways we think about the relation between academic and vocational education and the relation in our lives between education and work. He thought that we need to avoid the sharp break we often assume between the two, which would require rethinking both. We can return to these matters after looking more closely at Dewey's social and political philosophy, and to do that we must understand his approach to democracy.

EDUCATION AND DEMOCRACY

Dewey thought, as did Plato and Rousseau, that a fulfilled human life and a defensible society require each other; one cannot exist without the other. Plato put this idea in terms of justice and proposed how to achieve a just individual and a just society. Rousseau put it in terms of the natural development of the individual and the functioning of the general will. Dewey understands it in terms of democracy, which means that in order to understand how education is related to a fulfilled life and a justifiable society, it is necessary to grapple with the nature of democracy.

Perhaps the single most important point to realize about Dewey's treatment of democracy is that for him democracy is not primarily or most critically a form of government and political decision-making. To allow him to put the point, "Democracy is more than a form of government; it is primarily a mode of associated living, of conjoint communicated experience" (DE 93). Dewey certainly thought that a democratic form of government and distribution of political power is valuable and important, if for no other reason than that it provides people with the opportunity to exercise some ideally intelligent control over the social and political conditions of our lives. That control is diluted considerably in a large political entity with many voters, but it is still better to have this input than not, he thought. It is also not clear whether voting in elections, as is the common form in contemporary liberal democracies of exercising one's democratic entitlements, is the only or necessarily the best way of having such political input. But this is a question we do not have to consider here. For our purposes, we should be clear that Dewey held most dear democratic forms of politics of the sort with which we are familiar.

However, he was convinced that the greater value of democracy is not confined to elections and periodically making partisan political choices. In his view, democracy is a broader social arrangement, one that he thought was most important. The reason, he said, is that "democratic social arrangements promote a better quality of human experience, one which is more widely accessible and enjoyed, than do non-democratic or anti-democratic forms of social life" (EE 18).

In *Democracy and Education*, Dewey gives as clear an account of what he means by democracy, and why it is important, as anywhere in his vast corpus of writings. As was his habit, consistent with his pragmatist sense that our ideas arise and are justified in experience, Dewey developed definitions not out of thin air or in the abstract, but he drew them from relevant features of experience. In the case of democracy, though, a definition serves not simply to describe a situation but also to offer an ideal, something to which to aspire. In that case, it is necessary not only to draw the conception from experience but also to do so in a way that does not simply reproduce what already is the case. If we were to do that, then we would simply be claiming that what already is the case it what ultimately ought to be, in which case no growth is possible. But if no growth is possible, then our conception offers no useful ideal toward which to strive. On pragmatist grounds, an idea that cannot accomplish anything is no idea at all. The way to resolve this evident dilemma is to draw from experience those features that point to what we can erect as an ideal condition.

In the case of democracy, Dewey says that we can draw our conception of a functioning ideal from two characteristics that we find in existing societies. The first is that in any social group, "even in a gang of thieves," he says, there is some interest held in common by the members of the group. The second feature we find in existing social groups is interaction and communication with members of other social groups. "From these two traits," Dewey says, "we derive our standard" (DE 89).

The mere presence of these two traits, though, is not enough to constitute a democratic social or political arrangement because, as Dewey himself points out, non-democratic social groups, and whole societies, have some common interests among their members. The question becomes how many and varied those shared interests are, and Dewey offers two interesting examples to illustrate his point. Even in a "despotically governed state," he notes, people have a number of things or interests in common, but they are limited in important respects by the conditions under which they are governed. If they are governed primarily by fear, which has been the case in many places at many times, then they do not have the opportunity to develop the broad range of common interests that come from shared social and political responsibility. This is one of the underlying reasons that despotism is contrary to the free development of people in the society. Even if a despot can make informed and well-crafted decisions and judgments, the lack of access that the citizens have to the shared responsibility of governance and decision-making, and therefore to the common interests that such responsibility presupposes, renders the social and political environment inadequate to the development of its people and therefore to the justification of the state. Democracy, by contrast, because it assumes the presence of shared social and political responsibility, both engenders and reinforces a broader and more varied range of common interests.

A second example that Dewey uses to clarify why he thinks that common interests are relevant to understanding democracy has to do with class divisions in society (DE 90–91). Because a limited number and variety of shared interests militate against the intellectual growth that comes from developing and exercising the capabilities we have individually and in concert, the limits placed on us by the imbalances created by class divisions are also hostile to democracy. As Dewey puts it, "The more activity is restricted to a few definite lines—as it is when there are rigid class lines preventing adequate interplay of experiences—the more action tends to become routine on the part of the class at a disadvantage, and capricious, aimless, and explosive on the part of the class having the material advantage." This point applies to any class divisions in a society. It could apply equally to the power and authority that a traditional aristocracy has over bourgeois and working classes, and it applies to the class distinctions between capitalists and wage laborers. If one class of people controls the means by which another class of people lives, then the ruling class dictates what the weaker class must do in order to live as well as the others' purposes and ends. The ruling class, in other words, determines for workers not only what they must do in order to live but also the values and ends that become enshrined in the society's structures and institutions. Consequently, as in the case of a despotism, the opportunities for the majority of people, and it is always the majority that finds itself in the weaker position with respect to class differentiation, to exercise their potential and to engage intellectually and in practice with the responsibilities of shared governance is often severely limited. The result is, again, that the range of shared interests is truncated, and so consequently is individual and social development. Dewey's point is that even in a society that has a democratic form of electoral politics, the unequal distribution of power that results from class divisions undermines the democratic character of the society. Democracy and class divisions of this kind are not compatible, and we can see why that is the case when we realize how important shared interests are for a democracy.

But this is still only one of the two traits that Dewey uses to define democracy, the second being the pursuit of common interests by the members of one group with members of others. Even a "gang of thieves," Dewey said, have shared interests with one another, but by the nature of that group, its members must cut themselves off from others. The character of the members of the group is stunted because they cannot expand and enrich their own experience beyond the group's narrow concerns. A social entity that can offer its members the opportunity to grow in these ways is one that encourages the pursuit, perhaps even intentional creation, of shared interests beyond the group. There are social groups of all kinds, defined by many factors—geography, politics, gender, race, nationality, citizenship, profession, religion, hobbies, and many more. Any such group that tries to cut itself off from others is endangering its own strength and the experience of its members. A strong community, by contrast, and Dewey thought that a democratic community would be the strongest in this sense, is one in which its members seek and act on shared interests with others. One of the implications of this view is that such frequently encountered social phenomena as nationalism, sexism, racism, militarism, imperialism, and any behavior that impedes the pursuit of common interests across borders is inimical to democracy.

It should be clear that democracy in Dewey's sense is not limited to the presence of political parties and periodic, uncoerced voting. It is also not limited to the standards of liberal democratic societies with which we are familiar—equality, freedom of speech, religious belief and practice, and the press, as well as the general principles of the rule of law and all that such principles imply. These are important, as is uncoerced voting, but they are not enough. Democracy is a form of living together that promotes individual experiential enrichment through the pursuit and expression of common communicated interests, and the purposes and meanings that we find in them or create through them. Dewey uses the term "democratic ideal" to refer to this conception, and he describes it this way: "The two elements in our criterion both point to democracy. The first signifies not only more numerous and more varied points of shared common interest, but greater reliance upon the recognition of mutual interests as a factor in social control. The second means not only freer interaction between social groups . . . but change in social habit—its continuous readjustment through meeting the new situations produced by varied intercourse" (DE 92).

If we take this ideal seriously, and Dewey clearly thinks that we should, then we have to think through its implications for education. On the face of it, there are two general reasons that education is of paramount importance for such a democracy. The first, and Dewey calls it the superficial reason, is that education for democracy is critical because the electorate needs to be knowledgeable. It is fair to say, as Dewey would have, that a polity in which the electorate makes its decisions based on superficial considerations, unfounded prejudice, or simply misinformation is bound in the long run to suffer, as are its citizens. From Dewey's point of view, though, there is a more important reason that democracy requires education. Since democracy is a mode of living that is characterized by shared interests and ever widening communication, a democratic society must educate toward these ends.

We should take care to note at this point that Dewey would want us to think about what this means in the context of our own society and educational systems. A moment's reflection will make it clear that there are many aspects of modern liberal democracies, including those in the United States, Europe, and nations around the world that are similarly organized, that do not meet the standard. All of them are characterized by the unequal distribution of wealth and power along class lines, and that is not consistent with the democratic ideal; all of them suffer to one degree or another from racism, both social in the structural, systemic sense and on a personal level, which is also inconsistent with the ideal; all of them also either flirt with or embrace a nationalism that in some measure cuts them off from other communities; and in more or less serious ways, all of them remain, as they have always been, sexist. None of this is consistent with the democratic ideal, and yet we want our schools to educate for democracy. How, we might ask, is that supposed to be possible?

Dewey engages this question, specifically with respect to the problem of nationalism. It has been common for a long time for countries to expect their public schools to have national interests function as an educational goal. Children are taught the values of the nation, usually in some idealized form, and are expected to embrace those values as they grow into members of the national community. In one obvious sense, this is entirely appropriate, in that we can expect members of a community to enculturate our young people to be part of "us." When we specify the kind of community, or nation, we wish ours to be, a serious problem comes into focus. In Dewey's words, "One of the fundamental problems of education in and for a democratic society is set by the conflict of a nationalistic and a wider social aim" (DE 103). There appear to be contrary tendencies within the situation we find ourselves. On the one hand, science, technology, and many other aspects of contemporary life point toward increased interaction and collaboration, even worldwide. At the same time, nationalism tends toward less interaction and communication. Democracy requires the former and is impeded by the latter. So, "Is it possible for an educational system to be conducted by a national state and yet the full social ends of the educative process not be restricted, constrained, and corrupted?" The problem is expressed both internally and in relation to a nation's relations with other nations: "Internally, the question has to face the tendencies, due to present economic conditions, which split society into classes some of which are made merely tools for the higher culture of others. Externally, the question is concerned with the reconciliation of national loyalty, of patriotism, with superior devotion to the things which unite men in common ends, irrespective of national political boundaries" (DE 104).

Given the nature of democracy as Dewey understands it, the problem for education is becoming clearer. Disparities of wealth and power that derive from class distinctions are inconsistent with democratic social relations. How, then, in the public schools do we educate children to take their places in our society without reproducing the anti-democratic character of its class divisions, and without allowing the prevailing fact of class disparities to distort the educative reconstruction of experience? At the international level, democratic values expect of us that we promote interactive, collaborative, and communicative engagement with other nations and their people, and that we do so on the basis of respect even when we have fundamental disagreements with them. Democracy in Dewey's sense is internationalist. How, in the public schools, do we square that democratic internationalism with educating for national interests? Dewey thinks that because they are the basis of democracy, the virtue of common interests internally and internationalism externally trumps whatever value there may be in class divisions and nationalism, no matter how familiar the latter may be to us.

Much of what Dewey thinks about the goals, methods, and content of education requires a reconstruction of experience, as we have defined experience, that is oriented toward the creation of democratic individuals and a democratic society, as we have defined democracy. Even in the earliest years of the Laboratory School, Dewey urged its administrators and teachers to experiment with ways to construct classroom environments and activities, regardless of the topics of instruction, to promote learning in experience. He was also committed even then to identifying the most effective methods whereby children's creativity and problem-solving skills could be nurtured. As a general matter, this implies helping children develop control over their own experiences and purposes. Even much later, he would write that "The ideal aim of education is creation of power of self-control" (EE 41). This has a flavor of Rousseau in it, but for Dewey the relevant concepts have distinctive meanings. Self-control in the sense that Dewey means it implies the intelligent direction of one's own experience, and intelligent direction in turn assumes that the child can identify the goal or goals of a particular activity, learn to organize her experience, perhaps experimentally, toward those ends, and recognize the fulfillment of a project or activity. This is the sort of intelligent control, taught via the reconstruction of experience, that will foster for a child the problem-solving habits of mind and growth toward ever new and richer experience. Classrooms can be organized to develop such self-control and in principle even whole schools can be so organized, at least to some significant extent.[2]

In this context, we may return to the dichotomies in education that were introduced earlier. Recall that the pairs of concepts that concerned Dewey were labor and leisure, theory and practice, physical and humane studies, and finally self and world. Our understanding of Dewey will be enhanced if we look briefly at each.

The first dichotomy is labor and leisure, which derives from traditional class distinctions. Now that it is clear the extent to which Dewey thought that disparities of wealth and power that derive from class differences badly undermine democratic social relations, we can see why he is as concerned as he is with lingering remnants in education of the labor–leisure disjunction. It was common in Dewey's time, and it is common today, to hear it said that the primary role of education is to prepare people for the workforce. On the one hand, this idea is understandable, in that all parents want their children to be able to fend for themselves, and socially we want our compatriots to be as able as possible to provide for themselves. The problem, though, is that education for work trains a person in a skill, but if education is largely limited to that training, then the skill learned is put to use under the control of someone else. Education organized toward this end perpetuates class-based inequalities, it undermines democracy, and it deprives children so educated of the potential of their own experience.

While we all need to learn skills and abilities that will help us get along in our lives, we are in no way obliged, Dewey thought, to educate for class subservience and inferiority, and to undermine human development in doing so. On the contrary, the schools and their classrooms are precisely the social location in which debilitating class distinction can be overcome. This would require a rough equality of educational opportunity, and Dewey thought that such equality was possible and in fact necessary for successful education. And in addition to the egalitarian potential of schools and classrooms, we have at our social disposal technological achievements that make possible a more equitable distribution of work and play, labor and leisure, in people's lives. In fact, he thought that a more egalitarian education is the first big step in this direction: "There is already an opportunity for an education which, keeping in mind the larger features of work, will reconcile liberal nurture with training in social serviceableness, with ability to share efficiently and happily in occupations which are productive. And such an education will of itself tend to do away with the evils of the existing economic situation" (DE 269).

The traditional dichotomy between labor and leisure is too easily reinforced by the way we have tended to distinguish between theory and practice. This is a long-standing division, as we have seen it built into Plato's distinction between the important theoretical learning required for the rulers by contrast with the training for an occupation that he thought appropriate for the bulk of the population. In Plato's hands, theory, or the use of reason, can reach the most important and valuable knowledge, while practice is merely the repetitive activity that we go through in the "daily grind," we might say. Of course, things changed over time. Experimentalism and the rise of the scientific method put knowledge from experience in a new and more valued light, though we have yet to unleash its potential. Initially, the newly discovered value of practice was processed through the lens of the sort of passive conceptions of experience that characterized early empiricism. Dewey's revised understanding of experience, however, can free our sense of practice and its relation to theory to allow for a fuller appreciation of both. As reconstructed along the lines Dewey proposes, experience enables us to realize that theory and practice cannot be sharply differentiated, and they certainly do not constitute a moral hierarchy. And, again, it is the educational process in which this advance can come to fruition: "It is not the business of the school to transport youth from an environment of activity into one of cramped study of the records of other men's learnings; but to transport them from an environment of relatively chance activities (accidental in the relation they bear to insight and thought) into one of activities selected with reference to guidance of learning" (DE 283).

Dewey makes a comparable point when considering specific content, and it is also tied to his philosophical differences with traditional conceptions—in this case, of nature and knowledge. For various reasons, the study of nature in the sense of the physical world and the study of human affairs have been regarded as largely different enterprises, and there has at times been hostility between them. Dewey is here telling a European story, and we should recognize (even if he did not) that the details would differ if we were to consider other intellectual traditions. In Europe, though, nature was for centuries regarded as something God had made available to humankind, so that there was a divinely endorsed relation between the two. With the rise of scientific cognitive possibilities, nature became something we could investigate directly for the purpose, as Francis Bacon said, of exploiting it. This meant that we came to rely less and less on tradition for our understanding of the world, and more on our direct inquiry. One consequence is that, as Dewey put it, science doomed feudalism, but it enabled capitalism. Unfortunately, capitalism soon revealed a certain hostility to human interests, both in its degradation of the conditions of people's life and work and in its reduction of human value to pecuniary ends, as if the most important values in life were to be delineated in financial terms. A backlash was inevitable, and on the intellectual level that backlash took the form of Romanticism, which tended to regard science as hostile to human concerns.

As far as Dewey is concerned, this is an untenable position to hold, and his conception of experience as the mutually constitutive interaction of the individual with her environment provides a desirable alternative. As he put it, the only legitimate distinction that can be made between nature and human being is between the conditions we need to deal with in order to achieve our aims, and the aims themselves. It is incumbent on education to reintegrate the study of nature with the study of human being (DE 294). For one thing, such an integration is how reality works, as his conception of experience makes clear; for another, the success of our experience in enriching our growth toward more and more fruitful experience requires that we appreciate the integration of nature and humanity, or, to put it slightly differently, the natural character of human beings.

When Dewey talks about the dichotomy between the self and world, he has in mind primarily the relation of individuals to one another, and his concern is of a piece with the other damaging distinctions he discusses. One of the advantages of the modern period, the rise of science (and, for that matter, the rise of capitalism) is that they produced an intellectual and social environment where the individual began to matter more than it had. The problem has been that the individual was conceived as a mind more or less cut off from others. This, in a way, is Rousseau's lone individual, Emile by himself growing up in his natural surroundings, or Robinson Crusoe alone on his island. The modern period unleashed the individual, but the individual was ill conceived as an atomic entity, a mind cut off from the world. As far as Dewey is concerned, his conception of experience as the interaction of individual with the environment breaks through this traditional notion of the atomic individual. Human individuals are, he insists, social beings, a condition built into our experiential natures. If we are constituted by our relations with our environments, if other people are among those environments, and if those relations are mutually constitutive, then each of us is a social being by our natures in that we are constitutive elements of one another.

With this point in mind, Dewey asks us to stop thinking of ourselves as minds cut off from one another. Mind, he says, is not an entity but a function, and it is a function that operates in experience. To the extent that education can be described as the ongoing development of our minds (and in some ways it can be so described), then it has to take into account the social nature of individuals. It also has to take into account that to develop a mind as an experiential function requires not that it be filled with information but that its exercise in experience be fostered and guided. We also want education to promote free individuals, which means to provide the conditions that enable individuals to develop, grow, and act (DE 310–311). In this respect, education meets both its individual and its social expectations because a democratic society requires free individuals who operate for ends of their own construction, in concert with others as circumstances dictate, rather than be dominated by others.

For Dewey, all of these dichotomies culminate, interestingly enough, in the issue of vocational education, and the reason is that we have failed, he thinks, to understand and appreciate the integration of learning for knowing and learning for doing. We have made a mistake in thinking that educating for a vocation is something of less value than educating for other ends, that it is something that is strictly pecuniary, and indeed that it is something that can be divorced at all from other sorts of learning and education. We need, he says, a new way of thinking about what a vocation is: "A vocation means nothing but such a direction of life activities as renders them perceptibly significant to a person because of the consequences they accomplish, and also useful to his associates" (DE 316). The opposite of vocation is not something like "knowledge for its own sake" but aimlessness. To avoid both lack of direction and subservience to the purposes of others, education must walk a narrow path. It is never appropriate to let people become mere appendages to machines, or, in less industrial contexts, simply "employees," and an education that sees itself that way has already failed. We need rather to understand that the dominant vocation of all people is life, which is to say intellectual and moral growth, and Dewey means this to apply in all the contexts of our lives, from our work to our families to all of our aspirations. Schools correctly organized can help achieve this, but to do so we also need to realize that a different sort of society than ours is required, one in which everyone will be occupied in activities that better bind people together (DE 326). There are powerful interests in society that may be, and almost certainly will be, opposed to this, which is one more feature of our environing conditions that define our experience and pose the challenges a genuinely democratic education faces.

EDUCATIONAL PRINCIPLES

At a highly general level, the goals of education as Dewey understands them are similar to Plato and Rousseau's approaches. When we look more closely, though, there are distinct differences. All three of them are convinced that education is central to the proper and prosperous development of an individual and society as a whole. Of course, many aspects of our lives are critical for a healthy life and a strong society, but education, they all think, is uniquely central. If education misfires in any systematic way or to an extensive degree, then individuals' lives and the character of a society can go very wrong. This is the reason that all of the figures we have studied are as concerned as they are with understanding how education can be done right and what would count as being done right.

Dewey recognized the similarities between himself and his predecessors, but he thought that they had for the most part got the details wrong. It is generally the goal of education to enable the health of individuals and society, but in Dewey's hands this means not just any kind of society or just any sort of person but specifically a democratic society and the sort of people who can make such a society work. Because a democratic society is characterized by shared interests among its members, and by the pursuit of shared interests with others beyond one's own communities, education has to be so organized that it leads in those directions. Taking the importance of shared interests seriously means that we aspire to, and act to bring about and sustain, a society in which collaboration with one another in the resolution of our many problems, both domestic and international, is enabled and encouraged. However we select topics for instruction, or methods of instruction, or organizational principles for our schools and classrooms, this is the general goal toward which it all should be pointing.

And of course, the consequences of those decisions are felt not simply on society generally but more directly on the individuals—children, students, teachers, staff, administrators, school board members, families—who are the stakeholders in the educational process. To put the point crudely, education creates not just societies but also the people who constitute them. If the preferable society is one rooted in the importance of shared interests, then it can prosper only to the degree that its members appreciate the significance of those interests and know how to express and promote them. Such people are open to experience and to new experiences; they are creative in the pursuit of their own interests and those they hold in common with their neighbors; they organize their interests and the activities to pursue them based not on rigid and dogmatic ideological assumptions, political or otherwise, but on the understanding that we all have concerns in common and that whatever else we may disagree about, to advance our common interests requires some meaningful degree of communication and collaboration with one another. This sort of person is what Dewey means by a democratic person, and it is the sort of person he has in mind when he says that education amounts to the reconstruction of experience to enable growth in the sense of further and enriched experience. The democratic person does not close herself off but opens herself out. That is how we solve problems and advance common interests; that is how we are able to exercise the intelligent direction of experience that constitutes a fulfilled individual life and a strong, healthy community. We are, however, not born this way. Education, and education rightly conducted, is required to help make it all happen.

Unlike both Plato and Rousseau, Dewey believed that all people should be educated in roughly the same way. He understood, of course, that people, younger and older, differ from one another in ways that can affect and be affected by the educational process. But he rejected the idea that any of those differences imply, or even justify, unequal education or unequal access to educational opportunities. Dewey had no use for Plato's kind of "tracking" or for Rousseau's gender discrimination in education. He was so convinced of the need for a rough equality of educational experience for all people that he argued that the schools are actually the one social institution that can overcome, even if somewhat artificially, the inequalities that prevail outside the school. In fact, he was convinced that the only way we will be able to overcome the inequality in the distribution of wealth and power, as well as the inequalities rooted in gender, racial, religious, and other divisions that prevail in the society as a whole, is if the schools embody the sort of equality that a democratic society requires.

Dewey's intense interest in how schools and classrooms organize themselves points to another difference between his approach to education and that of his forbears. Neither Plato nor Rousseau spoke about schools of the sort we are familiar with. Such schools and school systems did not exist in Plato's time, nor did they exist in Rousseau's, though one gets a clear sense from Rousseau that even if they had existed, he would not have trusted them. Dewey thought differently about the schools, so much so that he may place more weight on them than they can bear. Whether that is the case or not, Dewey argued that the schools are where a society supplies the commonality of experience that can engender the developed intelligence and habits of mind that individuals and the society need.

As important and necessary as the schools are, though, he would not have wanted us to think that education is or should be restricted to school settings. We have seen that Dewey was opposed to rigid distinctions and dichotomies among the various aspects of our lives. He believed, for example, that it is a mistake to think of art as something that is to be found in museums and concert halls, and nowhere else. He argued in his book *Art as Experience*, in fact, that art signifies a basic feature of our lives, and that it permeates not only our private, individual lives but also our public lives, as well as the social structures that organize them. Just consider the degree to which design pervades everything we see and do, from how we dress and prepare ourselves every day to how we organize and decorate our homes, to the organization of the physical infrastructure of our communities. Our lives are shot through with aesthetic features, and Dewey made much of this point.

He has largely the same idea about education, which can be restricted to schools no more than art can be confined to museums and concert halls. This is what is implied by his idea that education consists of a reconstruction of experience. Education, we might say, inhabits experience, and it does so whether we are in the schools or not. It is common in our day to talk about lifelong learning, usually in the sense of people being interested in learning new things and having new experiences throughout their lives. Dewey would have endorsed this idea, though he would have wanted us to realize that lifelong learning can be limited to special classes for retirees no more than education early in life can be limited to the schools. The ongoing educational character of experience is available outside of schools and throughout our lives, and in any context, just as the aesthetic is. That education occurs as an ongoing feature of our lives can be taken advantage of by people only if we can realize that it is in fact related to our ability to forge our experience in the resolution of the problems we face and in the pursuit of the shared interests that constitute our social lives. This, in the end, is the reason that Dewey so heavily emphasizes the reconstruction of experience as the general character of education. We have available to us the learning we need to live our lives fruitfully as "works in progress," as we might say today, but only if we are the sort of people who have cultivated the intelligence, skills, and habits of mind and life to take advantage of it. To become such people, though, we need an education that moves us in those directions.

The sort of education that can move us in those directions is what Dewey describes in his extensive comments on content and method. If read superficially, his comments on how to approach content in education (as well as the methods through which we teach) can sound rather anodyne, even if somewhat unique in his formulation, especially if we do not attend to the details. If we do attend to the richer meaning of his ideas, though, we can begin to see how much of a challenge they pose to our typical ways of organizing the instruction we provide in our schools. With respect to content, one of the themes Dewey focuses on is the integration of subject matter. He argues, as we have seen, that the study of nature should be integrated with the study of human affairs, and that we need better to account in our curriculum for the integration of the self and the world. He makes further points along these lines, but they concern methods more than content, so we can focus for the moment on these two.

For various reasons, some more understandable than others, we have tended for the purpose of instruction and study to divide the world into distinct fields or subjects. In one way this makes sense, in that there are clearly significant differences between, for example, biology and politics, or between history and art. Each attends to different aspects of our world and our experience, and each requires distinctive approaches in our study of them. In those ways, they are distinct fields of study. The problem comes when we treat them as if they are unrelated phenomena, which of course they are not. Biology, or at any rate ideas we might hold about biology, can have meaningful connections with political matters. What we know about human gestation in utero, to select one obvious illustration, has a great deal to do with political debate and public policy. Stem cell research offers another example, as does climate science and related political activities. We can make comparable points about the relation of history and art. On the face of it, they seem to be different enterprises altogether, but on closer examination it turns out that art and history (and here I mean the social and political history that is typically the subject matter of classes and textbooks in history) intersect regularly. To pick illustrations arbitrarily, one cannot adequately understand Nazi Germany without a sense of why the Nazis were concerned with what they called "degenerate" art and how they dealt with that concern. To offer a different example, not only is the Marseillaise the French national anthem, but it often carries with it a sense of national identity that can carry a people through difficult times. For a fictional representation of this point, recall the famous scene from *Casablanca* in which the band plays and the patrons of the café sing the song as an act of political resistance.

Such examples can be multiplied indefinitely, and taken together, they make Dewey's point about the integration of subject matter. The pedagogical implication is not hard to grasp. We see the integration in such examples, and in any case we know, from Dewey's naturalism and his transactionalism, that reality is constituted by situations and that situations are sets of relations that constitute one another. In that case, no aspect of our experience can be isolated. On the contrary, we can expect that biology and politics will influence one another, as will history and art. In that case, to treat any of them as largely distinct topics or subjects of study is to condemn ourselves not to understand them adequately. If that is true, then we should not be teaching them as if they were unrelated to one another.

Dewey is also concerned that in our educational content we integrate the vocational aspects of our lives. Some people may say that we already do this when we organize the educational experience to prepare people for jobs they will, or may, do later in their lives. Dewey, though, thinks this is precisely the wrong thing to do, and it surely is not what he means by treating education vocationally. First, education is never simply a means to some extrinsic end, so thinking of it as preparation for a job distorts it from the start. Second, conceiving of a vocation simply in terms of a job we may do in the future distorts even our understanding of that to which we dedicate ourselves. Vocations are important, Dewey thought, and we typically have many of them, in the sense that a vocation suggests a direction of sustained attention and energy that embodies value for us. In this sense, a vocation in the sense of employment is a significant feature of our lives, and, ideally, we are able to engage employment that commands such a sense of importance. But employment is not the only such aspect of experience. One may have a vocational sense of one's place as a citizen, for example, or a spouse or parent, or an artist or athlete. Vocations in the sense of a meaningful and coordinated direction of experience are much of what enriches our experience and lives. In this sense, it is tragic to restrict vocation as we do to employment, and it multiplies the tragedy when we conceive of education for vocations as a kind of "applied" education as opposed to something "purer." There is no meaningful education that is not integrated with and in experience, and that integration, at its best, takes account of the many vocations that may move us over the course of our lives.

To extend the general idea of integration, Dewey also wants to see the content of education and schooling be directed toward developing a sense of the relation of the world as experienced to the world as ideally conceived. In other words, a satisfactory education enables us not simply to grasp the world intellectually but also to engage it morally as we construct, individually and collectively, the future. Children need to learn that the existent and the desirable are elements of one another. Our ideals cannot be abstractly drawn in such a way that they are unrealistic, and our understanding of what currently exists is never adequate if we are not inclined to ask of it whether it ought to be. The ideal in relation to the real is another of the traditional dichotomies that Dewey would have us overcome, in our lives generally, of course, but perhaps more fundamentally in education.

Dewey's interest in one's intelligent guidance of experience toward growth and enrichment drove his conception of the principles that he thought should guide the educational process. Learning, we will recall, does not mean gathering information. There is nothing wrong with information, of course, and it is always valuable to have command over a good deal of it.

But to understand education primarily as a process whereby one consumes information is to misunderstand it woefully. For one thing, most of us forget most of the information we take in, as children and for the rest of our lives as well. For another, it is relatively easy for most of us (at least those of us with access to the internet) to acquire any information we need or want at any time. If education were simply or primarily a matter of consuming information, then we are wasting children's time and a huge amount of social resources by maintaining school systems and requiring children to spend their time in them.

But as we now know, Dewey would want to say to us that education is not about information but about the guiding of experience toward intelligent self-control and the ongoing growth of experience in its richness and efficacy. How we do this from day to day, year to year, and lesson to lesson involves decisions made by teachers, administrators, and others, including children and students. Dewey offers no magic pill or secret formula. He does, however, offer principles that he thinks can guide us in making those day-to-day decisions. First, it is critical that we organize the schools and the educational experience such that the detrimental consequences of disparities in wealth and opportunity are overcome. If we do not do this, Dewey believed, then we are overlooking one of the necessary conditions of social progress. The schools, he thought, do not exist simply to induct us into our worlds; they exist to enable us to appropriate our worlds and move them forward. In a society like ours, one that is characterized by debilitating class divisions, this cannot be done unless those consequences are mitigated. In this sense, Dewey would have endorsed a description of education properly conducted as progressive, even if he had some misgivings about educational reforms so named that were introduced in his lifetime, and sometimes in his name.

Organizing the schools and classrooms to overcome class distinctions, assuming that it can be done to some meaningful extent, is only the first step in educating for enriched experience. The second principle that will guide the decision educators and teachers make is that a child's time in the classroom, to be genuinely educative, has to consist of experiences that are structured and guided by teachers. Presumably, there is no one way to do this sort of thing, though Dewey is insistent that education should be neither routine nor capricious. A school day can be structured in any number of ways; classrooms can be physically organized in various configurations; children may spend fixed or variable amounts of time on tasks; teachers may at times set projects for students and at other times guide children in the design of their own; the relative amount of time spent on providing information and facilitating problem-solving activities can differ from occasion to occasion; children may work alone or together; evaluation can presumably be undertaken in any number of ways. Dewey did not want to insist on any one way to manage any of these methodological concerns. How the decisions are made in any given case can depend on a range of factors: the expertise of a teacher, or the expectations of parents, unique social circumstances, the talents and interests of children and students, and any number of other factors. What Dewey does insist on, though, is that the guiding principle we put to work in making those decisions is to assist a child in the enrichment of her experience, and in the ongoing development of her capacity to guide her own experience toward greater and wider possibilities.

Those possibilities grow over time, due to a child's own growth in maturity and competence, and as a result, the details of the educational experience will grow accordingly. The principle, however, remains the same. One of the important dimensions of this development over time is that as the relevant abstract and practical concerns of a child become more complex and sophisticated, the necessity that theory and practice, as well as study and work, be fully integrated becomes an increasingly critical factor in educational methodology. Because education is an aspect of experience, and because experience at its most rewarding is educative, it is never wise to reinforce the commonly made distinction between education, or schooling, and work. Dewey captures some of this in his discussion of the place of vocation in education, but for similar reasons, he thought that the world of work, or what he calls "industry and commerce," should be brought into the schools to enhance the educational process. Again, how this is done is up to teachers and their colleagues in the schools. They know best how to manage the extant circumstances at any time and place. But Dewey would want the principle to be clear. As an educational matter, it is not wise to treat the world outside of the school as something else entirely, even if the school, as he wants it to be, is an intentionally designed environment. The school and its social context have to be integrated if the children and students are to have valuable and educative experiences, just as the many disparate topics in the curriculum require integration.

Dewey was convinced, for the philosophical and practical reasons we have surveyed, that if such principles as these guide the schools, at all levels, then it would be possible to achieve an education (and educational systems) suitable for the development of intelligent and responsible individuals and for the maintenance of a democratic society. His ideas have had numerous supporters, and perhaps an equally large number of detractors, over the years. Dewey was politically progressive, we may say, much to the dismay of more conservatively minded philosophers and educators. Some of them have advanced reasonable objections and alternatives to his ideas, many of which he engaged in his own lifetime. In some cases, the criticism has not been reasonable, at times objecting to ideas Dewey never advocated and teaching styles or principles he never espoused. This process will, no doubt, continue as long as Dewey's ideas remain of interest, and that is likely to be for a very long time.

His ideas have also been criticized by those who think that he was not progressive enough. The point was made at the beginning of the chapter that Dewey was not a revolutionary, though he often advanced goals (for example, the overcoming of class differentiations not only in the schools but also in society as a whole) that would appear to be revolutionary. There seems to be a disconnect in this regard. Dewey knew that there are powerful interests in the society that would be hostile to the sort of reforms he proposed; however, he also thought not only that education could overcome these obstacles but also that it is the only way the obstacles can be overcome. Dewey was never an advocate of, for example, Karl Marx's view of class-based revolution as a viable—perhaps even necessary—means to correct social ills. It is not that he thought the ills did not need correction; rather, he believed that violent revolution could be justified only as a last resort. Aside from all of the undesirable consequence of violence, the main reason Dewey objected to violence as a method of solving social problems is that he was convinced that once we reach for violence, we have effectively abandoned the method of intelligence. Our default approach to social ills should be the application of intelligence in experience. That is why education as the reconstruction of experience is so important.

Some educators have thought that Dewey missed too much in this sort of analysis. One of them was Paulo Freire, to whose pedagogical ideas we can now turn.

CHAPTER 4

Domination and Liberation

Freire's *Pedagogy of the Oppressed*

Teaching is a political act. In some sense, this statement is true for Plato, Rousseau, and Dewey, in that they regard education as pointing toward the republic, the general will, and democracy, respectively. For Paulo Freire, though, the very act of teaching is inherently political, and in the act of teaching we invariably engender oppressive or liberating consequences for our students, ourselves, and our societies. What this means, what Freire's background philosophical conditions for it are, and how he justifies his conceptions are the topics to be explored in this chapter.

Freire also shares with our other figures, at a highly general level, a sense of the strength of the impact of education on individuals. Plato takes education as the way individuals can be raised to fulfill their individual natures, as determined by the class of "soul" that defines each of them; Rousseau thinks that education is the way to enable each individual's natural traits, including her innate goodness, to flourish; and Dewey wants education to help individuals develop the self-control through which they can guide their own experience to an experientially richer life. In Freire's case, education properly conducted is the path by which an individual achieves critical consciousness. This is one of the most important concepts in Freire's view of education, and we will develop its meaning and import as the chapter proceeds.

There are several books in which Freire developed his philosophy of education, including *Education for Critical Consciousness*, *Learning to Question: A Pedagogy of Liberation*, and *Pedagogy of Hope*. The most central and important of his books, however, and the one around which the others revolve, is *Pedagogy of the Oppressed*, and this is the work on which our study will focus.[1] We do not need many biographical details at this point, but it will be helpful for the reader to know that *Pedagogy of the Oppressed* explores ideas that Freire developed primarily while teaching literacy to impoverished peasants in northeastern Brazil, his native country. The book was written and published while Freire was in exile, having been expelled from the country soon after a military dictatorship took power in 1964. His experiences teaching the rural poor, and his arrest and expulsion for advocating freedom for the poor, are the background social conditions that have had an impact on the book and Freire's philosophy generally.

We may begin by citing two passages from early in the book in which Freire sets the terms of his analysis. He begins with a consideration of what it is to be human, or to live a genuinely human life. He states the issue in terms of the "problem of humanization," which, he says, "has always . . . been humankind's central problem." Humanization is so central to our lives, in fact, that he refers to it as "the people's vocation" (PO 25). In the second passage, Freire offers what he calls the "central problem" for his approach to education: "How can the oppressed, as divided, unauthentic beings, participate in developing the pedagogy of their liberation" (PO 30).

These two passages provide the terms and concepts out of which Freire develops his philosophy of education: humanization, vocation, oppression, authenticity, pedagogy, and freedom. There are indeed a number of assumptions implicit in the language he uses and in the way he frames the issues. Consider the idea that our vocation as people is humanization. First, he means the word "vocation" in the sense of a calling—that is, each of us, whatever else we may do with our lives, has humanization as a fundamental calling, which is to say something that, by virtue of being alive, we are oriented to do. Specifically, we are oriented or called to make ourselves human. Clearly, Freire means something more by the terms "human" and "humanization" than simply being biological *Homo sapiens*. The biological condition is a point of departure, but "humanization" is something to be accomplished or achieved. Being human in this sense—and we have yet to fill out the details of what that is—is something that requires effort on our part as well as appropriate social conditions.

It is also something that can fail to happen and may not be achieved for one reason or the other. Any number of things can go wrong. Perhaps we simply do not know what to do or how; perhaps we have not received the appropriate guidance, or the guidance we have received points us in the wrong directions; and, importantly, perhaps our social, economic, political, or cultural conditions impede our humanization. When we fail to achieve humanization, we fail thereby to live "authentic" lives; we are alienated from our own natures, from our vocation as human beings. When such inauthenticity and alienation is the result of social, economic, political, or cultural conditions that impede our humanization, we are suffering from oppression. In that case, it becomes a necessary feature of our lives, because it is necessary for us to pursue our vocation of humanization, to liberate ourselves from the oppression that generates our inauthenticity and alienation. If for whatever reason (and there are several possible causes) we do not pursue our own freedom, and thereby accept our oppressed condition, we are accepting life as alienated beings, deprived, by force or through our own contrivance (or both), of our own humanity.

Because it is so central a feature of our lives, education (in the sense of schooling, to be sure, but more important in the sense of upbringing) plays a critical role in our humanization. It can impede the process, in which case it is a tool of oppression, or it can contribute to the process, in which case it is a liberating activity. Freire was convinced that education cannot, in this respect, be neutral. It contributes necessarily to our oppression or to our freedom. This is not to say that individual teachers necessarily see the situation this way. In fact, almost certainly, most teachers do not see themselves in this way. But whether or not individual teachers or school administrators understand it, education in its structure, goals, and methods contributes either to oppression or to freedom. In this respect, Freire wants to make both a normative and a descriptive claim. Normatively, he holds that because education is central to our lives, and because our vocation as human beings is to achieve authenticity, education ought to have as its goal contributing to our own humanization. Descriptively, Freire's interest is in understanding in some detail what it is about the structure and methods of education that can be oppressive. Once we understand this, it becomes possible to articulate how education can avoid contributing to people's oppression and can become instead a tool for liberation. This is the overarching point of a pedagogy of the oppressed.

LIBERATION, AUTHENTICITY, AND LOVE

In order to understand how Freire goes about this analysis of education, it is necessary to understand his context, both social and intellectual. Freire was educated and began his pedagogical work in Brazil, so his social environment was conditioned by the history of Brazil specifically and of Latin America generally. We cannot go into this history in any detail, but there are several general features that should be highlighted. Most important, the history of Latin America from the very late fifteenth century through the end of the nineteenth century is a history of European colonization and rule. Every part of South and Central America, and all of North America as well, was divided for rule and economic exploitation by the major European powers—Spain, Portugal, England, France, and the Netherlands. In the mid-eighteenth century, England drove France out of much of North America, and by the end of the century, England itself had been driven from the Atlantic colonies of North America that lay south of Canada and north of the Caribbean. By the turn of the twentieth century, through a long and rather circuitous process of resistance and rebellion, Spain and Portugal had been driven from their colonies in South and Central America. However, direct colonial domination from Spain and Portugal was replaced, to a large extent, by less direct domination by the United States. The United States had already early in the nineteenth century declared in the Monroe Doctrine that much of Latin America fell within its "sphere of influence" and that it alone, therefore, had the right to influence events in that region.

The control that the United States exerted over much of Latin America after the departure of the Spanish and Portuguese had much the same purpose as had their colonial rule, which was to make the resources of the region, both natural and human, available for exploitation. The Spanish and Portuguese had done this in the name of "civilizing" the region, while the United States did it in the name of freedom and economic development. The result was largely the same in both cases: the wealth of the region was siphoned off to the dominant country, and the people were subjected to whatever rule seemed to be necessary to ensure their compliance. Sometimes that rule was imposed through direct military invasion, from Cuba at the end of the nineteenth century to Panama at the end of the twentieth, and continued threats (for example, against Venezuela) are being made as this book is being written in 2021. In most cases, though, the United States installed or sustained governments throughout Latin America that pursued policies that complemented US desires and interests. There are too many cases of such moments to mention, but time and again, and often to violent effect, the United States has tried, usually successfully, to dictate the internal affairs of Latin American countries.

If much of the twentieth century is characterized by the imposition of brutal dictatorships in Latin America, it is no less characterized by popular resistance. Resistance, subversion, rebellion, and revolution have been as common over the past century as have the oppressive regimes against which they are directed. Sometimes they have failed, and sometimes they have succeeded; sometimes they have distorted their own purposes and methods, while often they have provided freedom and development for millions of people. We will have occasion to refer to the idea of themes again later in the chapter, but it may be noted now that Freire held that one can identify what he calls historical epochs and that each such epoch can be characterized by one or more themes. The contemporary period in Latin America that we have been describing is one such epoch, and Freire says of this epoch that its theme is *domination* and its correlative task is *liberation* (PO 84). In light of even the cursory overview just offered, one can understand why he would say this. The imposition of oppressive rule on millions of people across Latin America has been relentless throughout this period, and it requires a certain act of willful avoidance to overlook it.

It is important to realize that the point is not to list invasions, coups, and exploitive economic arrangements. It is important to be aware of them, of course, but it is necessary to dig a bit deeper in order to appreciate why and how such events constitute a denial or negation of people's humanity. The first and most obvious point is the grinding poverty to which huge portions of the population of Latin America are subjected. This is true elsewhere in the world as well, but our focus here is on Latin America. From the farms of southern Mexico through the barrios of Managua, to the hillsides visible from downtown Caracas, to the rural villages of northeastern Brazil, where Freire taught, to the *favelas* of Rio de Janeiro, and well into the Southern Cone, there are living conditions more dire and tenuous than most people elsewhere in the world, including the United States, can imagine. Whether people in these places work in fields or factories, if they are fortunate enough to have regular work at all, the conditions of their labor can be burdensome, the controls under which they work are often brutal, the wages they receive are meager, and the opportunities available for education or self-improvement at any point in people's lives are minimal at best. Lives are lived, and lost, in such circumstances generation after generation.

These are the places, and the people, that Freire has in mind when he talks about oppression. It is not hard to see why such conditions generate for him a concern with humanization. By imposing such conditions on people, by denying them control over the conditions of their own work and lives, and by removing possibilities for a more developed future, the economic and political leaders responsible are effectively denying to the population the conditions of their own humanity. By now, we can see that this point is not unique to Freire, even if the precise terms in which he frames it are his. Rousseau had something similar in mind when he urged that Emile, during his childhood and education, not be subject to the strictures of an unjust society, and Dewey made a comparable point by emphasizing the necessity for people to control their own purposes and goals. For Rousseau and Dewey, too, these were conditions of living a genuinely human life. In fact, Plato had pointed out millennia ago how distorting to individuals and to their societies excessive wealth and dire poverty are.

Freire wants to help us to understand the same thing, while the drama of his language is proportional to the depth of the deprivation, and the consequent challenge, as he sees them. Oppressed people have their humanity denied them as they struggle with the conditions of their poverty and political repression. If humanization is people's vocation, then there is no choice but to struggle against the oppressive conditions imposed on them. We can expect nothing less, in fact. The situation is often complicated by the fact that the oppression is often justified in the language of freedom, rights, free markets, free speech, and all the other values with which we are familiar. What is often not noticed, however, and Freire is determined that we see this point, is that as valuable as these ideals are, when they are used to justify the actions of the oppressors they are simultaneously denied to the oppressed. If we are to speak in the language of rights, for example, the factory owner's right to exercise his capital as he thinks fit runs directly up against the workers' need for a livable wage, decent living and working conditions, education for their children, decent health care, and other features of normal life that many of us take for granted. As ironic as it may sound, the language of freedom and justice is a tool used to deny freedom and justice to millions of people. This fact, coupled with the desperate nature of the poverty to which so many people are subjected, serves only to deepen the problem of dehumanization and alienation. For Freire, this is not a mere disagreement over policies and practices; it is, rather, a much deeper question of existential entitlement on the part of the oppressed, and the fact that the very humanity of the oppressed is being denied them. There is no justification for such an existential crime, which makes the role of education all the more important. If education cannot be neutral, then it is either complicit in the existential crime or a means to overcome it. Freire, obviously, is urging the latter on us.

Four intellectual strains were available to Freire in his efforts to understand this situation, analyze its details, and develop an alternative pedagogy that can respond to it. The four were Marxism, existentialism, anti-colonial theory, and liberation theology. We are not able to delve into any of them in detail, but it will help to understand Freire if one has a flavor of them. We can begin with Marxism.

For better or worse, Marxism is rather out of fashion just now, but that was not the case in the 1960s, 1970s, and 1980s, when Freire's philosophy of education was being developed, implemented, and disseminated. On the contrary, Marxism was easily the most influential explanation available for the suffering so many people felt at the hands of their economic and political leaders, for how best to respond to those conditions, and for possible alternative economic, social, and political arrangements. To understand why Marxism was as influential as it was, aside from its intellectual merits, it is important to grasp the degree to which the dominant ideas and practices of liberal democracies had been discredited in many parts of the world.

In the developing world generally, which is to say Latin America, Africa, and South and Southeast Asia, dictatorial regimes were in place, some military and some civilian, that made no pretense of endorsing equality, freedom, and rights for all their people. It was clear to anyone who wanted to respond to the prevalent conditions of oppression that such dictatorial, authoritarian, and in some cases overtly fascist situations offered no solutions. More telling, though, was the fact that for many people who were resisting their economic and social repression, no solutions were forthcoming from the liberal democratic world either. The nations of North America, Europe, Japan, and other liberal states may have seen their own traditions as providing viable options, but that was in no way clear to many of those who were on the front lines in the opposition to oppression. On the face of it, liberal democracies should have been able to offer solutions, at least in theory (if not always smoothly in practice). The commitments to equality, justice, civil liberties, and economic opportunities that characterize the liberal democratic world ought, in principle, to provide options in the response to oppressive conditions. This was the reason, for example, that early in the struggle of the Vietnamese people against French colonial rule, beginning in the 1940s, the Vietnamese leader Ho Chi Minh based some of his ideas on the founding documents of the American republic in its own anti-colonial struggles, and he even thought that his efforts would have American support. He was tragically mistaken in that assumption, and it is instructive to consider what went wrong.

The basic problem was that the liberal democratic nations that had given birth to the ideals of liberty, equality, and justice had become the centers of colonial and imperial power. That France had initiated the themes of *liberté, égalité,* and *fraternité* in its own revolution in 1789 did not prevent it from using its power to repress its colonial subjects for its own economic interests. The same can be said about the United Kingdom, the Netherlands, Belgium, and, in its own way, the United States.

But the problem was not simply that liberal democracies had become the masters and ruled in what they regarded as their interests regardless of the consequences for subject peoples; they also did so in the name of the very values and moral commitments that they were violating. The values of freedom, equality, justice, and human rights had been weaponized, we might say today, and they were being directed against efforts to overcome oppression in the developing world. If, for example, one is helping a group of factory workers to respond to the overweening power of the factory owners and administrators, and if the state is supporting the owners in the name of their rights and freedom, then there is little point in appealing to the state on the workers' behalf in the name of those same rights and freedoms. In such a case, the rights and freedoms apply to one segment of the population and not to the rest. Invariably, they are used to support the interests of those who hold economic and political power against those who do not. From the point of view of the oppressed, then, such values as rights, freedoms, equality, and justice cannot serve as liberating tools when those responsible for the oppression are using them against you. This is precisely what many people in the postwar developing world saw in the liberal democracies of the time.

This was a problem of economic class, and the prevailing ideas of the liberal democracies, given their colonial and imperialist positions, were serving the interests of the ruling classes in the home countries and in most of the rest of the world. The many millions of people around the world who were suffering in this situation needed an analysis of the conditions they found themselves in, and they found the class analysis they needed in Marxism. There are many versions of Marxism, but they all share a set of core ideas. Marx had argued that since the emergence of agriculture and the creation of cities thousands of years ago, societies have been characterized by class distinctions based primarily on the control of productive wealth. A range of explanations have been offered for this development, and they tend to be related to the creation of a surplus that settled agriculture and life in cities engendered. Whatever the causes, class stratification developed such that one set of people tended to accumulate greater wealth and power, and this ruling class became able to dominate its society. Wealth tends to accumulate, again for a range of possible reasons, and over time the ruling class becomes a relatively small segment of the population. The net effect of this is that a minority accumulates a disproportionate amount of wealth and power, and the subservient classes (the majority) find themselves under the domination of the ruling class. In such a circumstance, the ruling class has as its interest to maintain its wealth and power, even at the expense of the subservient classes. Conversely, the subservient classes find themselves with interests that contradict those of the ruling class. A great deal of detail is being overlooked here, but this is the basic Marxist idea.

Moreover, the ruling class invariably establishes the social institutions that support its interests, even when they are inconsistent with or contradict the interests of the subservient, or working, classes. In the ancient world, for example, such legal and political systems as there existed were designed to protect the wealth and power of the propertied elite. This is the reason why in most ancient societies around the world the propertied class held political as well as economic power. This has remained the case throughout history, even when the details change to accord with different sorts of social structures. In medieval Europe, for example, the details of the relationship between the landed aristocracy and the rest of the population differed from those of ancient societies, and the details of the social and political structures differed accordingly. Despite the differences, the economic elite, the wealthy minority, continued to control political power.

Marx argued that when the feudal system in Europe broke down in the early modern period, to be replaced by what is now commonly called capitalism, the details of the class relations changed again but not the general structure of power. Capitalism is characterized by mobility, of both capital and labor, and in this respect the details of the relation between those who control capital and those who sell their labor differ considerably from what had come before, and over the years social institutions were generated to acknowledge those differences. For example, systems of ownership of productive capital, and the legal institutions that enable them, now must accommodate the mobility of capital and the contractual nature of the relation between capital and labor. What has not changed, however, is that the minority of the population that controls the bulk of the productive wealth in a capitalist society continues to exercise the greater political power and the working classes, whose interests remain largely inconsistent with those of the capitalists, remain for the most part at their mercy.

These points convey Marxist economic and social analysis, but it is equally important to see that there is a correlative ideological analysis. Marx argued that in order to sustain its wealth and power, the ruling class not only constructs social institutions in its interests but also drives the dominant ideas of its society such that the ideas serve its interests rather than those of the majority working class.

When the American revolutionaries, for example, emphasized in the Declaration of Independence that "all men are created equal" and the centrality of human rights, specifically the rights to life, liberty, and the pursuit of happiness, they understood those values in terms that were consistent with their own class interests. There were disagreements among themselves on various matters, but, for the most part, the Founders did not believe that, for example, men without property were equal to men with property, nor did they believe that liberty for the propertied meant the same thing as liberty for those without property. Eventually, these differences became apparent to a growing number of newly independent Americans, and the result in some cases was several popular rebellions. The point is that the meaning and import of the historically important commitment to the values of equality, freedom, and rights was from the beginning oriented toward the interests of the ruling class rather than to those of the majority.

Times change, and the details of how these ideas are applied change as well. Ownership of property, for example, is no longer a condition of political participation in liberal democracies. Some features have changed relatively little, though. When, for example, workers challenge a company that decides to move its facility to another city or country, thus eliminating jobs and possibly destroying a community, one typically finds that the owner's rights to the mobility of his capital are more important than any interests of the members of the community. In the end, the ideas still mean largely what the ruling class needs them to mean.

This is even more starkly the case in the developing world, where, as a rule, far fewer legal and political protections for workers are in place. When the values of rights and equality are structured to support the ruling class, one cannot expect the liberal democracies, from which those same ideas derive, to offer any help. On the contrary, they typically align themselves with the local ruling classes, so that oppressed peoples throughout the developing world have found themselves fighting not only their local oppressors but also the enablers from the capitals of the liberal democracies themselves. Under these circumstances, it is small wonder that many people struggling for the interests of working people have turned to Marxist analysis and socialism for answers and support.

This was the analytic milieu in which Freire approached the problems of education, or, better to say, it was part of his intellectual environment. He was also influenced, as many at the time were, by the existentialism that was then prominent, especially in the writings of Jean-Paul Sartre. We can say very little about this here, but it is important to bring this up because it helps to explain a dimension of Freire's understanding of oppression that we do not find in most other Marxist and socialist thinkers, and that is his concern with authenticity and humanization. From Freire's perspective, the oppression he saw around him is not simply a systemic denial of the material conditions necessary for a comfortable (or even decent) life. It is, in addition, a systemic denial of the very humanity of the people who suffer; it denies them the necessary conditions of living a genuinely human life. This is the existential crime mentioned earlier, and one gets the distinct impression when reading Freire that he regarded this as perhaps the worst feature of oppression. Material suffering is bad enough, but to have the capacity for one's humanity denied, especially when it is done in the name of freedom, justice, and rights, is an unbearable travesty, and nothing even resembling a humane circumstance. It is important to understand this level of seriousness of the problem, because without understanding it, Freire's anger and passion can seem exaggerated. But if our humanity is at stake, then there is nothing exaggerated about a pedagogy of the oppressed.

The idea of authenticity rests on the prior idea that there is something distinctive about human beings generally and about people as individuals. One could trace the history of the idea in detail, though for us it will be enough to point out two prior conceptions out of which the idea of individual human uniqueness derived. In earlier epochs in Europe, and to this day in some cultures around the world, the social order and its dominant moral commitments framed individual life, not only in the sense that it made biological life possible but also, and equally important, in the sense that it was social relations that gave individual lives meaning and purpose. In such a situation, one, for example, did not choose one's profession, or religion, or often even one's spouse. These were all aspects of the social world that conditioned each member of it.

With the rise of what we now call the "modern" world in Europe, a gradual process certainly, but in full swing by the seventeenth century, the constitutive character of the society fades away (at least in theory), and the individual begins to be prominent. This can be seen in the nature of the Protestant reaction to the power of Rome, wherein the Protestants argued that the Church was not necessary or even desirable, because each individual should have a direct relation to God. At roughly the same time, thinking about the relation of the individual and society had been reversed. Where earlier, it was the social structure that conditioned the nature of individuals, it was now thought that individuals constitute the society, and we begin to see such ideas as the social contract, and the idea that the state derives its legitimacy from the consent of the governed. This is the same process that generated the modern ideas of individual freedoms and rights. The centrality of the individual also found expression in economic theory, in which in the late eighteenth century Adam Smith could argue that economic activity must be understood as a process wherein countless individuals interact with one another, each seeking her own individual purposes.

The second general idea is that the human individual, even when understood to be more central than her social relations, is distinct in nature or character from other kinds of individuals. We are obviously distinct from inert objects like rocks, even though like rocks we are in some measure material beings. We are also distinct from other organic beings in that we can do things that, for example, trees and plants presumably cannot do. We have some degree of conscious awareness, a trait that it appears we have in common with at least some other animals. But even other animals that are aware of their surroundings and can feel pain and even emotion, are not, again presumably, self-aware, and they are not capable of the kind of cognitive, aesthetic, and political development that define human individuals.

The distinctiveness of conscious human beings began to play a role in people's thinking about the world at the same time as modern religious, social, political, and economic ideas began to emerge. Individual consciousness began to be seen as the source of what is important in life. The French philosopher Descartes did not say "I socialize, therefore I am," but "I think, I am," and he understood thinking as an internal process that each individual undertakes independently from others. The story gets more complicated from there, and we will skip it for the most part. Eventually, people began to wonder about this distinctive human individual and to speculate about what it is that is so unique. This is the point, specifically in the early twentieth century, at which the idea of authenticity comes into focus, first in the hands of the German philosopher Martin Heidegger, and by the middle years of the century in the work of the French writers Jean-Paul Sartre and Simone de Beauvoir. It is from them, especially Sartre, that Freire absorbed the idea.

Heidegger argued that a human being is unlike other beings in that she is never only an object for others. Sartre put the point in what may be more accessible terms when he said that the human individual is radically free, by which he meant that we are constantly making choices about our lives—among other things, about what we value, about what we do, about what we aspire to, and about how we treat others. The authentic person is one who embraces this radical freedom and thereby takes responsibility for her life and her choices. To fail to accept one's own freedom is to alienate oneself from one's radical freedom, from one's own existential condition, and thereby to live an inauthentic life. When we choose to live inauthentically, we are living in what Sartre called "bad faith." But when our social and material circumstances are such that our radical freedom is curtailed and our choices truncated, and when those circumstances prohibit us from making the choices about our own values and aspirations, it is our very humanity that is being denied. Bad faith, in Sartre's sense, is the refusal to live a human life and thus a kind of self-determined alienation, but an alienation from our own human freedom that is imposed on us by a social, cultural, economic, and political order is a material and existential oppression. This is how Freire understood what he saw around him.[2]

A third influence enriches the picture even further, and I refer here specifically to the analyses of the colonial environment and people's resistance to it that was emerging in the 1950s and 1960s. The two figures on whom Freire draws are Albert Memmi and Franz Fanon. Memmi's most influential nonfiction work was *The Colonizer and the Colonized* (1957) to which Sartre contributed the preface, and Fanon was universally known for his *Wretched of the Earth* (1961).[3] Both books, written by authors who were familiar with colonial environments—in their cases, the French colonial world of northern Africa—concerned themselves not only with the material, social, and political aspects of colonialism but also with the effect that colonialism has on its victims. From them, Freire took the idea that an oppressed people can internalize the conditions and terms of their own oppression.

What Sartre had called bad faith, which is the denial of one's own freedom, can occur even among those whose freedom is denied them by their oppressors. Even the oppressed can engage in bad faith and deny both their own inherent freedom and their oppression. This happens when people accept as their own the values, perspectives, and interests of those who oppress them—for example, when people who are poor by virtue of underdevelopment accept the insistence of the ruling class that they are poor because of their own shortcomings. It can also happen when the oppressed accept an ideology that attempts to justify their oppression to them, perhaps with promises of a better life after death. Freire understood that if domination is to be overcome and liberation achieved, the internal oppressor—the bad faith that the victims of oppression impose on themselves, what he refers to as people's "fear of freedom"—has to be addressed. His effort in this regard is what he calls in Portuguese *conscientização*, which can best be translated into English as coming to consciousness or raising one's consciousness. The idea, and this is a central aspect of Freire's pedagogy, is that people who are victimized by oppression, and perhaps especially those who have internalized the oppressor, can only choose their own freedom if

they can come to see the oppressive nature of their circumstances, understand their freedom to reject it, and embrace their own power to overcome
it. Freire's pedagogy is an effort to articulate how this might be done.

Before we can look at the pedagogical details, there is one additional factor that needs to be taken into account in order to understand Freire's own
sense of what he was dealing with and his approach to it. The final influence is what we I have referred to as liberation theology. To ascribe to Freire
an interest in liberation theology is in one sense to make an attribution
avant la lettre, since the term itself was coined only in 1971 by the Peruvian
Catholic theologian Gustavo Gutiérrez in his book *A Theology of Liberation*.[4]
The ideas, however, had been percolating, especially in Latin America, from
the late 1950s. The ideas to which the term "liberation theology" refers were
immensely influential in the 1970s and 1980s, in Latin America certainly,
but elsewhere as well. Many theologians and activist Catholic priests and
nuns, some of whom moved south from North America, played important
roles in the political movements and revolutions during those years and, in
fact, held leadership positions in revolutionary governments (for example,
in Nicaragua during the early Sandinista years of the 1980s).

As with the other intellectual influences, we are obliged to make a long
story short. The basic idea of liberation theology was that a serious and
committed Christianity had to take the side of the poor. Traditionally, the
church's approach to the poor was at most to try to ameliorate their suffering, either materially or spiritually, but it stopped well short of attempting
to eliminate the causes of that suffering. The liberation theologians and
their followers felt that this reluctance to address causes is unacceptable.
It is all well and good "to render unto Caesar what is Caesar's," but not
when Caesar is actively immiserating his people. To allow such immiser-
ation to go unchallenged is effectively to be complicitous in the oppression, and for that there is no justification in Christianity. Some advocates
of such a "liberation Christianity," to coin a phrase, took up arms in rebellions and revolutions, and others took a more pacifist commitment. In
all cases, though, they argued that the Christian injunction to love meant
to side with the poor, and, reciprocally, to side with the poor meant to act
with them in a loving context.

Freire comes to his work in precisely the same spirit. We have already
seen that he embraced the Marxism of a class analysis, so that he understood the oppression that he saw as the result of a capitalist system that
was exercised by a ruling class to defend its interests against those of the
working majority. Liberation theology also tended to accept the same Marxist analysis, much to the consternation of Church leaders of the time in
Rome and elsewhere. Freire was more disposed to enrich his Marxism with
French existentialism, while the liberation theologians took their spiritual
guidance from traditional Christianity. But they agreed on the centrality of

love. Freire makes the point explicitly: "Because love is an act of courage, not of fear, love is commitment to others. No matter where the oppressed are found, the act of love is commitment to their cause—the cause of liberation. And this commitment, because it is loving, is dialogical" (PO 70). We will turn in a moment to what Freire means by the term "dialogical," but for now the point is the centrality of love to the engagement with people and to pedagogy. In this respect, Freire shares with the liberation theologians not only a commitment to the poor but also an understanding of the ground of that commitment.

It should be somewhat clearer at this point how Freire understood the conditions he saw around him, why he thought that pedagogy has no choice but to engage itself with those conditions, and the general terms on which that must occur. With that clearer understanding, it is possible now to look more closely at the details of the pedagogy he thought was able to take on such a weighty task.

BANKING, PROBLEM-POSING, AND DIALOGUE

An initial point that should be made concerns the applicability of Freire's pedagogical ideas, especially since the conditions in which he developed them seem to be so distant from conditions in the more developed world. His pedagogy, one might say, even if appropriate for an oppressed peasantry and industrial working class in the developing world, hardly seems suitable for a modern urban or suburban classroom. This is a legitimate concern, and one that needs to be answered if the study of Freire's pedagogy is to be more than a merely academic exercise.

First, we should realize that the "uniqueness" feature of Freire's context is actually something that he shares with the other philosophers whom we have considered. They are all in unique contexts. Plato's ancient Athens is surely unique, certainly by comparison with anything anywhere in the world today. We can say more or less the same about Rousseau. Dewey's context, which is the modern classroom, is much closer to the schooling those of us in developed parts of the world recognize, but then that means that anyone in less developed or more economically exploited parts of the world might wonder whether Dewey has anything to say to them.

So, we are faced with a bit of a conundrum. Either there is some way for us to reach out of our immediate environments to understand the perspective of others, and possibly to imagine ways to apply their insights in our own times and places, or we are all condemned to benefit only from those who are largely the same as us. If the latter were true, then it would be impossible for us to understand anything about (or learn anything from) history, or anthropology, or literature, or painting. The meaning and value of all of those enterprises would be restricted to their own environs, and little more than closed books to us. But that clearly is not so, because all of us have had occasions in which we have gleaned something that was not previously clear from a historical event or a compelling piece of fiction. Indeed, the whole point of such undertakings is to take ourselves, even if at times reluctantly, out of ourselves, thereby benefiting from the rest of the world.

The situation with educational theory is no different. Notwithstanding the differences among us and Plato, Rousseau, Dewey, and Freire, there is also a great deal that we have in common. It is in the end that commonality that allows us *entrée* into one another's world, and that creates the conditions that enable us to learn from them, and from others in our own time. It is precisely the generality of philosophical inquiry (which is to say that though its material may be bound by time and place, its aspirations are not) that makes it available to us, and to others in any time and place, to learn from and draw on. Freire's pedagogy can and should be approached in the same spirit, and for the same reasons.

A second consideration, one that follows from the first, is that Freire is not providing formulas for how to teach peasants in northeastern Brazil, or, better, he is not only doing that. He can be quite specific in his methodological recommendations, which are in fact built on his experience teaching literacy to Brazilian peasants, but even in the greatest specificity, there are general principles that may be extracted and applied in other circumstances. Again, the same is true for Plato, Rousseau, and Dewey. Despite Plato's argument for having philosophers run the state, we are not likely, and with good enough reason, to follow him down that road. But there are principles implicit in Plato's recommendation—for example, that good leaders ideally are people of wisdom and insight and in possession of habits of mind and behavior that are conducive to understanding and sound judgment. Plato has a point, regardless of the political standing of philosophers. The same is true for Rousseau. We are not going to follow many of his prescriptions or specific methods in our educational practices, but we can certainly be mindful of the ways that social relations can distort the children we work with, which is the general point behind the details of Rousseau's pedagogy. In the same spirit, when considering Freire, we do not want simply to ask whether specific methodological proposals can be applied in a classroom, although in some cases they can be, but what are the general principles that drive the details and whether we can benefit from a greater understanding of them.

There is one final point as a preparation for a closer look at Freire's pedagogy, which is that we would do well to keep in mind at least the possibility that the experience in modern urban and suburban classrooms (and in whole contemporary societies, for that matter) may not be as far from the conditions that Freire saw as we may initially think. For one thing, even in the midst of some degree of wealth and comfort, there is often a debilitating poverty and oppression that can easily be overlooked and passed by. If that is so, then we would all do well—assuming that we take our educational responsibilities seriously, whatever they may be—to make a genuine effort not only to face that uncomfortable fact but also to understand and make some attempt to ameliorate it. This sort of thing can reveal itself in many ways, from some children coming to school hungry or ill clothed to the effects of disparities of educational opportunity from one town or school district to the next. If we look further afield from our own neighborhoods, problems like these can be even greater.

The oppression in our midst, moreover, may apply to ourselves, whether we have realized it or not. Freire's concern, after all, is in the long run with humanization, and education of the kind that he devoted himself to has as its purpose the enabling of our common vocation to achieve our own humanity. The obstacles to that end are everywhere, not simply in grinding poverty and overt political oppression. They can be found in the inability to control the circumstances of our lives (for example, at work), which is a problem that plagues many or most of us. Even many people who are reasonably comfortable materially are only months away from serious problems and even desperation if they lose their income for one reason or another; for many, especially in a country like the United States where health care is so expensive, sometimes medical needs go unmet for lack of available funds; often we are virtually compelled to work in alienating jobs because our material circumstances give us no real choice; and, increasingly for many, it is necessary for material reasons to continue to work well into an age in which ideally we could finally relax and enjoy the leisure that a lifetime of labor has earned. The vocation of humanization applies to all of us, and it is an ongoing project toward which Freire may have something to teach us.

Freire's initial recommendation concerns a preposition. His is a pedagogy of the oppressed, but he wants to be sure from the start that we realize that the mechanisms of this pedagogy are not *for* the oppressed but *with* them. If we want to help people achieve their humanity, the first thing we need to do is to stop telling them what they need, or how they should think, or what they should do. One form that oppression takes is a condition of passive malleability, wherein people allow others, typically others with more power or authority, to define them, to tell them what they should do and what they need. Those who are passive in this way allow others to shape their lives and even to supply its content. If as teachers we approach our task in that way—even if we do so with the best of intentions—we are simply reinforcing the alienation and oppression of our students, whoever they are.

The most common form of manipulation of this kind in education is what Freire calls the banking method of teaching. He is here emphasizing a point that had been made repeatedly over the years, from as early as the

Republic. Recall that Plato had said that the point of education is not "to put knowledge into the souls that lack it" but to "turn the soul" toward knowledge and wisdom; Rousseau argued that it is pointless, even detrimental, to fill children with information, most of which in due course they will forget, and it is far preferable to allow them to learn from and in experience; Dewey also thought it far better to provide children with the opportunity to discover things on their own than to feed it to them, even if their discovery requires guidance from us.

Freire's idea is in the same tradition, though he makes much more of the point than the others do. Not only does he highlight it more than the others had, but his objection to teaching in the form of providing information also cuts more deeply than the reasons the others had to resist it. They all thought that teaching in this way is not only bad pedagogy (in the sense that students will learn better in other ways) but also dangerous because, for one reason or another, it impedes children's development. For Freire, the danger is that teaching this way contributes to the oppression of the students and consequently works against the proper purposes of education. This is an important feature of Freire's pedagogy, and we need to dwell on it a bit.

The teacher–student relationship, he thought, is fraught with danger from the start, in that it can too easily embody a kind of contradiction. If the teacher understands herself (or is understood by her students) to be the specialist who knows what the students need and will provide it, the experiential balance in the relationship is already off kilter. The problem primarily is that in such a situation the teacher assumes an active role and requires the passivity of the students. Such passivity, as we have already seen, is a mark of the oppressive conditions that characterize the lives of so many people. Others—supervisors, bosses, political leaders—make the decisions that condition people's lives. By assuming an active role in the classroom and expecting passivity among the students, teachers are simply placing themselves among the ranks of those who, knowingly or not, deny people their humanity. The fact is, Freire thought, that genuine learning only takes place when students merge the passive and the active, in what he calls, using a term that was common at the time, praxis.

Most of us express a vague sense of the importance of activity for learning when we ask students to write a point down rather than just listen to it, or when we say to one another and to students that when they must organize their thoughts and ideas in an essay they will master the material much better. In these moments, we are recognizing that activity is essential in the learning process. Freire would have agreed, but he also thought that praxis, the merger of reflection that is active and activity that is reflective, is even more vitally important: "Functionally, oppression is domesticating. To no longer be prey to its force, one must emerge from it and turn upon it. This can be done only by means of the praxis: reflection and action upon the world in order to transform it" (PO 33).

Students—and the rest of us, for that matter—may not regularly accomplish this condition, but to aim short of it is for education to abrogate its humanizing responsibility: "For apart from inquiry, apart from the praxis, individuals cannot be truly human. Knowledge emerges only through invention and re-invention, through the restless, impatient, continuing, hopeful inquiry human beings pursue in the world, with the world, and with each other" (PO 53). Education as banking, as making deposits of information in students' minds, is the opposite of praxis and undermines the educational purposes of learning and acquiring knowledge. When teaching is done primarily by conveying information, "the teacher issues communiqués and makes deposits which the students patiently receive, memorize, and repeat . . . in which the scope of action allowed to the students extends only as far as receiving, filing, and storing the deposits . . . in the last analysis, it is the people themselves who are filed away through lack of creativity, transformation, and knowledge" (PO 53).

Freire is quite specific about the traits of the banking method of teaching that he thinks are the reason it is so seriously flawed:

a) the teacher teaches and the students are taught;
b) the teacher knows everything and the students know nothing;
c) the teacher thinks and the students are thought about;
d) the teacher talks and the students listen—meekly;
e) the teacher disciplines and the students are disciplined;
f) the teacher chooses and enforces his choice, and the students comply;
g) the teacher acts and the students have the illusion of acting through the action of the teacher;
h) the teacher chooses the program content, and the students (who were not consulted) adapt to it;
i) the teacher confuses the authority of knowledge with his or her own professional authority, which she and he sets in opposition to the freedom of the students;
j) the teacher is the Subject of the learning process, while the pupils are mere objects (PO 54).

The more passive students are, the less they develop critical consciousness, which in the end serves the interests of the oppressors. If the social, economic, political, and cultural structures are in place largely to support the interests of the ruling class (which is what Freire thought to be the case), then the last thing the ruling class (or what he frequently simply calls "the oppressors") wants is a population that does not calmly accept the conditions they are in and the ideological justifications provided for them.

When teachers underscore the passivity of students through the banking method, they serve the interests of the ruling class and contribute to the oppression, albeit often unwittingly, of the students and their communities. Echoing a point that Dewey had made, though with a slightly different emphasis, Freire says that the banking concept of teaching assumes a dichotomy between people and the world by positing people as spectators. The world around them, or the powerful people in it, act while they passively watch and absorb the results. People are thereby trained not to be the masters of their own lives but to adapt to their oppression: "The more completely the majority adapt to the purposes which the dominant minority prescribe for them (thereby depriving them of the right to their own purposes), the more easily the minority can continue to prescribe" (PO 57).

These are the reasons that the contradiction between teachers and students created by the assumption of the teacher's activity and the students' passivity is exacerbated by the banking approach to teaching. The necessary alternative, again in a turn of phrase that to a degree is reminiscent of Dewey, is "problem-posing" education. The first step into this conception is to think of the teacher's relation to the student not, as the banking method would have it, as one in which the teacher dictates and the student absorbs, but rather as a sort of partnership. This idea may be somewhat easier to picture in the case of educating adults, as Freire was doing, but undoubtedly, with the application of a bit of imagination and creativity, a teacher can approach even young children in this spirit. It would depend, of course, on what Freire means by "partnership."

A critical component of the concept of a partnership between teacher and student is communication, the importance of which from Freire's point of view cannot be overstated. Its importance lies, first, in the fact that communication is a necessary condition of cognition: "Authentic thinking, thinking that is concerned about *reality*, does not take place in ivory tower isolation, but only in communication" (PO 58). The second reason for the significance of communication is that it is a condition not only of cognition but also of meaning, in fact "only through communication can human life hold meaning" (PO 58). We should notice that implicit in this point is that Freire's conception of the nature of the human individual is, as we have seen in other respects, quite different from the view of the individual that arose in the early modern period, and that still dominates thinking in the liberal democracies that hold the most power and influence. In those ways of understanding the world, the individual is an atomized entity, abstracted from her social relations. In that conception, thinking, learning, and knowing are internal, individualized processes, and it would make no sense to say of such an individual that communication is necessary for thinking or for meaning. To say that it is necessary is to signal that one has in mind a different idea of the individual. For Freire, communication is necessary for thinking and meaning because human life is inherently social. *Robinson Crusoe* meant something to the eighteenth-century mind, and, as we saw, it meant a great deal to Rousseau, but for Freire the idea of an isolated human being is a contradiction in terms. People need communication because we need one another to be human. This is another reason that the banking method of teaching is so detrimental, in that it consists not of communicative engagement between teacher and student but of the issuing, as Freire puts it, of communiqués. Moreover, communication in the sense of the engagement of individuals with one another in the process of learning and the development of meaning is no less possible between an adult and children than among adults alone. If communication is possible in the education of children, so is the partnership that Freire believes necessary to avoid contributing to injustice and oppression.

If such a partnership is possible in contemporary primary and secondary school classrooms, then so is the problem-posing pedagogy that assumes such a partnership and that Freire advocates. Because "liberating education consists in acts of cognition, not transferals of information" (PO 60), and because cognition occurs in communicative relations rather than "in" individual minds, genuine education takes place in the meaningful communication between teacher and student—and among students themselves, we might add.

Freire also provides a bit of a twist to our understanding of subject matter, one that turns out to have fairly expansive ramifications. As he puts it, liberating education "is a learning situation in which the cognizable object (far from being the end of the cognitive act) intermediates the cognitive actors—teacher on the one hand and students on the other" (PO 60).

We need to consider briefly what this claim amounts to. It is common to think of the point of a pedagogical experience (leaving aside for the moment other longer-term goals of education) as enabling a student to understand the subject matter, whatever it is at the moment. Imagine, for example, a lesson in American history—specifically, on the origins of the Civil War, though we could use any topic from any discipline to make the point. Our inclination as teachers is to think of the point of the lesson that, as a result of it, students will understand to some (possibly even minimal) extent why there was a civil war in the United States. If we think about the lesson and its purpose in this way, we are regarding the "cognizable object" (in this case, the Civil War and its origins) as "the end of the cognitive act," which is to say the purpose of the lesson. But this, Freire wants us to realize, is the wrong way to think about subject matter. The value of the subject matter, on the contrary, is that it is the occasion of the communicative engagement of the teacher with the students and of the students with one another. For example, the topic of the origins of the Civil War is an opportunity for all of us to talk about aspects of our own lives, and the lives of our ancestors, that might generate such events. We might wonder together whether anything goes wrong in our own communities that could create such a disruption; we might wonder together whether we can imagine anything worth fighting and dying for, and why; we can wonder together whether what appear to be the circumstances that led to the Civil War may have left imprints on our societies and communities that are visible to us.

Many teachers do this sort of thing as a matter of course, but they often do not realize the full import of what we are doing and thereby pull up short of a genuinely liberating experience and situation. By treating the object as an "intermediary" or occasion for communicative interaction, we are able to value the communication rather than conveying information as the educational event. This is enriching for students, even very young children, because by engaging them as agents in relation to the subject matter, we enable them to take control of it; it is in this regard an empowering event. The "cognizable object" in this case is not another burden that weighs on the child's mind and serves as one more obligation but an occasion to dig into one's world, which is one way to describe inquiry, the result of which is greater understanding of oneself, one's world, and, in the process, the subject matter. The example of a profound historical event may seem ideally tailored to this sort of pedagogy, and perhaps it is, but the same approach can be taken to any topic. A lesson on gravity can relatively easily be handled this way, in that, in the process of describing and illustrating what gravity is, we can consider with students what it means in their lives, about how the balls they throw behave and why, about airplanes, and how the control of gravity enables the experiences of their lives. It is a question not of what the subject matter is but of engaging with it as a way of triggering the agency of the children in relation to it. A novel, or a painting, or a song, or an equation, or a frog, or a chemistry experiment, or anything else we wish to teach, can have the same liberating result if we approach it as an intermediary in the communicative relation between teacher and student. This is the significant upshot of Freire's brief remark about the "cognizable object."

This also helps us to see why Freire uses the term "problem-posing" as the pedagogy that is the appropriate alternative to banking. The communicative engagement with students in the process of spinning out the meaning of any subject matter is a process wherein the teacher encourages the student, even if indirectly, to approach her own experience from a position of power. It is in this sense that problems are posed by this method of teaching. But for Freire, this is only the beginning of the process. It is an important beginning because it enables us to overcome the dichotomy or contradiction between teacher and student. Moreover, in the process of communicative interaction, the teacher and the students are sharing not only ideas and observations but also their pedagogical roles themselves. Teachers are becoming students in that they are learning, and students are becoming teachers in that they are realizing, or uncovering, aspects of their experience that they then share with the teacher and the other students.

All of this is critically important for a liberating education, and it is enabled by dialogue, which is a feature of the communicative situation on which Freire places a great deal of emphasis. As he puts it at one point, "The students—no longer docile listeners—are now critical co-investigators in dialogue with the teacher. . . . The role of the problem-posing educator is to create, together with the students, the conditions under which knowledge at the level of the *doxa* is superseded by true knowledge, at the level of *logos*" (PO 62). The two Greek words *doxa* (which means "opinion") and *logos* (which means "word," or "thought," or "discourse") convey a difference not so much in cognitive confidence but in depth of understanding. Freire means to say here that the traditional way of approaching content in the educational experience can, and does, give students ideas or conceptions of things, which he describes as *doxa*. They are, though, somewhat superficial because they tend to lack for the students meaning and lived import. Problem-posing pedagogy, by contrast, which has at its heart dialogue between teacher and students, enables students to grasp not simply an idea of something but also its meaning and import and, most important, its meaning and import in the student's own experience. This is a much more profound grasp of a subject matter, and Freire describes it as *logos*, or "true knowledge." A pedagogy that opens for students the possibility of grasping their world and their lives as agents, and which allows them gradually to develop an understanding of themselves as powerful individuals who under the right circumstances can knead their understanding into their own experience and lives, is enabled by dialogue.

The caveat "under the right circumstances" is of course critical, because one of the assumptions of Freire's analysis is that in the contemporary world many people, probably the vast majority, in fact, do not have the right circumstances available to them. They do not have the opportunity to transform *doxa* into *logos*, which is to say that they do not have the opportunity for genuine education, knowledge, and inquiry, and they do not have the opportunity as a consequence of the oppressive conditions under which they must live. This is an intolerable situation, Freire thinks. An empowering education "bases itself on creativity and stimulates true reflection and action upon reality, thereby responding to the vocation of persons as beings who are authentic only when engaged in inquiry and creative transformation" (PO 65). The denial of such an opportunity to people, at any age, is an attack on people's very humanity: "Any situation in which some individuals prevent others from engaging in the process of inquiry is one of violence"

(PO 66). A dialogic education is probably not a sufficient response to such violence, but it is, Freire argues, a necessary one.

Dialogue is by definition at least a two-way process in which people engage one another in a meaning-generating communication. At the heart of dialogue, Freire points out, is the word. But words are not simply tools with which one conveys ideas. Freire's conception of language, and his epistemology, are more complicated than that. First, and in this respect he again sounds a bit like the pragmatists, ideas are not reflections of reality, largely because unless they are simply shadowy and fleeting images; ideas invariably have an active and transformative dimension to them. In fact, the truth of ideas, in what is a fairly radical epistemological point of view, lies in their transformative power. To say of an idea that is of no use to anyone in the ongoing construction of their experience that it is true is to offer a pointless attribution. The meaning and value of ideas lie in their transformative power in action. Second, language in that case is a component of the transformative process. Perhaps it is better to say that meaningful language is a component of the transformative process.

We are, here, returning to the concept of praxis. Reflection and inquiry, insofar as they are meaningful, must have an active side, simply because meaningful ideas and language are active. The word in a dialogical context is, as Freire wants to put it, a convergence of reflection and action. To make the point, he acknowledges that it is possible to have language without transformative action, as well as action without reflection. Language, or reflection, without transformative action is, he says, mere verbalism, while action without reflection is what he calls activism. Neither verbalism nor activism in the sense in which Freire uses them are desirable conditions. Verbalism divorces language from its transformative power, and activism divorces power from the reflective dimension that gives it direction (PO 68–69). Praxis is the convergence of the two, and educational dialogue—if it is liberating—is praxis.

Dialogue is the communicative engagement of people with one another to "name the world." This can only happen, however, if people are not simply repeating the terms of another, because in that case they are merely reporting the world as others have named it, so to speak. In genuine dialogue, people must take control of their language and name their world with their words, not others'. The importance of this process is not to be underestimated: "To exist, humanly, is to *name* the world, to change it. Once named, the world in its turn reappears to the namers as a problem and requires of them a new *naming*. . . . Dialogue is thus an existential necessity" (PO 69). This is the reason that a liberating pedagogy cannot be "for" the oppressed. To engage in genuine dialogue, people must be able to take an active part in the process. It is not a process undertaken for people but with them.

Freire at this point focuses on the affective relation a teacher must have with students, presumably with students of any age: "Dialogue cannot exist, however, in the absence of a profound love for the world and for people. The naming of the world, which is an act of creation and re-creation, is not possible if it is not infused with love" (PO 70). Furthermore, dialogue requires a teacher's humility. One cannot, he says, participate in an educative communication, in dialogue, if one treats one's students as ignorant, or unworthy, or in general engages them with arrogance. Humility is required, as is faith: "Dialogue further requires an intense faith in humankind, faith in their power to make and remake, to create and re-create, faith in their vocation to be more fully human" (PO 71). And he warms to the theme, making the further case that because it requires love, humility, and faith, the dialogical, educational relation rests on mutual trust between teacher and student. Moreover, such a situation is one imbued with hope, specifically hope in the student's capacity for her own development and the creative construction of her life (PO 72–73). Dialogue and education do not reside in resignation or futility, or, as we might put it, simply "going through the motions."

This all sounds quite nice, but it can have a ring of naïveté about it, especially for teachers who are accustomed to dealing with unruly or uncooperative students. We should realize, though, that Freire worked in the most difficult of circumstances, and he was not likely to think in naïve and cliched terms. So what, we may ask, is realistic in his injunctions to teachers to love, trust, and hope? Freire understood as well as anyone that students may not cooperate in the effort that a teacher is undertaking. In his case, working as he was with adults who were typically poor and, in many respects, downtrodden, he often encountered people whom he might have described as having internalized the oppressor. Sometimes the poor accept the terms in which the oppressor describes them and see themselves as unworthy of anything better; sometimes they simply do not see that anything else or more is possible for them. In such cases, Freire would think and speak as closely with people as they would allow and approach them in ways that we will briefly describe in a moment.

A typical primary or secondary school classroom is a different matter, of course, and student resistance can take different forms. The principles for pedagogical progress, though, are similar, even if their application in practice depends on the skill of the teacher. Freire's point is not that students can be expected to be cooperative all the time, and as long as a teacher has the right affective attitudes, teaching and learning will be smooth and effective. He knew better than that. His point, rather, is that whatever difficulties are encountered and however they are dealt with by teachers, in the end, a pedagogy that contributes to the humanization and empowerment of students, at any age, can only be one that assumes love, faith, trust, and hope. There is nothing naïve about that.

Because Freire's own circumstances were unique, and quite different from those in which most teachers in elementary and secondary schools find themselves, it is best merely to highlight the fairly detailed account he gives of the teaching methods he developed. The first moment of a dialogical education is for what Freire at this point refers to as the "teacher-students" to decide what they will talk about. They need to decide together what the content of their experience will be. As challenging as this might be, especially in devising a way for the spirit of it to be applicable to a room full of children, one can readily see the point. For an educational experience to be humanizing and empowering, its content cannot be imposed by the teacher on the student. The student has to have a hand in what will happen and how. Also, successful pedagogy does not happen in the abstract but arises from the lived conditions of the students. Freire held that in the discussions teachers and students have, certain "themes" of or in their lives will emerge. These themes form the framework in which people understand themselves and their lives. For the adults with whom Freire worked, such themes may be work, or frustration, or family, or any number of other features of their lives. For children, the "themes" that emerge in discussion with them, whatever they may be, are what the children notice, and what they are thinking about, and there is always something on children's minds; they are the "generative themes" that condition much of their experience and its meaning for them. All people's lives, including children's, are meaningful for them, and what generates the meaning at any given point are the themes that Freire urges we identify.

Whether with adults or with children, these themes serve as the point of departure in developing the content of the educational experience. The themes can be explored with students, and when this is done, what tends to happen is that people identify difficulties, or obstacles, or problems in their experience related to the themes. Freire refers to these as "limit situations," and they help the teacher to clarify how to work with the students toward greater control over them. He puts the point a bit abstractly, but it is worth hearing his own words: "Humans . . . because they are aware of themselves and thus of the world—because they are *conscious beings*—exist in a dialectical relationship between the determination of limits and their own freedom" (PO 80). In plainer language, we and our limits condition each other, and in the right circumstances, and the teacher's goal is to create those circumstances in the pedagogical experience, students can begin to take control over the limits as they understand them. As Freire puts it, "it is not the limit-situations in and of themselves which create a climate of hopelessness, but rather how they are perceived by women and men at a given historical moment" (PO 80). The ways we engage our limits contributes to the power they have over us, and to our developing abilities to address and overcome them.

Any attempt to apply such methods to children is likely to be less ambitious than it might be with adults. Children's ability to reflect on their own experience and observations is limited, but at any level, it is developed enough to work with and to provide the teacher a pedagogically pregnant entrée into the child's experience. With adults, it is possible to analyze their experiences, and their themes, in greater depth. In either case, the teacher may want or need to enable themes to emerge through a process that Freire calls "decoding." We might, to give an example that could work with children or adults, show people a photo, perhaps of their neighborhood or someplace nearby, and discuss what we can see in the photo—the buildings and their conditions, perhaps, or the people and what they are doing. From there, discussion can, and in Freire's experience often does, lead to a clearer expression of the themes that are conditioning people's experiences. This is the process of decoding and is often successful because with it the teacher and students move from the abstract to the concrete, and meaning is more evident in the concrete.

Freire identifies stages in the process, but that is a level of detail on which we do not need to focus. The important thing is that the principles are clear. When we treat our students as humanizing, authentic beings who have not only the ability but also the right to frame their experience and its meaning on their own terms, we are in a position to create educationally viable experience. When teacher and students collaborate on the details of that experience, the students' agency is supported, allowing them to approach their experience and its limits as something over which they have some control. In that way, content can be generated, and it can be studied in a way that enables knowledge of the subject in the richer sense of knowledge, as praxis, that Freire believes to be critical. This is the dialogical education that can begin to chip away at oppressive conditions, and to which all students, in their capacity for authenticity, are entitled.

REVOLUTIONARY PEDAGOGY

Freire understood as well as did Plato, Rousseau, and Dewey that education is part of a much larger project—the growth and development of individuals, and the structural maintenance and development of their societies. Also like them, he realized from both study and his own experience that the way education is conducted in a society is at any time a function of prevailing structures and the ideas that reinforce them. And he shared with them the idea that in one way or another, prevailing social structures and ideas are ill serving people and their individual and social possibilities. The situation can be better, and education is an essential ingredient in the creation of better lives and a better world.

Unlike the other three, however, Freire was unequivocally committed to a revolutionary process that he thought necessary for the kind of individual and social development, which he in turn thought was the birthright of all people. In his day, and perhaps in ours, the revolutionary alternative that was available to him was some form or other of socialism. It sometimes seems as if there are as many versions of socialism as there are socialists, and maybe more, since people change their minds from time to time, but there is no point in our wading into that muddy stream. One reason we do not need to do so is that Freire himself did not worry about those details. For him, there are general aspects of the present human circumstance, and the viable alternative, the articulation of which is sufficient for understanding the directions in which education should turn, and how it might do so. In drawing this account of Freire's philosophy of education to a close, it will be helpful to review his sense of the current social problem and its attendant distortions of education, by contrast with a preferable alternative and the educational designs necessary to achieve it.

The larger social problem is that in most (if not all) contemporary societies, productive property, wealth, and power are concentrated in the hands of a relatively small segment of the population. The interests of those people, or of that class of people, are to maintain their property, wealth, and power, and these interests in many ways conflict with the interests of the majority of the population that controls a relatively small proportion of productive property, wealth, and power. The economic class that controls property and wealth exerts, by virtue of its wealth and attendant power, an extraordinary amount of control over its society, the state, and the dominant ideas of its time. In whatever form the state takes, and the specific forms may differ from one country to another, the legal structure and the policies in place invariably reinforce the interests of the dominant class. Sometimes there is resistance from the majority, and the ruling class is compelled to revise its laws or policies in the face of that resistance. An example of this has been the gradual extension over the past few centuries of the right to vote, from only propertied males to unpropertied males, to women, and to citizens generally, regardless of religion, race, and other increasingly irrelevant characteristics. There are many examples, but in all such cases, the result in the end is that the ruling class devises a way to make the necessary adjustment while retaining the bulk of its property, wealth, and power.

The same class also uses its wealth and power to craft and to reinforce the ideas that prevail in a society, so that those ideas contribute to the maintenance of their power and control. The idea of freedom, for example, is understood to reinforce the ruling class's freedom to own, put to use, and dispose of its property as it pleases; the idea of freedom is not, however, universally understood to reinforce a worker's effort to resist the conditions of labor under which she has to work. In such a case, the worker is told that she has the freedom not to work in a place that does not have conditions that suit her. The problem, of course, is that in conditions in which the worker has no control over property and wealth, that freedom is entirely hollow. She cannot live without an income, so her freedom is constrained by the very conditions that are established by the ruling class to reinforce their freedom. The very idea of freedom is interpreted in such a way that it supports the interests of the propertied minority and works against the interests of the majority.

People are taught, usually from a young age, that such a situation is natural and good for everyone. For example, some economists will say, against all evidence, that the increasing concentration of wealth in the hands of those who already control most of it is actually good for everyone, because these are the people who will use that wealth as productive capital and thereby create more jobs and more wealth. Aside from the fact that it generally does not work out that way, such a claim presumes that the prevailing social and economic order is justified as long as it enables the majority to put food on the table. Such economists (and the many politicians, journalists, scholars, and others who spread and try to justify such ideas) rarely ask the rather obvious question, which is whether simply having jobs is the end toward which social policy should strive and thus be the goal of people's lives. Those who control the wealth and power would never settle simply for jobs as the culmination of their lives; yet they and their defenders seem to think that everyone else should settle for that.

Freire's philosophy of education is intended to address two issues, given this state of affairs: how the ruling class uses education to control the majority and how education may be reconceived to function in the interests of the majority of the people. With respect to the first, there are several general features of an oppressive education, which is education that militates against majority interests in support of the power and wealth of the ruling class, that Freire takes the trouble to specify. They are, in the order in which he describes them in the final chapter of *Pedagogy of the Oppressed*, conquest, divide and rule, manipulation, and cultural invasion. We may review how an anti-dialogical education expresses these traits, after which we may look at the general features of a liberating education, which he says are cooperation, unity for liberation, organization, and cultural synthesis. Note, if it is not obvious on the face of it, that these two lists present four pairs of opposites, such that what oppressive education promotes is specifically rejected by what a liberating pedagogy embraces.

The primary goal of an oppressive education is to reinforce the status quo that supports the interests of the ruling class. In order to achieve this, the population as a whole must be rendered passive and accepting of the economic, social, and political conditions in which it finds itself. If the majority of people can be induced to accept passively their own conditions and circumstances (even against their own interests), then, in principle, the ruling class is able to maintain control over the society, thereby increasing its wealth and power. Education achieves such oppressive results through its methods, its content, and its use of different approaches for different segments of the population. The "why" of oppressive education should be clear, and we can review now the "how," "what," and "who" of an education designed to deny the majority of people their humanity.

The most effective way to create a passive, compliant population is to treat them as naturally passive from the outset, and this is precisely what the "banking" method of education does. By treating people, and this is as true of children as it is of adults, as passive receptacles into which "deposits" are made by some person or persons in authority, students are denied the agency that is a necessary feature of their full humanity. It assumes from the start, and expects the students to internalize, that the students are empty to begin with, and therefore are to be provided with whatever they are told they need; that the teacher, or the principal, or the school system, or the legislature, knows what the students need, and the students do not; that knowledge is simply "filing away" information, the use of which is often obscure or invisible; that students are supposed simply to accept the information they receive and do nothing with it but hand it back on exams. Such a method, we have seen Freire argue, is essentially dehumanizing for the students because, first, it divorces inquiry from practice, thereby distorting the nature of knowledge itself, and second, it thereby undermines students' agency. To the extent that students accept this passivity, their capacity to develop as authentic human beings is denied.

The way content is understood in this process is no less debilitating. When the object of inquiry is treated as something simply to be accepted and retained, it is turned into dead matter, so to speak. It is small wonder, we might notice, that so many children and students regard with disdain the content of their schooling. If it is given to them as inert information, we can hardly expect it to seem alive to them. Freire thinks, though, that this is precisely the point, at least as far as those who craft the educational process to fit ruling class interests are concerned. An inert subject matter reinforces the students' passivity, thereby contributing to the denial of their authentic development.

It is, finally, worth noting how education as a component of the ruling class's control of the society handles the question of "whom" to educate, and in this respect, Freire maintains a view similar to Dewey's approach to the question, and quite different from Plato's. If it is assumed that the goal of education is to support the existing social, economic, and political order, then schooling will be organized differently for different groups of people. Most people do not control any productive wealth, any capital, and therefore, in order to live, will need to "earn a living." They are, in the essentially inhumane parlance that is common in contemporary economic, political, and educational worlds, "human resources." The economic world needs those human resources, but it needs them only for certain functions, which is to say that it needs them to do certain jobs and perform a generally narrow range of functions. These are the people, the vast majority, who are told that the purpose of their education is for them to "get a job," and whom schools and universities have in mind when they refer to their own purposes as preparing a future work force. This conception of the possible futures these people may have, and of the education that is made available to them, does little more than truncate people's potential and support their ongoing manipulation by the ruling class. Of course, some small proportion of the population will be needed in various positions to manage the economy, and these people tend to receive a different sort of education, one designed not so much to "get a job" but to foster the kind of intelligence that is required to understand and to manage things. This is the reason that the economic, political, and cultural elite, who insist that the schools should be preparing people for future work, send their own children to other kinds of schools, ones that offer a much different sort of education. In all of this, it seems nowhere to be considered that the people who are to be little more than human resources are entitled to no less control over their lives than is anyone else.

Against all of this, Freire posits the contrary values of cooperation, unity for liberation, organization, and cultural synthesis. These are the values that address the second main issue, which is how education can function as a liberating experience and in the interests of the majority of people. The goal is clear, which is that education is not to prepare people to fit into preexisting slots in the economy but to accomplish an awareness of the conditions around them and of their own potential that will enable them to achieve their own humanity. The method by which this can be accomplished is, in contrast to the passivity of the banking method, a dialogical engagement of teacher with students in which the activity and agency of the students is underscored. This is a method in which the essential value of knowledge is properly understood and accounted for, in that the point in a dialogical process is not to receive and store information. The point, rather, is to inquire in such a way that the process is conducted in the context of the inquirer's own needs and purposes, which allows the inquiry to be related to the inquirer's action. The method enables praxis, which Freire regards as a necessary feature of genuine learning and knowledge.

A pedagogy of liberation revises not only the methods of education but also its approach to content. Rather than being the inert object of study that characterizes much of traditional education, subject matter here is understood as a means through which the teacher and student communicate and engage the world together. Freire insists that the student be actively involved in the selection of content, and it is important that his reason for this be clear. It is not a matter of a student simply choosing to study this or that because one topic is more interesting than another. The point, rather, is that through communication, through dialogue, the teacher and student together identify the themes of a student's life and experience through which a subject matter will have meaning and import. Once such features of a student's experience are identified, her selection of the object of study, which is done with a teacher, is undertaken in a way that contributes to the meaningfulness for the student of the pedagogical experience. The object of study thus possesses a meaning and impact that it would not otherwise have. Moreover, the knowledge of the object of study that is achieved in the process of inquiry is likely to be far deeper and richer than it would be through traditional education, if only because its meaning is far more evident to the student.

Finally, a pedagogy of liberation will not separate students into those who deserve to understand the world and those who are to be "human resources." If the purpose of education is to achieve a level of conscious understanding of the conditions around one, such that people are better able to take some measure of control over their lives, then that purpose applies equally to all people. If the vocation of people is humanization, as Freire believes it to be, then it would be monstrous to act as if some people are more entitled to their humanity than are others. A pedagogy of and with the oppressed is designed to avoid alienation in the pedagogical experience itself and to enable an understanding of oneself and one's conditions that will allow all people to collaborate in overcoming alienation in society as a whole.

This, as we have said, is a revolutionary pedagogy, and Freire is quite clear about that. He aspires to a society that is organized in the interest of all people, not only the wealthy and powerful, and one in which intellectual and cultural expressions are understood not in limited and distorted ways but such that they speak to the needs and interests of people generally. These are, of course, relatively long-term aspirations, and it would be unrealistic to expect that a single classroom or school system would manage these results quickly. But an education that aims at anything less is not a liberating pedagogy and not worthy of the name.

PART II

CHAPTER 5

Education and Its Problems

We can begin by taking a page from the pragmatist philosopher's idea that thinking tends to begin in the context of problems. In that spirit, thinking about issues in education, including general philosophical issues of education, can best be grounded not in abstract analyses or definitions but in the current problems that education and educators face. There will be an inclination, which we shall try our best to resist, to wander off into discussions of policy, either to criticize or to propose. The temptation to discuss policy is understandable, since in many cases it is precisely a change in policy that is necessary to solve a problem. There are several reasons, though, to resist the temptation. First, policies may have to differ from place to place and time to time, even in the face of a problem that is more or less common. For example, though adequate funding may be a problem for schools and school systems nearly everywhere, the best way to respond to it may well differ from place to place. It is impossible to discuss policy meaningfully, therefore, without too narrow a focus on one or another location or time. Second, policy discussions invariably involve a complex interaction of economic, social, and political factors. The detailed, empirical analyses that would be required to understand problems in light of possible policy options, even if we were to limit ourselves to a specific place, are far beyond the scope of a philosophical analysis. Third, the nature of policy-related problems, and policy-oriented possibilities, differs widely from country to country. We would not want to engage in an analysis that can only be relevant for Americans or Europeans. It is unfortunate enough that the intellectual background of our study has been limited to European inflected philosophical considerations. It would not be valuable to compound that shortcoming by talking about problems only in a European or American context.

We are embarked, then, on an inquiry that can have bearing not only for one country or one region but also for education more generally. Moreover, we are interested not in an empirical examination of problems that might lend themselves to policy recommendations but in a more normative project that identifies general principles that recommend themselves for our endorsement. Even so, the principles we articulate and justify, in order to be meaningful, have to connect with the problems we face. If they do not, then they are not good for much and, to that extent, fail one of the criteria for justification. Consider again the problem of inadequate finances. While appropriate policy solutions in any case would depend on political and other details of the case, it is possible to identify principles to which one could appeal in identifying appropriate policies. These are not yet recommendations, because no justification has been offered, but if one were to endorse the principle that education is a social (and not only a private) good, then one would reach for certain policies rather than others. The philosophical question for us, then, would be whether education should be regarded as a social or strictly private good. Presumably, the justification that would make most plausible the principle that education is a social and not strictly a private good would apply not only in New York, or Germany, or Bangladesh, but everywhere. How it would be applied or implemented is likely to differ from place to place, but not the principle; even if we allow for the need to tweak a principle from place to place or time to time, we can presume that a principle is applicable across places and times. Philosophic principles are not Platonic forms, but they are the sort of ideas that, in the absence of sufficient evidence to the contrary, can be expected to apply quite broadly.

That education is a social as well as a personal good, which is a claim for which an argument will be made in due course, is one such principle, and there are many more. To identify those principles, and to make the arguments that justify them, requires bringing into the discussion the more general philosophical matters that we have seen other philosophers engage with. We will do this in the two chapters that follow this one, which means that the articulations and justification of the principles, which is to say the articulation and justification of a fuller philosophy of education, must wait until then. Our concern now, to return to the original proposal, is to identify the problems that a philosophy of education can help us address.

THE GOALS OF EDUCATION

The financial problem is a good place to start. There is never sufficient funding for education, at any level, no matter how wealthy the school, or school district, or state, or country, or university may be. There is also, by the way, never sufficient funding for several other important social phenomena—for example, the arts or health care. The reason there is never sufficient funding for education, as in the other cases, is not necessarily that funding sources are stingy. The reason there is never enough money is that there is always more on which we could spend money, regardless of how much is available at any one point. There are always more and different sorts of artistic projects that can be pursued and that need financial support. Similarly, it is always possible to improve one's health, or the conditions related to public health, or to invest in more extensive medical research, and so additional funding would always be desirable, regardless of how healthy we already are, or how advanced a public health regime is already in place. As far as education is concerned, imagine, for example, that a music teacher would like to have her students perform a certain musical show, and she is told by the school administrators that she should select a simpler production because there is not enough money in the arts budget for the current year to produce the one she prefers. In this case, the teacher can reasonably say that there is not enough money to do what she thinks is best. The larger problem, though, is that even if there were enough money in the arts budget to mount that specific production, the teacher could easily (and eventually would) have in the future other good ideas that require even more extensive funding. Among creative people in education there is literally no limit to the new good ideas that will be proposed, which means that no matter how much funding is available, it will never be enough. Creativity will always outrun resources.

The fact that there is never enough money means that in addressing financial problems and making financial judgments, some principles of discrimination must be employed. One of the most important of them concerns what one is trying to achieve in the long run. A financial decision maker may want as a goal to balance a budget, but that is not a long-term consideration, and it may in fact in a given case be inconsistent with other, more general normative values. In making financial judgments, whatever other goals one may have in mind, an educator must appeal to the goals of the educational process itself. When a school board, for example, decides to eliminate extracurricular athletics, or instruction in the arts, because they are thought to be unnecessary, a specific conception of the goals of education is being applied, at least implicitly. If that goal or set of goals is justifiable, then so be it, but if it is not, a different goal or set of goals will (or at least should) be applied instead. Whichever goals one wants to appeal to, the point here is that some conception of what education is trying to achieve is playing a role, explicitly or implicitly, in financial decision-making. That schools, school systems, and educators of all sorts invariably deal with financial constraints means that there are financial problems, the resolution of which from day to day and case to case requires a reasonably clear and justifiable sense of the goals and purposes of education.

The question of educational finances relates not only to the funding of educational institutions but also to individuals' funding of their own education. This is a very different kind of problem in different places, and for different educational levels. In the current age, even minimally developed countries have some sort of publicly funded educational opportunities for their children. The details differ concerning how much schooling is publicly funded, and to what degree, but a problem of individual funding of primary, and usually secondary, education is not widespread. Nor is a problem of a student's private funding of her higher education. In most developed countries of the world, higher education is state supported, and in some cases students receive not only free tuition but also some (though often modest) stipend for living expenses.

There are other countries, however, where a student's funding of her higher education is or can be a most serious problem. There are some cases (Russia, for example) in which state funding of universities meets only part of the public's demand. In such cases, those who do not receive such support must bear the financial burden for themselves. In other cases, only a selected segment of the population is eligible for state-funded higher education, and the others take on the cost themselves. The United Arab Emirates is one such country, where there is state-subsidized higher education for citizens of the country, which seems reasonable, though one should understand that only roughly 10 percent of the resident population in the country are citizens. Of the other 90 percent, many were born there and are lifelong residents of the country, though formally they are citizens of other countries.

The serious problem of private funding of one's university level education arises in those countries where there is little or no public support. In Great Britain, or anyway in parts of it, there are tuition fees for higher education, which students or their families pay unless they receive some sort of scholarship assistance. The problem of private funding is most serious in the United States. There are several reasons for this, the details of which do not concern us here. In general, though, a larger proportion of American students attend residential colleges and universities than in other countries, which increases the cost, and there are considerable costs for universities in salaries and various facilities that are passed on to students. These factors are certainly a problem for students attending private universities, and in the United States there are many, because the cost of tuition alone tends to be high, notwithstanding discounts and scholarships that are often applied. Even for students attending public universities, however, the problem of funding is growing more dire currently, in large part because the various states, which independently of one another provide most of what public support that there is for higher education, have over the recent decades decreased a great deal of the support that they provide. The gap between cost and funding, then, has to be borne largely, though not exclusively, by tuition payments that are the responsibility of the student.

These developments in the United States have placed sometimes extreme financial pressure on students and their families, enough so that the issue has risen to become a national political topic. How one thinks that this problem should be addressed depends to some degree on the issue raised above, which is whether one thinks that higher education is a private or a social good. The answer to that question, in turn, is related to what one believes to be the purpose or purposes of higher education. It was determined long ago that primary and secondary education are a social good, so that their costs must be borne by the public, usually through taxation of residents in a given area, whether or not they have children who attend public schools. The question is now being posed in the national political conversation whether a similar approach should be taken to higher education, though to answer that question carefully, one must have a clear sense of what higher education is or can be for.

Other problems point in similar directions. In Tucson, Arizona, in recent memory, the local school district refused to allow *Pedagogy of the Oppressed* to be used in a secondary-level Mexican Studies program, and all available copies of the book were confiscated from the classrooms. There is censorship of some kind in schools around the world, for a wide range of reasons, and it happens at all levels of education, from primary through university. The censorship is not always of books but can be of speakers or images or ideas, or even single words. We may for the moment leave open the question whether any such cases of censorship are justified and, if so, which ones and for which reasons. The point at this juncture is that whether we reject all forms of censorship in the schools, or justify some and not others, we must (at least implicitly) be appealing to some sense of what we want education to accomplish. Should it be organized to protect students from some ideas, or should a wide range of ideas be made available to them? The answer one gives to such a question depends in part on what one thinks education should strive to achieve. If we think that education should mold students according to a predetermined type, as Plato did, then one might think that censorship is justified toward that end, as Plato also did. But if one thinks that in their education students should be guided to the ability to analyze critically whatever ideas they encounter, then perhaps one would not be inclined to endorse censorship. Whichever it is, and for the moment we leave it open, a conception of the goals of education is required to conduct a coherent analysis and to reach an intelligible answer.

Another question of current moment that is related to the goals of education is the role education, at all levels, may play in social life, especially in relation to acute social problems. On the one hand, given the centrality of education in the social life of any town, region, and country, it is easy to make a case that there is a role to play for education in the process of addressing serious social problems. Climate change comes to mind as an example of such a social problem, as do protracted wars, or matters of social justice and civil rights, whether the context is racial minorities in the United States, or the Roma in Europe, or the Shiite population in some Sunni-dominated countries, or the several national minorities in China, or religious minorities in India. There is no shortage of profoundly serious problems facing societies around the world, some of them, like climate change, held in common. Education at all levels can help to address such problems, whether through relevant research, or helping to educate the public, or providing institutional role models of how to handle certain problems. Some forms of assistance are appropriate for higher education, some for primary and secondary, contexts, but all could have one or another role to play.

On the other hand, it is sometimes argued, the schools are places for teaching, learning, and inquiry, not for activism. It may be, one could say, that whatever moral obligations may emerge from pressing social issues fall properly on individuals, or self-organized groups of individuals, but not on a social institution like education. It is traditionally held that the responsibility of education, or the long-term responsibility, is to knowledge and truth. If that is so, the argument runs, activism in the effort to advance any specific moral or political purpose is likely to be an impediment to education's overarching responsibility. The reason is simply that the priorities established by moral obligation and attendant activism can easily conflict in many cases with the obligation in inquiry to follow where the evidence or argument leads. If we have already decided what is true, and if we have adopted an activist's commitment to enacting that truth, then we have decided ahead of time on the result in ways that could prejudice the inquiry. It is better, some argue, for education to maintain itself, to the extent possible, apart from pressing social problems if it is to fulfill its responsibility to inquiry and learning.

Schools in any country, whether state-supported or privately maintained, can no more be genuinely removed from their social context than a university can in any reasonable sense be an "ivory tower." If that is so, then one is entitled to wonder about the adequacy of, on the one hand, the idea that schools should stay out of struggles related to social problems, as well as, on the other hand, the position of people like Dewey to the effect that schools should abstract from unjust social realities to create equitable educational opportunities for all. The point at this juncture is simply that the problem of the role of education in relation to social issues is tied to the question of the goal or goals of education. Saying that education should, in one way or another, play a part in the resolution of social problems commits one to the more general claim that one of the goals of education is to help forge a more just and defensible world. That may well be a valuable conception of education, but before it is accepted, it requires justification.

It is worthwhile to raise one more problem related to the goals of education, and that concerns the extent to which it is reasonable or realistic to expect state-sponsored education to aspire to goals or purposes that are more general than the interests that the state may identify for itself. All of our philosophical sources have pointed to this problem. In Plato's hands, properly organized and structured education is necessary for justice in the state, but it is equally true for him that the state's responsibility, through the wise leadership of the rulers, is to ensure an education that can provide for justice in individuals. For his part, Rousseau was so nervous about the determinantal effect that the state could be expected to have on education that he argues for a pedagogy abstracted from social circumstances. Dewey asked the question explicitly, because he knew that the democratic ends of education, which require students to be educated in critical understanding of their worlds, and in the inclination to pursue common interests beyond the confines of their groups, societies, and states, may well run contrary to state-identified interests. Freire was the most explicit in his treatment of the problem, in that, in his opinion, in a capitalist society the state can be expected to advance the interests of the ruling class, which by the nature of capitalist economic and social relations are contrary to the interests of the majority, in which case a state-funded education can be expected to contribute to oppression, and not to the proper liberating ends of an education that serves the humanizing interests of the majority.

It is not at all clear how this circle may be squared, regardless of the terms in which we state the problem. That the problem can be resolved at all (and, if so, how) depends to a large degree on what we think the goals of education ought to be. If one thinks—and this is probably the most commonly held view around the world at the current time—that the goal of education is to enable future generations to fit themselves into the economic and social roles that are made available to them given the current economic, social, and political conditions, then one can see a solution to the problem, even if the details might be difficult to enact in practice. Basically, one would try to identify the needs of the economy and society in its current form, and then organize education accordingly with respect to methods, content, and whatever differing educational details are appropriate for people heading for different roles in the society. But if one thinks differently about the goals of education (for example, along the lines of Dewey's or Freire's views), then the possibility of a solution to the problem is not so obvious, never mind how in practice it might be resolved even if in principle it can be. If one of the goals of education is to enable students to think and act in the pursuit of interests held in common with those beyond state borders, then it will require an enlightened state indeed to enable a public educational system to aspire to such ends. And in the case of a view like Freire's, for which education should aspire to ends that are directly contrary to the ends of the state, then it appears that education properly conducted is necessarily a subversive activity.

It is, of course, possible that we may in the end devise principles according to which the goals of education are constructed such that it may be possible to achieve both a reasonable degree of individual empowerment and a plausible consistency with some acceptable sense of state interests. If such an understanding of the goals of education is possible and desirable (and it is not yet clear that it would be), then a solution to the problem posed by state support may be available. We shall have to wait a bit before this analysis can be undertaken. The point for now is that contemporary education faces a very difficult problem insofar as it is state supported, and both the details of the problem and a possible solution depend on how one construes the purposes of education.

PEDAGOGICAL METHODS AND TESTING

We have considered four kinds of problems that are intrinsically related to the question of the goal or goals of education, and there are many more. There are also problems that are tied intimately to the issue of pedagogical methods. As we know by now, Plato, Rousseau, Dewey, and Freire all believed that the appropriate methodological model in education is not a teacher's delivery of information to students and the students' passive reception of that information. That all four of them rejected this model is not by itself sufficient evidence to conclude that the model is unacceptable, though the fact that some of the most important educational thinkers reject it should incline us to take the point seriously. All of them (to repeat observations made earlier) believed that such a method was not effective pedagogy, and, more important, it embodies a distorted understanding of what students can and should achieve in their education. They did not agree on what a proper understanding should be, but they were of one mind that a teacher conveying information to a student is not it.

A number of alternatives have been presented to us, and in subsequent chapters we will consider the issue carefully. It is worth noting at this point, though, that there seems to be a degree of exaggeration in the rejection of this traditional form of pedagogy. For one thing, there appear on the face of it to be countless instances where it is precisely the teacher's responsibility to pass information, of which she presumably has some command, to students, and that it is in the students' interest to receive that information and to incorporate it into their existing stock of data, conceptions, or understandings. Sometimes we want students to be aware of a particular detail or of a broad context, either of which might contribute to the student's understanding of and appreciation for whatever the topic of the moment might be. In such an instance, surely it is appropriate for a teacher to pass on information, ideally accompanied by an explanation of that information and its importance. In short, it is not difficult to make the argument that a well-crafted lecture may have considerable educational value.

For another, there is a nagging question about what especially Rousseau, Dewey, and Freire can plausibly think is the role of a teacher. It cannot be simply to let nature take its course, or to facilitate students' experience, or to dialogue with students. In themselves, none of those processes is reliably conducive to students' education. Rousseau, Dewey, and Freire do not say anything so simple minded, of course, but even given their more sophisticated accounts of the teacher's engagement with students to guide their efforts, there remains the question of the nature and extent of such guidance. All three of them argued that the teacher must create conditions in which the students' efforts produce viable educational results. Rousseau engineered specific events to steer Emile's natural development; Dewey's teachers structured problems so that students' experience in working through them would be educative; and Freire's teachers posed problems (for example, in the form of coding) that enabled the development of the students' themes.

If we take these ideas as rough guides, then we may conclude that teachers and students both must play active roles in the educational process. But even if this is the case, such active methods must be made to rest comfortably alongside the more direct activity on the teacher's part of conveying information to students. Teachers make decisions every day about how to balance these general approaches to pedagogical method, and no amount of philosophy will alleviate the need for them to continue to do so. Some amount of careful philosophy can, however, enable teachers to reach a balance that can be most effective and most defensible in light of the wide range of relevant factors in how we ought to interact with students. Again, the point is to develop clear and justifiable principles, rather than attempt to deliver a formula.

 Another problem related to method has to do with testing. Actually, there is more than one problem that emerges from testing. One of them concerns the reliability of standardized tests to gauge a student's academic accomplishments and level of achievement. Another concerns the extent to which standardized tests tend to embody cultural assumptions that can advantage one group of students relative to another. A third testing issue has to do with the frequent phenomenon of "teaching to the test" and whether that approach distorts the educational process. A fourth concerns the ubiquity of testing in contemporary schools and whether such a pedagogical approach enhances or inhibits learning. And to mention one more, there is the question of the possibility of placing too much weight on test results, which can easily have the consequence of derailing a student's education rather than enhancing it.

There is a raft of factors related to the role of testing in education. Some of them have to do with pedagogy, but others are psychological, social, and political. There has in recent decades been a growing tendency to believe that in order to minimize unacceptable bias in the judgments educators make about students' progress, it is best to eliminate as many occasions for judgment as possible. On such grounds, it is sometimes thought that standardized tests allow for greater "objectivity" in the evaluation of students' work. What is often overlooked is that if there is a problem of unacceptable bias, replacing educators' judgments with tests is not necessarily an improvement because the unacceptable bias can as easily appear in a test as it can in a qualitative evaluation. There are also psychological matters that can be relevant in the issue of testing. If students are anxious about tests (especially if a great deal depends on the results), it can easily happen that the student's nervousness impedes her ability to handle the test well, with the net effect that the results of the test do not accurately reflect her knowledge or abilities.

Social and political factors are no less relevant. For one thing, taxpayers may well put pressure on school boards and legislators, which flows downhill to school administrators and then to teachers, to demonstrate that the education provided to their children is effective. One of the simplest ways to do that, as long as most people agree that the results are meaningful, is testing. Even in such cases, administrative simplicity may not be the only or even the primary reason for a reliance on testing as a pedagogically justifiable evaluative method. If the political life and discourse in a country become unusually polarized, for example, it could well be that citizens cease to trust the evaluative judgments offered by teachers. They may be suspicious of teachers' competence, though probably more commonly they do not trust what and how the teacher is teaching. In such a case, it can easily be thought that a test, especially a standardized test, can compensate for any political or ideological bias that schools may embody and of which parents and citizens may be suspicious.

The idea of teaching to the test is an interesting one. It is typically claimed that to do so to some extent distorts the teaching and learning processes, and it is an argument against testing that it inclines teachers to structure curriculum in this way. There is something a bit odd about this objection, though. If the test is a reasonably good gauge of a student's knowledge and abilities, and if the test in fact tests the material and skills that we want students to have mastered, then one can plausibly wonder what is wrong with teaching to the test in such a case. If the test directs students' focus on those matters that we want them to pay attention to, then teaching to the test can seem to be precisely what we should be doing. If, however, we want to say that the test does not focus on the right material, and that is the reason that teaching to it damages the educational experience, then one wonders not why teachers teach to the test but why the tests are being given in the first place.

All of these factors in and approaches to testing are in one way or another controversial. Perhaps students would learn better without the pressure of tests; perhaps the professionalism of teachers should be respected and their judgments trusted more than they currently are. It may also be the case that underlying all these concerns with testing is a more general issue of what we want our pedagogical methods to achieve from one day to the next. If Dewey is right, for example, and the point of our teaching, not only in the long run but equally in specific instances, is to foster in our students a greater degree of control over their experience so that they learn to be able to guide their own lives, then it is hard to see how testing, especially extensive testing, can assist that effort. If our desire as teachers is for our students to learn, it may well be the case that our direction of their more active experience to learning a lesson is more effective or desirable than anything else. If that is so, then it is also quite possible that the more complex and messier processes of evaluation, rather than the presumed objectivity of testing, is the more appropriate way to gauge students' achievement. This will depend, to a considerable extent, on how we understand students' engagement with the material to be studied, with one another, and with the teacher, and all of this is related to how we understand experience and cognition generally. These larger philosophical questions will be addressed directly in the next chapter.

EDUCATIONAL EQUALITY AND TRACKING

We have far from exhausted the many problems that prevail in contemporary education. One of the more serious of them concerns whether to teach different people differently and on what defensible grounds (if any) we may do so. The primary form in which this problem appears is in the still commonly held idea that some students should be taught differently, or taught different material, depending on where they come from or on what they can be expected to do with their lives. This is the problem of tracking, which remains a pervasive feature of contemporary schooling in many countries, even if the term itself is used less frequently than it once was. The term "tracking" here is being used to refer to a range of ways that educational opportunities and experience are differentiated for students and a range of reasons for doing so. If we think of the term as referring to any kind of differentiation, then it would apply to cases as varied as making advanced experiences available for gifted students and segregating students on the basis of race or some other invidiously applied trait. It is safe to say that these two forms of the provision of varying educational opportunities differ widely, such that one may typically be acceptable while the other never is. Even the provision of special opportunities or classes for gifted students may be defensible in some cases and not others. It may be, for example, that at secondary or university levels, special courses or even special schools for more gifted or advanced students do not present a problem, while at a younger age such differentiation would.

The more pervasive form of tracking around the world, including in Europe and the United States, is the provision of varying opportunities for students depending on the economic and professional roles we expect them to fill when they have completed schooling. In some countries in Europe, distinctions are made among students even at primary school level that determine whether they will follow an academic or a more applied course of study. In the United States, the distinction has traditionally been made between academic and "vocational" education, and while the formal distinction is less common now than it once was, the educational differentiation is still made under other names and less rigidly. This is the sort of educational distinction that Plato thought was necessary for a just society and an appropriate developmental experience for children, on the grounds that people should learn what they will need to know, and people fulfilling different roles in society need to know different things and have different skills. This is also the distinction that Dewey argued directly against, on the grounds that to organize education around how people will make a living is to misunderstand the role education plays in people's lives and in their development. Education is properly oriented, he argued, toward vocation in a broader sense of developing the distinctly human capability of self-governance and the active direction of one's experience. In this respect, education as the enrichment of experience is appropriate for all students in the same degree and for the same reason. Freire, presumably, would have agreed, in that the vocation of people, as he put it, is humanization, and that applies to all people, regardless of whatever job they might do in the future.

Despite those objections, though, and despite the fact that formal tracking on the basis of an anticipated occupation is far less common and commonly defended than it used to be, tracking in precisely this sense remains a genuine problem, and its ramifications cut as deeply into the social fabric, and into individuals' lives, as they ever did. The problem is not that applied subjects may be offered to students. There is no good reason, on the face of it, to deny interested students the opportunity to study some applied subjects, even in their formal education. There are practical issues in the delivery of such subjects, and in how they are related to the other content a student is or should be expected to study, but learning in some detail about the various ways people "make a living" can be a most valuable form of education, whether a student eventually adopts one of them or not.

The contemporary problem of tracking, if we may continue to use the term, lies in the common (and, one gets the sense, growing) view that the purpose of education is to prepare people for occupations. If that is the case, then it would stand to reason that differing educational approaches and opportunities should be provided for students who are preparing for different occupations. On this reasoning, if an office manager needs different knowledge and skills than a programmer, and if education is basically preparation for an occupation, then the future manager should be educated differently from the future programmer. The same would presumably be true for all such distinctions—for example, between a future physician and a future plumber. There would, of course, be further questions in the application of this approach to education, such as the proper age at which the differentiation should be made would have to be determined. However such detailed issues would be resolved, the general idea that education is and should be oriented toward students' future occupations seems to have a firm grip at the current time. Plato, it appears, has carried the day.

The problem is particularly acute in higher education. Universities are frequently criticized for graduating students who are not "job-ready" or who are alleged not to have the knowledge and skills that employers require. Universities are told that they should develop degree programs that meet the current needs of the economy and of the various business sectors their students are likely to enter as employees. Governments, local and national, have taken to evaluating the success or adequacy of universities in part on the employment record of their graduates, and even on the salary levels that their graduates are earning at various points in their careers.

Students, wittingly or not, contribute to the problem. It is typical, perhaps because they are encouraged to do so by parents, friends, and guidance counselors, for students, when considering which university to attend, or which degree program to study, to believe that they need first to have an idea of which occupation they intend to enter when their schooling is complete. When asked what she would like to study, it is common for a student to say that she wants to do this or that after graduation and so should study some program or curriculum that is presumably tailored to that end. A student might imagine herself to be a manager in the future, and so will study business, or she may see herself as a designer or builder, and so study architecture or one or another form of engineering. Sometimes a student has difficulty deciding which degree program to study, and the common explanation offered by the student in that case is that she has not yet decided what she wants to do after graduation. One rarely hears a university student say that she wants to study a specific program or subject because it interests her.

This would all be familiar to anyone who spends time with secondary school students preparing for university or with university students. But why, one might ask, is any of this a problem? We can certainly understand why parents encourage their children to prepare as best they can for occupational and material success. For self-serving reasons, parents usually do not want their children to live in the basement forever. At a more generous level, parents typically want a good life for their children, and for most people, some degree of material and professional success is likely to be a necessary condition of a good life. Many people make the mistake of thinking that it will be a sufficient condition, but they are usually disabused of that notion in due time. In any case, it appears on the face of it to be reasonable to want professional success, and it would follow that it is necessary for people to learn whatever needs to be known to achieve that success. If that idea is right, then it seems natural and uncontroversial to look to education to provide the requisite knowledge and skills. In the end, what one needs for a specific job is likely to be made available from the employer, but formal education can be expected to provide what is necessary for a graduate to be ready to rise to an employer's expectations and meet the necessary requirements. Students, their families, and state leaders do not want to spend their resources on educational systems that do not meet these expectations or that do not meet them well enough. As a result, education is expected by nearly all its stakeholders to be occupationally oriented. So where, then, is the problem?

First, there is an insidious economic class dimension hiding in this point of view and the argument for it. When the claim is made that graduates of either secondary schools or universities should be "job-ready," the level of course depending on which jobs they are aiming at, the injunction can only apply to those who need to have a job in order to live. That certainly includes most people, but it does not include everyone. Some people are independently wealthy, perhaps as a result of inherited wealth, and they do not need a job in order to live and prosper. Some people, including many who are living on inherited wealth, own the companies, or they own a large proportion of shares in publicly traded companies and corporations, and they do not need a job because, basically, they own the jobs that other people need. There is also a set of people who will provide upper-level management of those companies and corporations, and who, though technically they are employees and so work for a wage, are so close in authority to the owners that their social situation is closer to that of the owners than to anyone else. We can also point to a set of people who have or can be expected to have extensive social and political authority, and who therefore do not need to prepare for a job in the way that the majority of people do. If education is oriented to preparing students for jobs and careers, and if these people do not need an education oriented in this way, then how do they stand in relation to education?

The answer is that for those people there are elite schools and universities that prepare them, and their children after them, to run and manage the companies, and to exercise political authority. Such students are not preparing for jobs. On the contrary, they are preparing for a life that, to a greater degree than for others, is under their own control and direction. This is where the vocational orientation of education converges with the traditional problem of tracking. There is one sort of education for the majority, those who need to "earn a living," and a different sort of education for those who already have a living by virtue of their position in society and do not need to earn it. That one sort of education is superior to the other is evident from the fact that parents of children who do not need to earn a living are highly unlikely to send their children for a vocationally oriented education. The education they receive at the private schools and more elite universities is more valuable for them. Tracking of this sort is a problem for education because on the face of it, there is no apparent reason that some subset of people is or should be entitled to an education that is demonstrably more valuable than what is available to the majority. To justify such an arrangement, it would have to be squared with the equality of opportunity that those of us in democratic societies claim to value.

A second problem with a vocationally oriented education is that it probably does not work, even if we were to limit our aspirations to training for a job. For one thing, there is no good reason to expect that an eighteen-year-old student is in a position to judge how she would like to spend her professional life. There may be a number of options that appear attractive at that point, but assuming that there are in fact options available to her, she is simply not mature enough to be expected to make a firm judgment on such a matter. If she prepares for a position that four or five years later she decides does not suit her, she may well have wasted her education—if her education is vocationally focused, that is. There is also the problem that the careers and positions that exist at a certain time are not necessarily the careers and positions that will be available later in a person's life. To educate for the existing economy is to educate for the past, not the future. The uncertainty of the future does not have to be a problem, though. The kind of education that is available to those who do not need to prepare for a job is the kind of education that prepares them to exercise a degree of intelligent control over their lives. This is also the sort of education that will help all students prepare for an uncertain future. If they are denied it, though, on the grounds that their school or university should make them "job-ready" when they graduate, then they are victims of a tracking in their education from which they are ill served.

The final reason that tracking of the sort we have described is a problem is that it risks being unreasonably selective in the focus it accords to education. Formal education cannot do all things, but it can do more things than job training, some of which are actually important. However else we describe it, the educational process is one from which we emerge into our adult lives, and our adult lives involve quite a bit more than the job or jobs that we have. In addition to being employees, we are spouses and parents, neighbors, and citizens. We do not expect education to teach us how to be good spouses and parents, but we might expect it to guide us in the development of habits of mind, background knowledge, and interpersonal sensibilities that we are likely to need as spouses and parents. We require the same abilities and sensibilities in how we will engage our neighbors, which ideally we do in ways that are conducive to both our development and happiness and theirs. And our role as citizen benefits from dimensions of education that help us to understand our own histories, the social issues that present themselves, the complex meaning of those issues on us individually and on our communities, the potential solutions to those problems, and the processes of rational evaluation that make it possible for us responsibly to participate in political decision-making. Education as job training, no matter how good it may be toward that end, does not do any of this. If we insist on understanding education primarily as job or career preparation, then we are unnecessarily denying ourselves, and more seriously our children, the education that can address the wider range of needs of their student and adult lives. That is a problem.

EDUCATIONAL CONTENT AND STATE EDUCATION

The issue of treating some students differently from others is necessarily related to the question of the content of education, which, just as the why, how, and who of education, presents a set of problems for us to consider. If we are willing to accept the idea that people who are destined for different "stations" in life (to use an old-fashioned but still serviceable term) may justifiably be provided with different sorts of educational opportunities, then we implicitly accept that the content of their education should or at least may differ. Schools and universities do not put it this way, in part, presumably, because there would be something embarrassingly elitist about saying so, but it seems clear that if the reason for education for most people is to prepare them for work, it would make sense that the content of their education would be determined accordingly. Students themselves often see it this way—for example, when they object to being asked to study something that it seems to them they "do not need." The idea that education ought to be useful is not itself mistaken, and we will attend to it in due course. When students object to studying something that they do not find useful, however, they are typically employing a fairly narrow understanding of what may be useful. Specifically, they have in mind what they expect to be directly applicable in their work or careers, or at most in whatever activities they can at that point in their lives imagine undertaking. If they cannot imagine putting algebra or British literature to use in their future careers or personal lives, then to them it is not useful, and they object to being asked to study it. In this respect, if we are suspicious of the idea that people should receive different educational opportunities depending on their future employment, we may say with Freire that such students have "internalized their oppressors" by wanting to be familiar only with what, in the limited range of their experience, they can imagine to be useful.

What, we may wonder, might be the differences between an education oriented solely or primarily toward students' future employment, and one for students who do not need to concern themselves with earning a living? If we think first about education for employment, one feature that comes to mind is the distinction between necessary items in the curriculum and those that might be considered to be "extra" or "frivolous." At primary and secondary levels, we can see this distinction brought to life when schools find themselves in financial difficulties. No school wants to do away with whatever it thinks necessary for its students, so if it must for budgetary reasons eliminate some subjects or activities, it will be those activities that are "extracurricular," and then those features of the curriculum that, they may say, can be eliminated without seriously damaging the students' education. These, more often than not, are subjects in the arts; presumably, aesthetic education is not especially important for students' education because, again presumably, it is not especially important for students' future lives. This, though all too common, is a singularly myopic conception of both education and life, and we will return to it in the next chapter. For now, we simply note that education in the arts appears to many to be, even if desirable, not necessary for students' futures. Other topics that may be deemed unnecessary, especially when budgets are threatened, are elective subjects that might otherwise be offered because they are thought to be potentially interesting and therefore of value for at least some students. This sort of thing tends not to happen at the primary level, but in secondary schools it is more likely. Some basic study in history and geography is likely to be regarded as necessary, even if some students may not be able to see why, but schools may, when they can, think it worthwhile to offer some number of social science electives (for example, in politics or sociology or psychology). Insofar as they are elective subjects to begin with, they are already understood to be more than is necessary for a students' future employment.

What is not extra or frivolous, at both primary and secondary levels, seems to include basic writing and reading, sufficient arithmetic to manage one's personal finances, some sense of the history of one's own region or country, and often not far beyond that, some degree of familiarity with natural science, and possibly the methods of experimental inquiry, and, when possible, some education in the arts. Beyond that, there is likely to be physical education and athletics, to some extent, and an effort to help students understand how to interact with one another calmly and to good effect. In American schools, there is likely to be little serious effort in other languages, though elsewhere in the world the study of second and third languages is more common. There is variety from school to school in how these subjects are taught, so students do not necessarily receive identical experiences, but the general approach is common. This is the information that students are presumed to need in their lives, and the subjects are typically taught in ways, as Freire noted, that underwrite the passivity and acceptance that is expected of them later in their lives.

The experience in schools that are not oriented to preparing their students to earn a living is likely to be rather different. Most important, the students in those schools will be expected to have different skills and dispositions than the students who will be one or another sort of employee. The students in the elite schools are those who will be responsible for managing the capital that drives the companies and corporations that employ everyone else; they will make the policies and laws, and staff the courts that will interpret them; they will manage the finances that will underwrite research and innovation in all spheres of the economy; they will people the boards that will define much of the cultural life of their respective countries and societies; they will be responsible for devising and maintaining the relations between their country and the others, whether in peaceful coexistence or in war.

It is clear that adults with those sorts of responsibilities need far more than a smattering of basic and useful information. Ideally, acknowledging of course that not all students achieve anything like the ideal, such students will learn not simply to read but also to read some of the most challenging, and thereby rewarding, history, philosophy, and literature that has been written; they will learn to analyze descriptions and arguments; they will learn to discern insight from nonsense; they will learn to devise solutions to problems, and how to test and evaluate them; they will learn to engage with people not only from their neighborhood but also from around the world, and not simply in one language; they will learn the heights of human aesthetic and cultural achievements, and why they are significant; and, perhaps most fundamentally, they will learn to be not the passive recipients of experience that others dictate to them but, when and where possible, to establish their own ends and to manage their experience consistent with their own judgments of what is possible and what is needed. The specific content and curriculum of a school, including primary, secondary, and

are some inherent?

tertiary levels, is determined with these ends in mind. There is of course a fairly wide range of options for specific material—for example, the number and precise subjects of history courses, or how much natural science and mathematics to teach, or on which pieces of world literature to focus. However any specific school makes such specific judgments, the content will point in the same direction.

One obvious question at this point, and it is here that the issue of educational content becomes a problem, is why only a small segment of the population should receive such an education. If these educational experiences and purposes are preferable for the economic elite and their children, then, on egalitarian grounds, it would seem that they are preferable for everyone. It is certainly true that not all students would be able to make the most of a curriculum of this kind, but then not all children of the wealthy and powerful make the most of what is offered them even now. So, the question is not whether all children and students, or even most, would rise to the occasion. The question, or problem, is whether we want the educational content we offer to vary to this extent, or whether we would prefer a greater equality of opportunity with respect to education.

There is, actually, already a clear sense that many educators are made uncomfortable by such differentiation in content, something that is especially evident in higher education. Most universities in the United States, and it is true to a somewhat lesser extent elsewhere in the world as well, build into their bachelor-level degree requirements a set of courses that is typically called "general education," or a "core curriculum." On the standard model, and there is ongoing debate among academic staff and administrators about what the details should be, students are required to complete courses, sometimes reaching as much as a third of their total studies, in a wide range of subjects that taken together provide students with a comprehensive exposure to the knowledge, skills, and intellectual achievements of humanity. Such dimensions of the curriculum are, we might say, a nod in the direction of a more egalitarian educational content than would be available without them. Whether such features of the curriculum successfully mitigate the inegalitarian aspects of content differentiation is open to debate, especially given the degree to which university students, and even many of their professors, fail to see the value of the studies required of them.

Another problem with respect to educational content has to do with the issue that was broached earlier about the role of the state in education. The question was raised in relation to the goals of education whether an educational process controlled and funded by the state can be expected to aspire to educational goals that may differ from those of the state itself. It is not difficult to see how this problem is expressed in the content decisions in classrooms. If we consider only the United States by way of illustration, though there is nothing uniquely American about this issue because the problem appears everywhere, there is an interminable debate about which interpretations of history should be taught in the schools. This is not a purely academic question, we may note, because curricular decisions on such issues have an impact on the publishing industry because of the size of the textbook market.

This description greatly oversimplifies the issue, but the problem is basically this: the state wants its citizens to learn the most complimentary interpretations of the nation or region's history, but such interpretations may differ considerably from studies that are less or differently politically biased or more scholarly. To give only one of many possible examples, the preferred interpretation of the Vietnam War of the 1960s and 1970s is that though the United States made some mistakes, even committing some criminal actions, the US effort was generally well intentioned and virtuous. This is also the interpretation that, through the policy decisions made by state departments of education, informs the most widely used American history textbooks. At least one study has shown, however, that the version of the war, including its buildup and its general goals, that is given in the textbooks is not consistent with the less politically charged version in the Pentagon Papers, which was commissioned and written by the Pentagon for its own internal use and to guide its military decision-making.[1] Another well-known example of this sort of thing is Howard Zinn's *A People's History of the United States*.[2] In this case, the argument is that American history is typically taught from the point of view of the economic ruling class and of white men, and that left out of this version of the story is an interpretation of that history from the perspectives of the working class, of racial minorities, and of women. In Zinn's hands, the latter story is quite different from the former.

In the Vietnam case, the problem is that the political purposes of those who make decisions for the state can manipulate a curriculum in such a way that students are deprived of an accurate (or at least an alternative) version of events. It is not that political leaders are trying to deceive students—or at least that is probably not the case. They are, in such situations, making judgments about curriculum and textbook content consistent with how they see things. In Zinn's case, the problem is that history is always written from some perspective, and different perspectives can result in quite different histories. The problem concerns what one can reasonably do about content in such cases. Presumably, we want students to be exposed to the most accurate and defensible understanding of historical events, but it is not clear that state officials can be expected to place that value over their own historical or political understandings. In the case of differing perspectives, it may be that the best we can offer students is an understanding that history is susceptible to interpretation, and that interpretations can differ widely. The difficulty in this case is that frequently, and this has been the situation with Zinn's analysis, the alternative interpretations conflict with received political opinion, and it often happens that powerful people do not want to allow interpretations that conflict with their own. Hence the problem.

It should also be pointed out, so that we are not too hard on political leaders, or on political leaders alone, that the same problem can occur in teaching that is religiously inflected. I can recall as a boy in a Catholic school classroom learning about the emperor Constantine's conversion to Christianity, and the picture in the textbook was of Constantine gazing at a vision of a cross in the sky. I do not recall any text suggesting that this vision was merely symbolic of Constantine's decision, nor that his decision may not have been the consequence of direct divine inspiration.

EDUCATION AND SOCIAL JUSTICE

Many of these themes taken together point to what is perhaps the most momentous issue in contemporary American education, and that is the relation of education to the general problem of social justice. This has been an ongoing issue in American education, and not surprisingly. The educational process, which is to say schooling, has been weighted with many different and quite possibly incompatible goals over the years. During the Progressive Era, for example, education was touted as a way to enculturate the children of immigrants. This was a social function, but not necessarily one that had anything to do with social justice. In our time, to offer a different example, it is thought by many people that the purpose of education and schooling is to prepare children to be employees, as was discussed above, on which view education's only or primary social function is as a support for economic development. As I write this, however, the most prominent public issue concerns the degree to which the schools and the educational process should or should not underwrite the struggle by Americans for justice in their own society.

In principle, there may be various forms of injustice against which people struggle. Social injustice may be grounded in economic class, or based on gender discrimination, or on racial discrimination, or any number of other possible issues. The larger question, though, is whether, and to what extent, education ought to have as a goal addressing problems of social injustice. Dewey, as we have seen, thought that it should, and he argued that the schools are a place where the economic inequality and injustice of the society might be minimized so that children could develop without the burdens imposed by that inequality. Freire, too, thought that the primary purpose of education is to overcome the consequences of the oppression and alienation that are so common in contemporary societies, including ours.

Each of us who is engaged in education at some level, from state education bodies to school boards to administrators to teachers, must face this question for ourselves. Until social injustices are a thing of the past, assuming that such a condition is even possible, we will have to deal with the challenge they pose for education. The specific form of social injustice that poses the immediate challenge will change over time, but the general problem will remain. Today, the form of social injustice that is most pressing in America is more than anything else based on race. There are those who believe that the schools should be teaching children and students about the ways in which racial injustice and oppression have permeated American history; the same people tend to urge on the schools the task of redressing these injustices to the extent possible. There are others in the country who with equal conviction believe that the schools should not focus on race in America, presumably because they think that to do so is to continue and even deepen the legacy of racial discrimination. In some states, legislatures have gone as far as prohibiting by law the teaching of racial themes. Whichever side of this debate and dispute one endorses, it is clear that it cannot be avoided.

How we think about the place of social justice among the goals of education will depend in part on whether we think that education is or should be a social good, and in part on how we understand justice in general. Our approaches and policies in specific instances will or ought to derive from the general principles we endorse, and, as we have been arguing throughout the book, those principles depend to some extent on our general philosophical ideas. We have seen, for example, that Plato's entire philosophy of education was couched within the overarching question of the nature of justice in both the individual and the society. Historically, the most influential thinkers have tended to consider justice an overarching concern, including Rousseau, Dewey, and Freire, as well as others such as Confucius and his followers. In the chapters that follow, we will suggest the approach to justice that is most consistent with the general philosophic conceptions that we endorse and clarify the general educational principles that are most appropriate. Those responsible for educational law, policy, and practice would be expected to do something comparable as they approach the problem of education and social justice in their own practice.

These are among the more serious and pervasive problems that a philosophy of education must consider. There are other aspects of education that were at times considered problems but have now been settled—for example, the education of women. When I began university studies in 1969, woman students in their first year had a curfew in the residence halls, but the men did not. For their part, there were many women students at the university I attended who were there, on their own account, to frequent the fraternity parties of a nearby university because, since the students there were likely to be doctors and lawyers in the future, they were good prospects as future husbands. Fortunately, those years are well behind us, and though there is a long way to go to reach gender equality, any "problem" of that kind has been settled—at least in principle.

There are other educational issues on which well-developed philosophical principles can have a bearing (for example, the question of the place of education, organized or otherwise, throughout one's life). This has to do with the "when" question in relation to education, and though it is a meaningful question, it does not present a problem of the first order with which we should feel obliged to deal. The "where" question, however, is a bit more pressing. As important as the countryside and the open air are, we are not likely to follow in any literal or strict way Rousseau's recommendations in this regard. There are, though, other issues that come up in the context of the location of educational experience, and it is an open question how much of a formal education would be better conducted outside the classroom. Dewey made the point that it would be pedagogically advantageous if students had some amount of systematic exposure to the working world, which he thought would help them develop a richer understanding of their social environment. Also, there has been for many years a growing interest at the university level in internships, which, when structured properly, can give students a deeper understanding of the sort of work toward which they aspire. There are also arguments to be made for the importance of an international experience in one's education, at either or both the secondary and the university levels. These considerations speak to the issue of the quality of the education students receive, and to that end need to be considered in the context of the development of philosophical principles.

Another issue that speaks to the quality of education (in this case having to do with method) concerns the proper role of technology in teaching and learning. More specifically, the prevailing problem, if we may consider it a problem, is the extent to which education should turn to some form of online experience. This question has been in the air for at least twenty-five years already (even longer if we add to it the topic of television and education from an earlier generation), but it has become especially charged after the coronavirus pandemic that began in late 2019. Online education has its champions (some of them provisional and some more absolute), and it has its detractors. The likelihood is that sooner rather than later the issue will become far less urgent, either because it will be regarded by the majority of educators to have been settled, one way or the other, or because a new technological possibility will emerge that will render the current debates moot, rather as the controversy over online teaching rendered earlier debates about television moot.[3] This situation suggests that though issues related to online teaching and learning are urgent just now, they are not as fundamental as the other problems that we have identified. Nonetheless, one would want the principles that constitute a philosophy of education to help one to make judgments concerning technology no less than other factors in educational controversies.

The review of Plato, Rousseau, Dewey, and Freire was intended to illustrate the claim that a systematic treatment of issues in the philosophy of education requires a specific consideration of broad philosophical issues that will enable the development of principles in terms of which to evaluate educational problems. In this chapter, we have brought into focus a number of educational problems, in the resolution of which we would want such principles to be of use. It remains now to undertake the broader philosophical thinking that will generate such principles and to articulate the consequences of their application to educational problems. In chapter 6, we will explore how best to understand reality in general, as well as related conceptions of knowledge and experience, and specify their implications for educational principles and the resolution of educational problems. In chapter 7, the focus will be on social and political theory, which is to say philosophically useful and defensible conceptions of society and the state, and the ramification of those conceptions for the analysis of the general problems of education that we have identified.

CHAPTER 6

Education in Context

Nature, Knowledge, and Experience

When Plato said that philosophers should rule the republic because only they were capable of the kind of education that rulers need, he drew that idea in large measure from his conceptions of the general nature of reality and knowledge. Plato thought that the most important features of reality, you will recall, are not in the physical world that we encounter in experience, but rather in an objective, unchanging, nonmaterial, world of ideas, or what he called the realm of the forms. Specifically, the most important of the forms were, first, the form of the good, followed by the forms of truth and justice. These forms, or ideas, are what constitute the meaning of goodness, truth, and justice, Plato believed. If we want to achieve goodness and justice in the society, we can only do so if decisions for the society are made by people who know what goodness and justice mean, and one can only know what they mean by knowing the ideal types or forms. Because these ideas or forms are not found in the material world, their study requires special skills that are possessed by only a small number of people. These people, who become the republic's rulers once they acquire the knowledge of the forms, must master the rational skills that Plato called dialectics, which is the process of reasoning from specific instances to first principles. This is the only way that knowledge of the forms is possible. Plato's understanding of education, or at any rate the education of the rulers, makes sense only in the context of these general metaphysical and epistemological conceptions.

Rousseau's idea that a child learns only through his direct experience requires, rather obviously, quite a different set of ideas about reality and knowledge. In his view, nature is the fundamental source of knowledge, and knowledge is obtained only through experience. We are rational beings, he thought, and much of what we know we reason to, but we reason to it from basic information that we glean from experience in and of nature. To know reality is to know how the world works, which is to say how its various components interact. As a product of his time and place, Rousseau understood nature by analogy with a machine, more or less, and to know it is to know how its many components fit together. The process by which we acquire this knowledge is, as a result, quite different in Rousseau's hands than it is in Plato's. Their differing views of reality and knowledge lead invariably to differing ideas about education.

Dewey went at all this in yet a different way. His reality is neither basically ideal, like Plato's, nor mechanically natural, as Rousseau had it. Dewey's image of reality is not as eternal ideas or as a massive machine, but as an ecosystem. Reality, in both its material and its nonmaterial elements, constitutes innumerable "situations," in which the components of the situation constitute one another's characteristics. A human being is similar to such a situation, as is a society, and a history, and a material object, and everything else that exists. Individual people are components of many such situations, which to one extent or another condition an individual's nature, just as she conditions the traits of the situations by virtue of her relations with them. This complex network of relations a person has with her environing conditions, both the give and the take, are her experience, and it is in the context of experience—one's engagement with the world—that knowledge arises. Knowledge, in this view, does not arise from experience, as Rousseau thought, but is rather embedded in experience. This is the reason that Dewey thought that education, to be meaningful and effective, must itself consist of guided experiences through which a child eventually gains a command of information about the world and a measure of control over it.

Freire also thought that knowledge occurred in the context of experience, though he went further than Dewey did in emphasizing the active aspect of knowledge. In his hands, it is not just that knowledge is to be understood as both active and passive but also that the active and passive aspects of knowledge condition each other in a liberating process. Understanding knowledge as passive in not simply a mistake but in fact contributes to the oppressive character of individual and social life. To achieve genuine knowledge is to understand the world through liberating action on it. Consequently, education, if it is to be liberating rather than oppressive, must engage the student in a process of praxis, in which the student achieves an awareness of her individual and social condition, and the wherewithal to address it.

Conceptions of reality and cognition, or what we may here call nature and knowledge, have been central to an understanding of education throughout the history of the effort to understand ourselves and the world, and they continue to be central. There are two questions before us now. One is how we might justifiably understand nature and knowledge, and experience as well, and the second is how that understanding informs educational theory.

NATURE AND ITS RELATIONS

In ancient Europe (at least in Plato's hands), reality was thought of as a set of fixed forms or types that were related to one another in a hierarchical fashion, with the fixed and eternal ideal forms at the top, and with the form of the good at the pinnacle; in modern Europe, reality was still understood as a set of fixed, eternal types, but there was greater emphasis on the physical world, which was thought of mechanically, as consisting of individual elements that interact with one another to produce nature. This began to change in the nineteenth century, and the full ramifications of that change are yet to be understood or accepted. It has become clear, though, that the old conceptions of reality as constituted by eternal and unchanging types, or of essentially unrelated atomistic elements, and of mechanical interactions of those elements, are no longer tenable. A different conception of nature and reality generally is required.

Challenges to the traditional world view came from many quarters. In the early nineteenth century, the German philosopher G. W. F. Hegel argued that the elements of both reality and thought are not atomistic and do not possess their traits independently, but they are in fact related to one another such that the relations make something what it is.[1] This is the idea that made its way by the end of the century into Dewey's concept of a situation. Hegel was an immensely important figure in the nineteenth century, and many philosophers, scientists, engineers, politicians, and writers who had an impact on how people thought about their world were influenced by him.

Even more influential, though, was Charles Darwin. When he published *The Origin of Species* in 1859, it sparked an intellectual revolution that is still reverberating. Since Plato, and more directly his student Aristotle, it was assumed that biological species were eternal and unchanging. In the Christian and then in the more modern versions of this idea, God had created all the biological species, and, like all other types of things, all individuals of a given species represent, more or less imperfectly, the unchanging ideal that defines the species. Species were Platonic forms, and they had only one origin, which was God's initial act of creation. Suddenly, Darwin presented a picture, accompanied by a broad range of evidence provided in excruciating detail, that species come into existence and go out of existence, and he articulated two processes—natural and sexual selection—through which the comings and goings of species happens. If this was right, then much of the intellectual edifice on the basis of which reality was understood would crumble. One can understand why Darwin's analysis was as controversial as it was, and why in many quarters it still is controversial.

Hegel had undermined the idea of nonrelational, atomistic individuals, and Darwin had toppled the assumption of unchanging and eternal types.

The third pillar of the traditional conception of nature, the assumption of elements interacting mechanically in absolute space and time according to fixed and universal natural laws, was undermined by late nineteenth- and early twentieth-century developments in physics. James Clerk Maxwell had demonstrated the inherent relations of electricity, magnetism, and light, and not long after, Albert Einstein's special and general relativity theories revised our understanding of the nature of time and space, showing, among other points, that gravity affects the character of space and that motion, specifically acceleration, is constitutively related to simultaneity. Subsequent developments in quantum physics, in the analyses of the behavior of atomic and subatomic particles, further broke down the assumptions of the mechanistic view of the material world in that it limited the applicability of the traditional laws of mechanics.

It is worth noting that the changes in the general conception of reality have had consequences in unexpected places. The idea that reality consists of independently defined and determined elements that interact according to definable laws or rules permeated the European world in the modern period. In the mid-seventeenth century, for example, the modern conception of nation-states and their relations was developed, according to which nations are entirely independent, sovereign entities, that devise and possess their own traits and interests independently of one another, and then enter into relations with one another in an effort each to seek its own interests. The theory of international relations to this day is an attempt to develop the principles according to which those interactions may be successfully carried out. The same idea, to somewhat greater effect, describes music in the Baroque period of the late seventeenth and early eighteenth centuries, as any student of counterpoint is, perhaps painfully, aware. Baroque music is characterized as a set of two or more independently defined and functioning melodic lines that interact according to the harmonic rules of counterpoint. By the late eighteenth century, the same general conception was applied in moral and social theory to the economic interactions of individuals. The Scottish moral philosopher Adam Smith, in his book *The Wealth of Nations*, argued that a society's economic life is best understood in terms of independent individuals, each with her own self-interest determined independently of the others, seeking to meet her interests in the marketplace, a process governed by the laws of the market, which Smith referred to as an "invisible hand."

As such assumptions of the mechanical view of nature were breaking down in philosophy, biology, and physics, their broader cultural impact was also being challenged. In music, for example, the harmonic principles that defined Baroque and classical music were being modified fundamentally (for example, by Richard Wagner's chromaticism) by the newly conceived harmonic coloration in the hands of Debussy and others, and most obviously by the development of atonal and serial composition techniques by, among others, Arnold Schoenberg and the Second Vienna School in the early twentieth century. Painting was shifting its assumptions as well, in the dissolution of the object at the hands of the French Impressionists, to the multi-perspectival works of Picasso, to the drip paintings of Jackson Pollock and others.

The absolutist, atomistic, and mechanistic assumptions about reality have been considered, challenged, revised, and in many instances replaced, and this has happened across our intellectual and cultural lives. One may reasonably wonder how and why such changes occur, and there have been a number of suggestions over the years. Our general thesis does not require us to answer the question, but a word or two about some possibilities may be in order. Hegel thought that among the constituents of every entity there are contradictory traits, and the tension generated by these contradictions explains how and why they change. Marx, not long after, applied this idea to economic life and argued that there are contradictions inherent in all economic systems, and the inherent contradictions created an instability that cannot be sustained. In capitalism, for example, he argued that there is a contradiction between the interests of capitalists, those who own productive property, and those who work for a wage. Eventually, he thought, this inherent contradiction would cause the system to be transformed into something else. In this respect, Marx was a consistent Hegelian. Unlike Hegel, though, Marx also thought that changes in social, political, intellectual, and cultural life are driven largely by the changes in economic structures. Feudalism needed ideas and systems that supported feudal economic structures and relations, and capitalism needs ideas and systems that support capitalist structures and relations.

Others, who are less convinced by the Hegelian approach, have suggested other explanations. The ancient Greek philosopher Heraclitus, for example, thought that change is the ongoing feature of nature and does not require an explanation. Others (we might mention Darwin as an example) thought that biological change happens because populations of organisms invariably grow to the point that they become too numerous for their environments to sustain. In this assumption he was following the ideas of the earlier British economist Thomas Malthus. He also thought that because of chance mutations in characteristics, some individuals will display traits that make them more or less adaptable to changing conditions. Because the environment cannot sustain the population, less well-adapted individuals will tend to reproduce at a lesser rate than those that are better adapted to the environmental conditions. Over time, this process explains, Darwin thought, most change in the biological sphere.

Other explanations are also possible. One might argue that changes in various fields, music or art, are the result at least in part of factors internal to the fields, without any necessary contradictions involved. For example, a cultural form such as music has at any time a number of possibilities among its traits. Various factors, pure chance among them, may contribute to which of those possibilities develop. There may not have been any features of classical music that required its transformation over the years into romantic styles, but the possibilities were inherent in the earlier forms, and for reasons that might differ from case to case, they responded to factors in the culture and society in such a way that the classical style died out and romantic styles arose. Or one might simply argue that there is no pattern to change, and that reality carries on as it does more or less by chance.

In whichever way one wishes to account for change, and for our purposes we do not need to resolve the question here (if indeed it can be resolved at all), there is an ongoing effort, and this applies in all fields of contemporary human endeavor, to sort out what comes after the atomistic and mechanistic conception of reality. There is no, or very little, convergence of opinion on the preferable alternatives to traditional ideas and practices, and that uncertainty is as true in physics and biology as it is in music, literature, or international affairs. The same is to be said of philosophy. If the metaphysics of Plato and Rousseau (and of very many others) can no longer be comfortably asserted, then we confront the obvious question how we can best understand nature, or reality in general, and our knowledge of it.

The initial clue to an answer is that if an atomistic, mechanistic worldview is no longer feasible, then presumably we need a view that is neither atomistic nor mechanistic, so we begin where Hegel pointed us, which is with a relational conception of reality and, presumably, everything in it.[2] This would mean that rather than think of entities as distinct, unrelated individuals that happen to interact with one another, like balls on a pool table or atoms in the void, we think of them as objects that are constituted by their relations. In fact, we have seen this general idea before, specifically in Dewey, where we explained his concept with the metaphor of an ecosystem. This is the same basic idea, though now it is necessary to drill a bit more deeply and clarify certain points that Dewey did not.

The shift from atomistic to relational entities is monumental. For one thing, it departs from the dominant view in the history of Western thought, notwithstanding Hegel, Darwin, and Einstein. Second, it departs from a number of assumptions we have built into our cultural way of seeing things. For example, we tend to assume that if we want to understand something, we need to identify its parts and components, and then analyze the components individually to understand each of them better. If we pursue this analytic process far enough, by analyzing the parts and components into their parts and components, and yet again if necessary, we will, we think, eventually understand all the pieces and therefore the whole. The problem with this idea of what it is to understand something is that it does not work. Consider a complex object, like the human eye, as an illustration of the point. The eye has many components, and there is certainly value in understanding each of them and the function of each. By understanding each, and its function, we do not thereby understand the eye, however; in fact, we do not really understand each component this way. The reason this analytic procedure does not produce knowledge of either the parts or the whole is that in abstracting the parts from the whole, we overlook their relations with one another. The nature and function of each part of the eye lies in its relations with the other parts, to such an extent, in fact, that it is reasonable to say, for example, that the cornea is not a cornea in the absence of an optical nerve because it requires the nerve to function, and its function is as much a part of its nature as any of its other traits. The relations among the rest of the eye's components are similarly critical for understanding them. Moreover, the eye itself is not simply the sum of its parts but also the sum of its parts in certain relations with one another. Both the components and the whole are relationally constituted.

A slightly more abstract way of saying this is that the components and functions are traits of the eye, which has two implications. First, the components have their own traits and characteristics by virtue of being traits of the complex entity, or simply "complex," that is the eye, in the sense that a cornea is not a cornea in isolation from its functional relations with other components of the eye; second, the eye is a complex that is constituted by its traits in certain relations with one another, in that without the right components in the right relations, there would be no eye. Nowhere in this picture is there any entity that is atomistic or that has its traits independently of its relations. We may also point out that just as the eye's components have their natures in part by virtue of being components of the eye, the eye also has its traits; it is what it is in part by virtue of more comprehensive complexes of which it is a trait. An extracted eye in a petri dish is a different sort of thing than a functioning eye in a live person. The nature of the eye itself is a functional matter, in that what it is, what it can do, and its meanings all derive from the relations in which the eye stands to its own constituents and to the broader, more comprehensive complexes that it helps to constitute.

The idea that entities are relationally constituted complexes applies to all entities of all kinds, including, among innumerable other sorts of things, material objects, ideas, people, histories, emotions, dreams, societies, fictional characters, living things, memories, and basically anything else that one can pick out or identify. One should also note that once we make the shift from understanding things as constituted independently from everything else to a view in which entities are relationally constituted, there are no longer any grounds on which to deny the existence or reality of anything that be identified. In other words, we can no longer say that this is real but that is not, or this is more real than that. An idea is no more or less real than a material object, a possibility no more or less real than an actuality, and a fictional character no more or less real than a nonfictional person. Each prevails in, or we may say is located in, some set or sets of relations; each has whatever traits that it has; each is related to some number of other complexes in a range of ways. We are sometimes tempted to think that one sort of thing is more real than another—a whole more real than its parts, or parts more real than the whole, or sometimes that individuals are more real than societies, or society more real than individuals. No such conception has any place in a world of relationally constituted complexes.

It may be possible to understand the idea better if we consider another example, one in fact that will help us when we talk about experience a few pages on. It is traditional in Western cultures to consider a human being, a person, to be an entity that has an essential, independently determined core or nature, which then has various relations with other persons and other objects in the world. This is the idea that is expressed when we say, for example, that a person has or is a soul. A soul (at least in the way it is traditionally understood) is not something the nature of which is determined by the person's relations or interactions with other people or things. One might say that the soul can be affected by such relations, but not that it is constituted by them. Such a soul is, traditionally, the core of the person, the essential nature of which remains constant through all the surface consequences of the person's relations with other people and things. It is what philosophers used to call the unchanging substance of a person, not to be confused with the attributes that the substance has.

In a relational understanding of the person, the traditional distinction between substance and its attributes, or between an essential nature and nonessential or accidental traits, no longer makes sense. On the contrary, a person is not an essence distinct from its relations, but rather it is constituted by those relations. We can illustrate this point by thinking of two different kinds of relations that constitute a person. The first is the set of entities that are themselves located by the complex that is the person. This would include parts or components of the person (for example, a person's organs), and it would also include a person's history, or a virus in the body, or the air one breathes, or perhaps even another person—for example, in the case of twins or, more obviously, conjoined twins. These are all traits that themselves prevail in the complex that is the person, though we cannot forget that they themselves are each complexes that locate their own traits. However, the person is relationally conditioned not only by the traits that she locates but also by the constitutive roles she plays in the complexes in which she is located as trait. Her family, for example, is as much a constitutive trait of the person she is as she is a constitutive trait of her family. In some measure, the person is who she is by virtue of her relations with members of the family and the family as a whole, and the family is what it is in some respects because she is one of its constitutive traits. And just as a family contributes to the nature of a person because she is a member of it, so, too, does her occupation, or hometown, or nationality, or circle of friends, or the books she reads.

There is probably a sense in which none of this is surprising, even if it has not been expressed in quite this way. Parents will often think of their children as part of themselves, for example, and the idea that one's children are genuinely constitutive of one's nature captures that sense. We are also likely to be comfortable with the idea that the broader complexes to which a person is related are constituted, at least in part, by that relation. One's family is an obvious illustration, but we may also consider a professional organization of which one is a member—for example, a teachers' union, or a legislature, or any such organization. On the one hand, the organization itself is not definable merely in terms of its constituent members, because it continues to exist even as its members come and go. The organization is a distinct entity, just as a person is a distinct entity, and not equivalent simply to any or all of its parts. At the same time, the organization is not equivalent to the set of its members either, because that would just be a collection of people. It is constituted not simply by its members, in part or in whole, but also by its members in certain relations with one another. There is no essence or substance of such an organization. Rather, it is a complex that is constituted by its relational traits, which include not only its members but also its history, its goals, its mission and values, and its own relations with other organizations.

The relational ontology that we are advocating simply takes this recognizable description and applies it to everything that exists, of any and every kind. As the reader may imagine, there is a great deal more that could and should be said to fill out and justify this conception, most of which would be too much of a distraction here, given our interest in articulating the general idea and exploring its implications for education. A couple points are worth mentioning, though, to make the idea more plausible. One of them is that though all entities are constituted by their relational constituents, not all of those constituents are equally relevant to the nature or character of the entity. Consider, again, a person as an illustration of the point. For any particular person, there is no way to distinguish from among all the elements that may be related to a person, those that are constitutively related and those that are not. Thus, it is senseless to say that there are relational traits or components of a person, but that they are not constitutive. All are constitutive. However, some are far more relevant, or we may say more important, to the person than others. To pick an obvious and noncontroversial example, my spouse is a far more relevant constitutive element of my life than is a particular stone in my garden. Both are entities that are related to me, and therefore constitutive, but one is by far more relevant to the person that I am than is the other. Constituent complexes may not be more or less related, but they may be, and generally are, more or less relevant. The relevance of a constitutive element, moreover, may become more or less strong over time or as circumstances change. The stone in my garden, though typically minimally relevant to me, becomes quite a bit more relevant to my life if, by design or chance, it strikes and breaks one of my windows.

In the same way, I may become more or less relevant to the nature of a complex of which I am a constituent element. If I am a member of a teachers' union, I am likely to be one of thousands of members, and in that case I am constitutively related to the union but minimally relevant to its nature and general character. However, if I am elected to a leadership position in the union, then my relevance grows accordingly. I would not be more related to the union, since relations do not admit of degrees, but I would be more relevant. This distinction between relationality and relevance is important because it allows us to accommodate the fact that lives change, and things become more or less important over time. Any philosophical conception must be able to fit the facts of whatever it is applied to, and ideally it would illuminate those facts. Otherwise, there is not much point to it. In the case of reality understood relationally, it can fit the demands of our lives in that it allows for such facts as changes in the relevance and import of things and events in our lives. At the same time, it helps us to make sense of features of our lives that are in fact much more difficult to square with the traditional, essentialist conception of a person. It allows us to understand that in a literal and quite meaningful sense, our child is a constituent of our lives, not just something external and merely attached to it. Our child contributes to who we are, and a relational ontology accounts for this fact. All other constituents do as well, though most of them do not do so in quite as meaningful and emotionally charged way as a child does. All of this counts toward the justification of a relational ontology. It is, in the ways described, coherent, plausible, and useful.

The other point that bears repeating, and some amount of development, is the idea that no complex is more real than any other. This is a point that is probably of greater importance in technical philosophy, but, as we shall see further on, it has its implications for education as well. Like the general idea of relationality, this one is a fairly sharp break from tradition. We are, for whatever reasons, used to thinking about some things as more real than other things. Philosophers have approached the world this way, as we saw in Plato, and scientists have as well. One may hear some physicists, for example, say that a table is not "really" solid, because it is "really nothing but" tiny particles moving about in mostly empty space at fantastically high speeds. When something like this is said, it implies that the subatomic context is more real than our normal experience. In this view, our ordinary experience is an illusion, and we can encounter reality, the "really real," only at the atomic and subatomic levels.

That such an idea is ever taken seriously is a mystery, since it flies in the face of everything we do all the time. It is, in fact, an incoherent idea. What is far more coherent is to understand things—in this case, material things—such that we can acknowledge the reality of both ordinary experience and the world of the very small and very fast. Neither is an illusion, in that both are highly pervasive complexes that have whatever traits they have, that interact with one another, that are constitutive of our lives and of the natures of countless other entities, and of which each of us (and innumerable other complexes as well) are constitutive elements. This is a far more coherent (and plausible) approach to reality than to assume that the table on which I am leaning is not "really" solid.

A further significant feature of this generous attitude toward reality is that it enables us to better understand the significance of the aesthetic features of our lives. We will say much more about the aesthetic dimension of experience in the next section, but for now we can consider the place of literature, and theater, in our lives. It is not uncommon for people to think that whatever is not material, or not "concrete," is somehow less real, more ephemeral, and therefore not really valuable or important. Sometimes people who think this way find it difficult to take literature or theater seriously, on the grounds that it is all an invention, and therefore not real. Since it is not real, this line of reasoning goes, it has nothing to teach us about ourselves or the world. A literary or theatrical construct is, presumably, unimportant because it is unreal, and it is unreal because it is imagined rather than concrete.

But if we have good reason to hold that because nothing is more real than anything else, from which it would follow that a literary or theatrical construct is no less real than a nonfictional person, then all of this changes. In this view, Harry Potter is no less real than any other boy, fictional or nonfictional. He has characteristics—for example, he wears glasses and has an intriguing scar on his forehead, his parents died when he was a baby, he is a student at Hogwarts, and, it turns out, he is destined for wizarding greatness. If we were to deny any of these attributes, we would be mistaken, and the reason we would be mistaken is that these attributes, and not any of their contraries, are true of Harry Potter, which is an assertion that would be nonsensical if he were not real. The reason Harry Potter is as real as any nonfictional boy is that the broad set of relations that constitutes the complex that is literature, what we might call the literary or fictional order, is no more or less real than the material order that we nonfictional complexes inhabit. Both have whatever traits that they have. They are not to be confused with one another, but they do interact with one another. The character of Harry Potter was a hugely relevant constitutive trait of the life of the actor

Daniel Radcliffe, not to mention his creator, the author J. K. Rowling. Harry and the whole of his fictional world have had various consequences in the nonfictional world. For years, that fictional world prompted probably millions of children to read more than they otherwise would have. It has also been a subject of controversy, specifically for people who, on religious grounds, found the idea of wizards and witches disturbing and did not want their children exposed to it. Apparently, from their point of view, wizards and witches are not entirely fictional.

To deny the reality of Harry Potter on the grounds that he and his world are fictional is, effectively, to acknowledge that one does not quite understand how life works. A fictional character can be important in ways we have ascribed to Harry Potter, but one can also be important in other significant ways. For more than four hundred years we have been considering what we may learn about human beings, and families, and aging, and leadership, from King Lear and his tribulations. That the play is a piece of fiction and that Lear is a fictional character does not render any of it insignificant, never mind unreal. An engagement with Lear, or with countless other fictional characters we might mention, is as rewarding and valuable as one allows it to be. If we were to insist that Lear is not real, and therefore think that engaging with him is pointless, we would thereby deny ourselves not only an opportunity for a rewarding literary and theatrical experience but also the chance to consider and learn a great deal about people, perhaps even about ourselves. And if we take that attitude to the literary and theatrical orders as a whole, then the disservice we do ourselves is little short of catastrophic. It is far more coherent, plausible, and useful to regard the fictional orders to be as real as the nonfictional, and that is made possible by the relational ontology that we are developing.

For our purposes, the more direct and extensive implications of this relational ontology are through the conception of experience that follows from it. In the next section we will explore that view of experience and its educational implications. Still, though, there are implications of the relational ontology for education and educational principles that we can discuss even now. The ontology has its most direct educational implications for curriculum. What I am about to say is a generalization, to which there are many exceptions in schools at all levels, but it remains the case that for the most part, we tend to think about distinct disciplines and subjects of instruction in isolation from one another. There are distinct disciplines, of course. History is not chemistry, music is not philosophy, and sociology is not exercise science. Where we go wrong is not in recognizing these differences but in treating them as if they were isolated from one another, like the balls on a pool table, rather than as elements in an ecosystem. It is not so much that the disciplines are constitutively related to one another, though they are, but that the aspects of the world that they study are constitutively related to one another, and if we treat them in isolation, we will never understand them well.

Suppose we are interested in Roman history, maybe the end of the Republican period and beginning of the empire, so the first century BCE. Certainly, we would study the actions of the leadership—Julius Caesar and Pompey, for example. We would need to have some understanding of the societies around the Italian peninsula, especially the Celtic tribes in Gaul and the Germanic tribes north of the Alps, as well as the geography of Europe. We would have to understand why Caesar was in Gaul with his troops, and why his famous crossing of the Rubicon as he returned to Rome with his troops had so much meaning for Roman politics. Some degree of understanding of Roman society would be important, so that we might comprehend why the leadership made efforts to placate the people of Rome. For this, some sense of sociology is necessary. We would also benefit from an appreciation of how the city itself was organized and the materials and engineering that was used to build roads and the aqueducts that brought water to the city from the nearby mountains. It is impossible, furthermore, to understand either Roman society or Roman politics without some sense of Roman religious beliefs and practices, not to mention the stories the Romans told themselves about their own origins and the values they derived from those stories. For that we need the poet Virgil, among others. In the middle of many of the developments of these years was Cicero, one of the most accomplished rhetoricians and philosophical Stoics of the ancient world. A reasonably firm grasp of Roman history of the time would require some familiarity with Cicero, his role in the Senate, and some of his writings.

The point is not to intimidate a teacher, or her students, but simply to make what may be the obvious point that there is not something called "history" that can be isolated from geography, engineering, sociology, religion, literature, philosophy, and politics. No matter which historical subject we wish to study, all of these factors contribute to constituting the subject matter. Every historian knows this, but we nevertheless continue to treat distinct subjects as if they stood in isolation. We teach English and literature in one class, and physical science in another, not to be confused with mathematics, or history and social studies, and art and music, if they are available at all, are treated as something else entirely. But if our world is not like this, then we cannot expect a curriculum so designed to provide our students access to the world in which we all live. And, in fact, they all too frequently grow to assume that these disciplines have nothing to do with one another. It is not unusual to hear a student object to being expected to learn something about history in an English class, or physics in a philosophy course, or literature in the study of music. This is most unfortunate, because, as we have been arguing, these various aspects of the world and of our lives are constitutively related to one another. We cannot properly understand Elizabethan literature without English history, or modern philosophy without modern physics, or Romantic music without Goethe.

The content of our curriculum, if we wish to state a general principle that would be implied by these considerations, should always be organized to emphasize relations rather than discrete bits of information or events. The bits of information and events are what they are, or were what they were, because of the relations among their constituents. If we do not emphasize those relations, then we make it far less likely that the information or events can be understood. For the most part, our curriculum is not organized this way now, so that it would require considerable revision, in some cases more than in others, to rethink the ways that we organize the content of instruction. This would certainly have to be done differently at different levels, given the expectations one could reasonably have of students at various stages in their own development and intellectual maturity. The general principle would be the same in all cases, though, from the earliest systematic instruction through graduate school.

There is a fairly wide range of possibilities here. One might imagine a school that has a specific theme (for example, a school of science or a school of the arts). In such a case, it would be possible to organize other subjects, all of them, to orbit around the general theme. In New York City, to give an example at the university level, at the Fashion Institute of Technology, courses in many subjects, such as economics or literature or history or sociology, are organized around fashion and the fashion industry. In this way, not only do students learn information, but they also learn it in relation to the subject of their general interest, which in turn makes it far more meaningful than it might be otherwise. At a more modest level, a school might organize smaller-scale learning communities, where a group of students study several disciplines for a period of time, perhaps a semester or a year, that are taught based on a specific theme (for example, climate, or technology, or local history). Such studies would require collaboration among the teachers who are participating, but it is not very difficult to organize and could be done at any level.

There would no doubt be structural revision that would be required to apply this principle extensively. Schools, and especially universities, might consider reorganizing their academic departments. This process would no doubt present various problems, political and otherwise, and it would be especially challenging at the university level, where so much of faculty personnel judgments are made based on discipline specific criteria. If the principle is appropriate, though, and our relational ontology suggests that it is, then we would want both curriculum and school structure to approach the relational model to whatever degree can be managed. As Plato and Rousseau both said about their principles, I do not mean to claim that the principle can be realized thoroughly, but I do claim that the closer we can get to the ideal realization of the principle, the better the educational experience will be.

A second curricular implication of the relational ontology follows from its commitment to the existential parity of any and all complexes. Each is whatever its constitutive traits make it, and each has whatever importance its context engenders. The specific broader, more pervasive context in which each entity or complex prevails is irrelevant with respect to its existence. To exist is to prevail in some context or other, regardless of what that context is. This means, as we have seen, that there is no sense to be given to the assumption that, for example, literature does not deal with reality, and therefore is less important than those subjects that do, which would be, presumably, the natural and social sciences. Not all disciplines are equally important for all others, or for any person at any given time, in the same way that not all traits are equally relevant for the complex in which they prevail. But just as no trait is entirely irrelevant, because all are constitutive, no discipline is inherently unimportant. We may not need to study any literature in order to learn the properties of steel, but we may well want to study some literary work if we are designing a building and there is a novel or some poetry that can help us understand residents' attitudes toward the area for which the building is planned. It will be most useful for an engineer or architect, to continue with the same illustration, to have learned why and how literature matters if we expect her to be able to benefit from it when the time comes.

The principle in this case is that any potential discipline or subject matter should be presumed to have some relevance and importance to people's lives and therefore deserves a place in the curriculum. Existential parity, we might say, implies parity in intellectual value among the subjects of study. As a practical matter, no school or university can be expected to build into its curriculum, or even to offer on a regular basis, all possible topics of study. Judgments to include or not, or to require or not, or to remove or not, any given subject are made regularly. What is being proposed here is not a formula by which to make such judgments but a specific principle, one implied by the relational ontology, that ought to guide them. Circumstances differ from school to school, or district to district, and from time to time, so we can expect that judgments and decisions will differ accordingly. But the principle holds and should guide those judgments as decision makers take account of the specific conditions of each unique circumstance. Regardless of those details, it remains the case that students, and the people who guide them, such as their parents, are much better served if they understand the value of the whole curriculum, from literature to music to science to mathematics, and if the schools can help them to see how these various subjects of study can figure importantly in people's lives. They all represent ways that we engage our world, and no understanding of the world can be adequate if it ignores any of them. To focus on literature and ignore history is to have a truncated and artificially constrained sense of things, but the same is true if one thinks that history can be understood without literature. The point simply has to be generalized to refer to all of the ways that we understand ourselves and our world.

The emphasis on the multiplicity of the relations in which each of us stands toward our worlds provides a convenient segue into a discussion of experience and knowledge. As we know from the study of Plato and others, a philosophical anthropology, which we will undertake as a theory of experience, and an epistemology, or theory of knowledge, are critical in a developed philosophy of education. As a consequence, we can expect a number of additional educational principles to emerge from them.

EXPERIENCE AND KNOWLEDGE

A relational ontology of the sort developed in the previous section has implications for how we understand experience and knowledge. We used the example of a person to help illustrate the meaning of constitutive relations, and now we need to focus on the implications of constitutive relations for our understanding of a person, specifically with respect to experience and knowledge. The first obvious point is that the traditional modernist concept of experience, which is the largely passive reception of sense data from the world around us, is no longer tenable.

If a person is constituted by the relations among the traits that it locates, and by the broader complexes of which it is a trait (which is what the general theory of relational constitution implies), then a person is by definition embedded in her components and in her environments. The point was made earlier that the idea of a person as an essential core, a substance or soul, has no meaning if entities are constituted relationally. A person, therefore, is defined by her complex engagement or interaction with everything that constitutes her. In this view, substance or soul is not the only traditional concept associated with the nature of a person that goes by the wayside. It also no longer makes sense to think of a person as, for example, a mind in a body. Technically, that sort of picture was never coherent, largely because minds are not the sort of thing that can be located in space, and so cannot literally be "in a body."

More recently, it has become common to think of mind as equivalent to brain, and brains, being physical objects, are located in space and, indeed, in bodies. The problem with this approach is that minds cannot be located in brains, for the same reason that they cannot be located in bodies generally, nor can minds be identical to brains. There are two reasons for this. First, many of the activities and processes that we associate with minds (for example, thinking or remembering) necessarily involve other entities (in these cases, ideas and memories) that are not material entities and therefore cannot be located in brains. Second, minds and their processes have traits that brains do not—indeed, cannot—have. A memory, for example, may be moving or disturbing or precious, but brains, as physical objects characterized primarily by neurochemical activity, cannot have any of those characteristics. Minds are not brains and are not in bodies. In fact, it makes very little sense to think of a person as inside a body at all. The relational ontology impels us to abandon even the commonly held idea that the body is some sort of border between the person, which is internal, and the rest of the world, which is external. The body is not a border between a person and the world, and the person is not inside a body looking out.

But if a person is not a substance or soul, nor a mind in a body, nor a brain in a body, and if the body does not separate the person from the world, then how are we to understand what a person is? The answer is that persons, like other living beings, are embedded in and constituted by their surroundings. It continues to be possible and reasonable to talk about mind and minds, largely because doing so remains the most convenient way to identify those aspects of human activity that we have traditionally considered mental—for example, thinking, remembering, or wanting. But mind, in this picture, is embodied, embedded, and in fact extended into the world of which each of us is a part. When I use a tool to perform some task, it is as much an exercise of mind as when I think a private thought.

Before turning to the details of a conception of experience, it is appropriate at this juncture to point out that the relational conception of the person that our general relational ontology implies is one that acknowledges the significance of a concept that is increasingly important in current literature on gender and other relations: the idea of intersectionality. The concept was first introduced in the late 1980s to make the point that there is a distinct sort of injustice directed at individuals who embody more than one category of systemic oppression. It is one thing to be a victim of racial injustice, and it is another to be the recipient of gender injustice, but if one is, for example, a black woman, then the situation is complicated by one's location in more than one relevant order of relations. This is what is meant by intersectionality. Since people are by definition complexes that are located in a range of orders of relations, such intersectionality is in the nature of what it is to be a person. When those orders of relations include more than one category of social injustice, then intersectionality helps us to understand both the nature of the injustice and how it may be addressed.

The contemporary American philosopher Kathleen Wallace has taken up this issue at the general and more specific levels. She has developed a detailed conception of a relational view of a person, and she has shown how the conception of intersectionality may be generalized to help us understand not only the nature of injustice but the nature of the person as well. Her point, and it is a valuable one, is that the concept of intersectionality, when generalized, enriches the feminist and other relevant approaches to women and others' social relations and the forms of social injustice they experience. Part of the argument she makes is that people who experience more than one form of injustice are likely to confront their inherent relationality more explicitly and directly than others of us who are not treated in similar ways. Without an appreciation of the relational character of one's life, it is more difficult than it might otherwise be to understand such multiple forms of oppression. The concept of intersectionality, which is implied by the relational conception of the person, helps bring to light aspects of that oppression.[3]

Human beings are sufficiently complex and elaborately developed, perhaps more so than any other living thing, that we interact with our surroundings in both passive and active ways. Some of these activities are automatic and largely unconscious (for example, breathing), and some are deliberate and systematic (building cities or writing books). The push and pull of the ongoing, mutually constitutive engagement of a person with her environment is what we mean by experience. To understand persons at a general, philosophical level, it is necessary to understand this ongoing interaction that is experience. Consequently, a theory of experience is a critical feature of a philosophical consideration that intends to have any implications for our lives, including any implications for education.

As one can readily see, this approach to experience is quite different from thinking of experience as the passive reception of sense data. But this is not the only difference between the traditional empiricist view of experience and ours. Another important difference between the two concerns the relation between experience and knowledge. Traditionally, it was standard to regard experience as a method for achieving knowledge. This, for example, was Rousseau's view of it, and it was the reason he advocated allowing Emile to engage the world as much as possible on his own. The more he interacts with the world around him, the more sensory impressions he has, which in turn supplies more material for his developing mind to process and transform into knowledge of the world. In this conception, knowledge is the broader category and experience, as the passive intake of information about the world, is a component of it.

Our conception of experience turns that picture on its head. If experience is not the passive intake of information about the world around us, then it cannot be understood to be a vehicle for knowledge. On the contrary, because it is the whole of a person's engagement with the world, experience is by far the broader category, of which knowledge is a component. Moreover, much of experience is not cognitive at all, although (as we will soon see) any experience can be, and yet knowledge is one among three of what we will call the dimensions of experience. Sometimes our engagement with the world is something we suffer (or preferably appreciate) and has no cognitive character to it, even if knowledge can be drawn from it. When a child stomps around in a puddle, splashing as much as she can, this is an experience that does not need cognitive features at all. Experience may not plausibly be thought of as either an avenue to or a less pervasive constituent of knowledge, nor as necessarily cognitive. The relation between experience and knowledge is more complex than that.

A closer look indicates that, far from being concerned primarily with knowledge, experience consists of three general features, which we will refer to as its cognitive, aesthetic, and political dimensions.[4] This picture of experience is rather complicated, because each of the dimensions of experience is a rich topic in itself, and because the three dimensions of experience are constitutively related to one another. A full development of experience, then, requires an account of the three dimensions, their relations with one another, as well as other features of experience that do not play as pervasive a role in experience as do the cognitive, aesthetic, and political. I refer here to such features of experience (I have elsewhere called them "constituents" of experience) as language, emotions, and imagination, which, as important as they are, nevertheless are not among the most pervasive dimensions of experience. To make the point quickly, we have said that not every experience is cognitive, though every experience can be. Of language, by contrast, we would have to say that not only are there are experiences that are not linguistic, but some cannot be. There is nothing linguistic about listening to a piece of music, for example, and any effort to provide a linguistic rendering of the experience is invariably a poor substitute for the original. Language is simply not a generic feature or dimension of experience, and the same may be said of emotions and of the role of imagination. These three aspects of our lives are significant enough to be considered constituents of experience, but they are not sufficiently pervasive to be considered among the dimensions of experience.

We must also note that in addition to the dimensions and constituents of experience, there are forms of experience, by which I mean the many and various kinds of experience people may have. We may distinguish any number of such forms of experience—for example, religious experience, political experience, social experience, sexual experience, military experience, or musical experience. Each of these forms of experience, and many others, opens us to some aspect of the complexity of and possibilities in our lives. They can be pleasing and enriching, educative or constraining, disconcerting or frightening. What we here call the forms of experience indicate the varied nature of the human engagement with the world. Woven throughout all of it, though, are the cognitive, aesthetic, and political dimensions of experience. They constitute the pervasive threads, to speak metaphorically,

of the complex fabric that is our experience. We must pass over most of the
detail here, but it will be sufficient to clarify the meaning and import of
the three dimensions of experience, the cognitive, aesthetic, and political,
because even that much will allow us to infer meaningful and significant
educational principles.

The cognitive, aesthetic, and political dimensions of experience correspond to knowledge, art, and power. The general idea is that knowledge, art,
and power are pervasive features of our lives, far more so than is generally
recognized. They are so pervasive, in fact, that any experience can elicit or
generate knowledge, any experience can have an aesthetic or artistic aspect,
and any experience can engage the power inherent in experience, which is
the ubiquitous human potential to act.

We will be able to be more explicit further on, but one can already get
a sense of how this way of approaching experience might have specific
implications for education. It becomes immediately obvious, for example, that knowledge is not something limited to bits of information but
is woven into, to continue the same metaphor, the aesthetic and political,
which is to say that knowledge is embedded in art and action as much as
anything else. It would also be clear on the face of it that if the aesthetic
is one of the dimensions of experience, and if the aesthetic dimension of
experience is associated with art, then art and the aesthetic are far from
frivolous or peripheral aspects of a curriculum. And it would also be
clear that if power (and therefore action) is threaded through experience,
then education cannot be a passive process. Plato, Rousseau, Dewey, and
Freire were right, it turns out, that to think about education as a matter
of conveying information is exactly the wrong conception to have. They
each had their own reasons for saying this. Our reason is that experience
is inherently active and imbued with power, and therefore if experience
is to be educative, to use Dewey's phrase, it must build students' active
engagement in the educational process.

We should dig a bit more deeply into the three dimensions of experience,
because doing so will allow us to draw more fruitful educational principles.
We can begin with any of the three because they are of equal pervasiveness
and therefore equal importance, so knowledge and the cognitive dimension
is as reasonable a place to begin as any other. It has been traditional, and
in some circles still quite common, to think of knowledge as associated
primarily, or even exclusively, with propositions. In other words, it has been
assumed that knowledge is propositional in the sense that it is in propositions, rather than in such things as pictures or actions, that knowledge is
conveyed. It has also been assumed that to know something is to have an
accurate description or account of it. People, of course, have distinguished
this sort of knowledge, which can be called "knowledge that," from what
is sometimes called "knowledge how." The assumption was that knowing

how to do something is a much or wholly different activity or process from knowing what something is or that "x" is true. This distinction was built into Plato's view of knowledge, which is why he placed little value on knowing how to do things—farming or building, for example—and much greater value on knowledge of the nature of things. The rulers, as Plato understood things, could not be people who had knowledge only of how to do things, because that is an inferior form of knowledge. The rulers had to have the more important knowledge, which is knowledge of the nature of things. Only they could guide the republic properly and safely. Some of his ideas about curriculum, and who needed to be taught what, rested on this approach to knowledge.

Once we begin to understand knowledge as a pervasive dimension of experience, and as in mutually constitutive relations with art and power, both of these conceptions of knowledge are left behind. Knowledge is woven throughout the fabric of experience, so it is misleading to associate it only or primarily with propositions. The fact is that entirely non-propositional moments in experience can be and often are as cognitively significant as propositions. The odd thing about all this is that in practice we already know it, but for some reason we lose sight of what we know when we begin to develop theories about it. Many of us, and perhaps all of us in one way or another, have come away from a work of art, for example, with a richer, or deeper, or clearer understanding of the relevant theme or topic. This is knowledge in art, and it happens all the time. Art does not have to be cognitive; sometimes it is expressive, or emotional, or inspirational, or devotional, or it engages some other aspect of experience. But all of art can be cognitive.

The illustrations are unending. If one wants to understand better, for example, how it felt to a Japanese person to live through the profound transformations of Japanese society in the Meiji period (the late nineteenth and early twentieth centuries), there is probably no more instructive source than the Japanese literature of the time. It cannot tell the whole story, but it tells some of it, and in a way that the best books of history, sociology, anthropology, psychology, or economics cannot do. Literature, and this is true of all art, is among the ways that we engage the world, and, more specifically, one of the ways that we engage the world cognitively. The same is true of a dance, a piece of music, or a painting, and again, this is not a radical claim, but something we have always known. Most of the art of Europe through the centuries (at least well into the modern period) was didactic, an effort to help people better understand the religious commitments that underlie their society. Some of it was more devotional than cognitive, but much of it was intended to teach and to convey knowledge and understanding. The approach to experience we have taken, which includes the idea that cognition is a dimension of experience, and therefore knowledge is more pervasive than it is often thought to be, is a corrective to much of traditional epistemology, and it allows us to acknowledge a common feature of our lives that is otherwise overlooked.

Just as the cognitive dimension of experience is related constitutively to the aesthetic dimension, which is a categorially more accurate way of saying that knowledge can have aesthetic traits and that art can be cognitive, so, too, is knowledge related to power, which is to say to action, in ways that have frequently been missed by epistemologists. In other words, the cognitive dimension of experience is also constitutively related to the political dimension. It is not only what we say that embodies knowledge but also what we do. This applies to much of what we do habitually, and even instinctively. A new mother can be uncertain and nervous about how best to handle her infant, but she also makes inferences and decisions based on her interactions with the baby, and the actions she takes, without thinking about them or putting them into propositions of any kind, are cognitively charged and, when they work, are examples of knowledge as legitimate as any other. The controlled bodily motions of a trained dancer, or the casting of an experienced fly fisherman, are instances of knowledge, and none of it has to be articulated in propositions. In fact, it probably could not be put into words. When I play a piece on the piano, one that I have practiced to some extent, it can plausibly and literally be said that I know the piece. This is not knowledge of the piece in the sense of a description of some kind, but it is knowledge of the piece as an action. And knowledge as action is no less knowledge than knowledge as description. Not every action is cognitively charged, just as not every work of art is, but just as art can be and often is cognitive, so, too, is action. Knowledge and power are entwined with one another, just as are knowledge and art.

In these ways, and in others a discussion of which we will have to forgo, knowledge functions differently in experience than philosophers have traditionally thought. This is certainly a different approach to knowledge from Plato and Rousseau's, though it has something in common with Dewey and Freire's. Dewey was especially concerned with how knowledge functions in experience; in fact, the view being developed here draws heavily from Dewey. And both he and Freire were adamant that knowledge is not primarily about gathering information but about action. When Freire spoke about praxis, or the necessity of inquiry for action and of action for inquiry, he was making a point similar to our idea that the cognitive and political dimensions of experience are mutually constitutive of one another, and that either abstracted from the other is a mere shadow of itself and devoid of much of its potential. Freire was not as concerned with a general theory of experience as we are, but there are nonetheless clear points of contact.

Dewey was more interested than Freire in a theory of experience, and ours draws a good deal of inspiration from his. In addition to his insistence that knowledge is meaningful and significant only in experience and experiential contexts, he was aware of the pervasiveness in experience of art. In fact, one of his more important and insightful books bears the title *Art as Experience*. Just as traditionally we have accepted conceptions of knowledge that are far too restrictive, we have done the same with art. One clear respect in which art is not limited to expression, never mind self-expression, is, as we have just discussed, in its cognitive capacity.

The claim is often made about art is that it is a matter of expression, or that through their art, artists express themselves. It was never clear to me what this means, but it is clear that whatever it means, artists can and do manage quite a bit more than simply "self-expression." Sometimes an artist is contributing to an ongoing engagement with some aspect of experience to which other artists have also contributed. Imagine an improvisational jazz band and the way its members hear the other members of the band and respond in their own playing. There is a performative give and take in this case in which each member of the band is contributing in a common direction. There may or may not be anything that any of them would call self-expression in such a situation, but it is surely art, at least when it is accomplished with some degree of skill and command of the musical material.

One of the more damaging restrictions we have placed on art through our common misconceptions is to think of it as belonging in museums, galleries, and concert halls. We have a tendency to make this sort of mistake in other aspects of our lives as well. We too often think that learning belongs only or primarily in schools, such that we artificially constrain the import of education; we also too commonly think that we have ethical responsibilities toward our family members and friends, but then suspend ethical considerations when we get to work. There are many other examples, from religious practice to political principles. In the case of art, by thinking of it as belonging primarily in museums, we miss how thoroughly imbued our normal experience is with aesthetic considerations. There are obvious examples of public art, such as cases of high art like Picasso in Daley Plaza in Chicago, but there are also examples of aesthetically rich murals and graffiti art; some people sing on the stage of the Met, while many of the rest of us restrict ourselves to singing in the shower, or maybe with a garage band; there is ballet in the Mariinsky Theater in St. Petersburg, and there is street dancing.

Aesthetic values and art, it turns out, are meaningful and important to all of us across the range of our experience. The clearest illustration of this is the degree to which our concern with design permeates our lives. We want the environments in which we move to be not only comfortable but also attractive. The criteria of attractiveness change from time to time and place to place, but we all look to achieve it in as many ways as possible. We organize the rooms in our homes to maximize efficiency, to be sure, but also to meet our aesthetic standards. We choose colors because we like how they look, or because they go well together; we care about how the walls look and what goes on them; we purchase furniture, other considerations such as price permitting, on aesthetic grounds as much as anything else; if we have a yard or garden, we arrange it and care for it so that it looks attractive and is a comfortable space to occupy. And the clearest illustration of the ubiquitous interest in design is in how we tend to ourselves and the way we look. Some people spend more time than others preparing themselves to leave home every morning, but practically everyone pays some attention to it. We attend to the clothes we wear and to how our hair looks because we want to be aesthetically pleasing enough at least to meet the expectations of others, if not to soothe our egos or to make specific impressions on certain people. Whatever the reasons, we apply design principles or organization and criteria of evaluation to ourselves every day, to our homes, to our neighborhoods, to our means of transportation, and to the extended environments in which we move.

This sort of thing is what it means to say that there is an aesthetic dimension of experience and that it is pervasive. It also indicates why it is a mistake to think of art as something that has its place in museums. What ends up in museums and concert halls is a refined expression of experience of the sort that we engage in all the time. In the same way, the knowledge that appears in books, libraries and schools is a refined version of a cognitive dimension of experience that characterizes our lives generally. Just as not everything we say or do counts as knowledge, not everything we say or do counts as art. Sometimes when we try to achieve knowledge, we fall short, in that we say something that is not true or fail to accomplish what we set out to do. Similarly, we may try and fail to create something of artistic merit. But whether what we are doing or undergoing in any particular case is an instance of knowledge or art, the cognitive and aesthetic dimensions of experience are no less pervasive in that all of our experience is susceptible to and capable of both.

The final piece of the theory of experience, for our purposes, is its political dimension. When we refer to the political dimension of experience, we refer to the pervasiveness of power, a point that requires some clarification. First, saying that power is pervasive in experience does not mean that everything we do is an exercise of power—or at least not a purposeful exercise of power. Just as the cognitive dimension is pervasive without implying that every experience involves knowledge, and the aesthetic experience is pervasive without implying that every experience is a matter of art, so the political is pervasive without every experience being an explicit exercise of power. The pervasiveness or ubiquity of power in experience derives from the relational character of experience. If experience is the constitutive push and pull of a person's life, then a person's life is necessarily having an impact on her surroundings. This is the feature of mutually constitutive relations from which the pervasiveness of power arises. We have said, though, that everything is related constitutively to something, so that in some sense every entity, not only the human and not only the organic, is characterized by power in this sense. It is true that every entity, because it prevails in mutually constitutive relations, is defined to some degree by its potential and possibilities. What distinguishes this general feature when it appears in human beings, however, is the degree to which people have the capacity to craft and direct that potential and those possibilities in the course of living. The power that characterizes our experience is not simply the mutually constitutive relations in which we prevail but also the fact that by virtue of the extensive potentialities of human being, by contrast with other beings, people have the capacity, the power, to control our lives and order our experience to meet our own goals and purposes.

A second point of clarification is that to speak of the exercise of power in experience is not to make a moral judgment. In itself, power is neither good nor bad, and in practice it can be either. Power is also not necessarily violence; in fact, it usually is not violence. Power can certainly be and often is destructive, but it can also be constructive. The creativity that is at the heart of the constitutive relations of a person to her environment is an expression of her power. Along the same lines, to say that experience has power as one of its fundamental dimensions does not mean to say anything about coercion or manipulation. People are certainly capable of coercion or manipulation, and exercise both far too often, but it would be false to say that the exercise of power in itself is always or even likely to be coercive or manipulative. Assisting a person, or helping to create the opportunity for another person to thrive, are examples of the exercise of power no less than coercion or manipulation. To say that power is a pervasive dimension of experience is not to make a moral claim at all. It points to the laudable as well as to the deplorable in our actions and, for that matter, to the merely quotidian.

The political dimension of experience is not about politics (or not solely about politics). Politics, in the sense in which we normally use the term, is the exercise of state power, or the pursuit of the capacity to exercise state power. Politics in its more common sense is one manifestation of power, but it is power only in a limited sense. We also use the word "politics" in reference to power in other than state contexts. One can speak, for example, of "office politics" or "academic politics." In both cases, as in "state politics," the term refers to the pursuit and exercise of power in the limited context of one's office or school. There is a tradition, then, of using the terms "politics" and "political" in broader contexts than the state, and it is this more general sense that we have in mind in identifying the political as a dimension of experience. Just as institutions of learning, such as schools, are refined instances of the cognitive dimension, and art institutions, such as museums, are refined instances of the aesthetic dimension, so state bodies such as parliaments and legal structures are refined instances of the political dimension that constitutes experience.

Power is one of the threads of the fabric of experience, and the form it takes in experience is a consequence of the human condition, or of what it means to be a person. This is a highly general claim, though, and it abstracts from specific conditions and circumstances. While it may be true to say that power pervades experience, it is also a fact that the exercise of power is often constrained by circumstances. Actually, it is always constrained by circumstances, in the sense that the parameters of one's situation influence one's possibilities and the power that one may exert. This is what Rousseau referred to when he said that natural conditions always limit what we can do. In itself, this is not a problem, and as Rousseau pointed out, we generally are able to acknowledge without resistance the unavoidable limits to our actions. It becomes a problem, and a serious one, when the constraints are such that we are unable to exercise the power that is at bottom definitive of our humanity. We have said that what characterizes power in human experience, and differentiates the human condition from other mutually constitutive sets of relations, is that power in human being is the potential to guide our purposes, craft the meanings of our actions, and generally direct the course of our lives. If and when we find ourselves in situations in which this potential is thwarted, then it is our humanity itself that is at stake. The less control we are able to implement over the conditions and meanings of our lives, the less of our human potential we are able to exercise.

We encounter constraints in nature generally, and we deal with them as best we can. It is the excessive constraints imposed by social relations in which the challenges to our humanity arise, primarily an artificially induced poverty and the complex set of social, political, economic, and ideological forces that contribute to and reinforce it. Here we have come, by a somewhat different route, to a conclusion that Freire had also reached, which is that the poverty in which huge segments of the human population are compelled to live, and the passivity with which they are expected, even coerced, to accept it, is a denial of people's humanity. For us, this point follows from the theory of experience itself, and it is unavoidable. The implications of this point for educational principles are significant, as they were for Freire, and we will turn to them in a moment.

There are points to be made, first, by way of final comments on the theory of experience. Experience, we have said, is the ongoing, mutually constitutive engagement of an individual with her environment, in both its passive and its active aspects. Experience, moreover, is characterized by three general dimensions. We have made a brief attempt to describe the cognitive, aesthetic, and political dimensions of experience and to offer some reasons to find the relevant ideas coherent, plausible, and useful. One point that bears emphasis, or reemphasis, is that these dimensions, though distinct and individually identifiable, are not isolated from one another. Each of them is in mutually constitutive relations with the others. For example, and to put the point in nontechnical language, we note that knowledge has the nature it has because it is interwoven with power. This is similar to a point that the pragmatists made, and that we saw in Dewey, which is the view that ideas are not descriptions of reality but tools that help us get things done. Knowledge has this character generally, which is to say that knowledge resides, we may say, in its role in our effort to make our way. This is part of what the traditional claim that "knowledge is power" means. Whatever else we may in a more developed epistemology need to say about knowledge, and about such related conceptions as truth and inquiry, its touchstone in experience will be its relation to our ability to accomplish our lives.

Comparable points must be kept in mind about the relations of all three dimensions to each of the others. Because the aesthetic is one of the dimensions of experience, it is therefore one of the ways in which we engage the world. It is one of the avenues, in other words, through which we learn about the world and through which we make our lives what they are. Art is as central to the nature of our experience as is knowledge, and power no less so. It is a central feature of being human that our experience is as active as it is passive, and the power that is implied by that activity is in turn central to knowledge and to the aesthetic features of our lives. All of these points have explicit bearing on educational principles, as we will now see.

EDUCATIONAL PRINCIPLES

It is commonly thought that education is a process whereby minds are filled with information and in which people learn some set of skills. That this way of thinking about education was unacceptable for Plato (at least for the rulers), Rousseau, Dewey, and Freire is clear. For our own reasons, it is also unacceptable for us. The picture of a person as a mind that can be "filled" with anything is incoherent. People are not minds that absorb information. We are complex beings who make our way in the world in and through the process of experience. And experience, in turn, is understood now as the mutually constitutive interaction of an individual with her environing contexts—material, biological, historical, social, and cultural, among others. These environing conditions constitute what and who each of us is, and each of us in turn contributes, more or less relevantly, to the nature of our environing conditions. A person is not a mind that is to be filled with information or trained to do this or that. A person is a being whose life is shaped through experience and who experiences through three dimensions—cognitive, aesthetic, and political. Whatever we say now about education must be applicable for persons understood this way.

We may think a bit more here about the goals of education. If it is not the purpose of education to fill minds with information and train people in some narrow set of tasks, in part because such conceptions are not consistent with the nature of a person as we have developed it, then the goals of education have to be reconceived in a way that is consistent with our idea of what a person is. In short, and here we draw on an idea that Dewey had developed, the nature of education is to enhance experience. Moreover, because our lives in their distinctively human character and meaning occur in and through experience, to enhance experience is to contribute to the capacity each of us has to master the conditions of our lives, to construct their meaning according to our own lights, and to guide the course of our lives in ways that are consistent with our own ends and purposes. This is a high ideal, no doubt rarely (if ever) achieved in practice. But given the nature of the person as we understand her, it is the ideal that defines the ends toward which the decisions we make about educational policies and practices should point.

The principle is also highly general, and it is meant to be so. The point is not to be as remote from daily experience as possible but to be sufficiently general that we allow for more than one way to articulate reasonable goals of education. It is sometimes tempting to think that we must distill our applicable goals to only one or two, but that is probably an unreasonable assumption. There are many goals and ends of education, and we do not necessarily have to adjudicate among them. For example, the British political philosopher Michael Oakeshott, whose thinking about educational philosophy has been insightful and influential, has made the point, among others, that "the idea of 'School' is that of an historic community of teacher and learners . . . devoted to initiating successive generations of newcomers to the human scene into the grandeurs and servitudes of being human." This is not a process that has a purpose, he goes on to say; rather, it is the very purpose of schooling and of education.[5] Surely, Oakeshott has a point here, if for no other reason than that it is clear that one of the things schools, and therefore education, can do is pass along to subsequent generations the legacies and accomplishment of our forebears. It makes eminent sense, then, to think of education as engaged in the sort of initiation to which Oakeshott points.

It cannot, however, be the only task, and this is why we need a principle that is sufficiently general to enable, even encourage, us to encompass in our sense of purposes some of the broad scope of which education is possible. If the general principle in relation to educational goals is to enrich experience, then our roles must go beyond inducting generations into the circle of distinctively human traditions and accomplishments. As enriching as that is, and it is surely enriching to be able to grasp and appreciate the constructions of meaning that are our intellectual legacy, there has to be more. First, learning is not primarily a matter of intellectual appropriation, primarily because learning has as much to do with putting knowledge and understanding to work as it does with simply grasping or appreciating it. Second, to put knowledge and understanding to work, one has to possess the mastery of one's conditions that comes from learning and doing within experience. It is not that Oakeshott is wrong; rather, we need to think more broadly if we want to grasp the greater purposes of which education is possible. Our principle has to be sufficiently general to accommodate Oakeshott's sense of education's goal alongside others.

One thoughtful contributor whose ideas are important to consider is the American philosopher John J. McDermott, who wrote a great deal about education throughout his career. McDermott was interested in the goals of education, but, unlike Oakeshott, he thought that in practice, schooling and pedagogy always need to place education in the lived experience of students. In many ways, his conception is similar to our own, especially in that he thought that for education to be able to enrich experience, which it should do, it has to concern itself with students' lives as currently lived. This emphasis on lived conditions allows him to make a more general claim about education and the direction of experience: "Pedagogy becomes . . . the twin effort to integrate the directions of experience with the total needs of the person and to cultivate the ability of an individual to generate new potentialities in his experiencing and to make new relationships so as to foster patterns of growth."[6] McDermott's emphasis differs from Oakeshott's, and both point not only to capacities of education but also to reasonable expectations we may have of it. Freire's concern with humanization is yet another, though consistent, emphasis that we would not want education to overlook. We should want a general principle of the goals of education that will allow us to accommodate these ideals, and others when they seem to us to merit it. The principle we have articulated in terms of education's role in enhancing experience allows for just this situation.

As important as the ideas of Oakeshott and McDermott are, the contemporary philosopher of education who has had some of the deepest insights is Nel Noddings, who is well known for her emphasis on care as the basis of a philosophy of education generally and moral education specifically. Though this is not the occasion to go into her ideas about care in any detail, it is well worth noting that the general conceptions that we have developed here about relationality and the nature of experience point directly to some to Noddings' ideas.[7]

In one of her books, Noddings describes her basic point as an approach to ethics that departs from the philosophical tradition. It has traditionally been the case, she points out, that we, or anyway philosophers, have assumed that to establish a firm ethical guide for our behavior we look to establish general principles, and then infer our actions from them. This was Immanuel Kant's approach, for example, when he worked his conceptual way to the principle that he called the Categorical Imperative, which is basically that we should act in such a way that we would want the reason for our action to be a general rule. Kant believed that he had given strong arguments for the acceptability of this principle, and his idea was that we ought to decide our actions according to it.

Noddings rejects this way of thinking about the basis of ethics, though not necessarily the principle itself, in much the same way that we have challenged the traditional understanding of knowledge. It is a mistake, we have said, to think of knowledge as largely propositional, and the reason it is a mistake is that knowledge is rooted at least as much in action as it is in inference. Noddings's point about ethics is similar. It is a mistake, she says, to think that our ethics has to be based on a principle from which we infer how to behave, and the reason it is a mistake is that to think this is to ignore the fact that much of our sense of how to behave derives from our relations with other people, not from rational inference. On these grounds, she proposes an ethics of caring and an approach to education based on caring more than on the dissemination of knowledge.[8]

There are several points worth noting here. The first, and most general, is that the value of caring derives not from some set of ideas but organically from the relationships in which we live. We do not draw inferences about whether to care for our children or our parents; we do it automatically as a result of the relations we have with those people. To put the point in our own terminology, Noddings's insight about caring presumes not a mechanistic but a relational understanding of the interaction among people, such that we adopt the commitment to caring as a consequence of both the constitutive relations in which we stand to the people in our lives and the strong relevance that those relations have to our own nature. At a slightly less general level, and related to the concept of experience that we have developed, an ethics of caring and an approach to education that is based on it recognizes that experience, and the understanding we acquire within it, is rooted at least as much in our actions as in our rationally determined inferences. Learning, in other words, is about doing no less than it is a rational exercise. Moreover, this feature of experience generally should be accommodated in the ways we understand and implement education.

Noddings, then, by appropriating a broadly relational understanding of human life, and an understanding of experience similar to ours (if *avant la lettre*), offers us a sense of the purposes of education and their bases that is profound and fruitful. And it is worth noticing that it is consistent with, one might even say implied by, the general ontological and epistemological concepts that we have developed.[9]

Several other points have been made in this chapter concerning educational principles implied by our general ontology and theory of experience, and it is sensible to expand them a bit here. The first two are related directly to the constitutive relationality of all things and deal with curriculum. Because reality is relational, and constitutively relational at that, the approach we take to educational content, to subject matter, should emphasize relations over data. There are, of course, bits of information, and some of them are worth knowing. But no bits of information, no data, contain their own meaning. Meaning is always couched in contexts, which means in relations. This is why, for example, the treatment of history as a list of names, dates, and events is worse than useless. Serious historians do not do this, but it can feel to students as if such lists are what they are presented with. If one is studying Roman history, to use an example we drew on earlier, one should know that Caesar and his troops crossed the Rubicon, why, and when. But those bits of information are meaningless if we do not know why Caesar was returning to Rome, why the Rubicon was so important, and why a successful general required approval of the Senate before bringing his troops into Italy. These relational contexts give meaning to names, dates, and events, and that is the case for all data. There is a great deal of data on a complex spreadsheet, but if one does not know how to read it, how it was collected, what organizational principles were applied, and what its possible applications are, the data are mute.

The importance of relationality for the curriculum applies not only to specific topics but also to the ways we treat whole subjects and disciplines. The point has already been made, so there is no need to rehearse it, but to the extent possible, it would be conducive to deeper and more meaningful learning if disciplines were approached in their interactions, and if schools and universities were organized that way. This was the point of the brief discussion above of the study of ancient Rome. Student learning would be enhanced, as would research. As a general rule of thumb, the deeper we dig into a topic, as we do in our research and scholarship, the easier it is to lose sight of how and why the topic matters, and to whom, and for which purposes. The centrality of relations, and their constitutive character, are, then, important to keep in mind not only for pedagogical reasons but also for our research and scholarship.

It was also pointed out, with the curriculum in mind, that we ought to be wary of assuming that some disciplines are inherently more valuable than others. If we are thinking with the aid of a viable philosophy of education, then this problem is less likely to happen. But if we are not, then there is an ever-present danger of thinking too narrowly about education and therefore about what is or is not important. If one thinks that the purpose of education is to make a student job-ready, it will be fairly easy to infer that such subjects as history or literature or philosophy, among many others, are unnecessary and a therefore a waste of time and their provision an unwarranted expense. If, however, we are able to take on board the understanding that fields of study are constitutively related to one another, then we will be much more likely to appreciate how engineering is related to ethics, and both to history, and all of them to mathematics. None of the ways that we have engaged the world, and given the world's complexity there are many, are irrelevant if the point is to help students comprehend and master their experience. Not all of it is relevant to all the rest at every point, but none of it is irrelevant or unimportant.

If one wants to learn to prove the Pythagorean Theorem, for example, there may be no need at that point to take on its history. But if one wants to understand the mathematics, and that is presumably why we teach it, then one does want to take on its history, and the relevant traits of Greek culture in the classical period, and what the role of the theorem has been, and who, two millennia later, Fermat was and why his theorem mattered as it did. To consider a related example, one way of understanding analytic geometry is to familiarize oneself with the mathematical meaning and uses of Cartesian coordinates; a related and complementary way of understanding it is to realize its applications in geography and mapping, and the reasons such applications were important in the early seventeenth century when Descartes developed the system and the European powers were extending their colonial reach around the world. Colonial expansion requires more extensive sailing, which requires bigger and better ships and more reliable means of navigation. Improved navigational techniques require better engineering and better optics, both of which require more advanced mathematics. This is the constitutively relational character of fields of study, and the more clearly we are able to accommodate such relations in the curriculum, the better will be the education of our students.

The theory of experience, too, offers implications for educational principles. We have just pointed out that relationality itself indicates the integration of subjects of study and our knowledge of them. If knowledge itself is a relational function, as the theory of experience indicates it is, then our efforts to accomplish knowledge, which is to say our teaching, has to take this into account. Specifically, knowledge is constitutively related to the other two dimensions of experience, the aesthetic and the political, and therefore to art and power, and this feature of knowledge has implications for teaching. Knowledge, we can now see, is not a product of propositions and propositional discourse alone but also emerges in art and in the constructive, perhaps even destructive, activity that expresses power. The education we provide our students will be enriched to the extent that we can embed the information we wish to teach, in principle in any subject, in the arts and in creative activity. We typically do the latter when we guide students through experiments in labs, and the better we understand why this sort of process is important for education and the acquisition of knowledge, the more carefully our pedagogy can embed it.

The same is true for teaching with and through art. We may, for example, ordinarily teach students about war through texts and photos, both of which are perfectly sensible sources for teachers to use. But if we want students to understand the impact of war on civilian populations, then they may achieve a much more viscerally powerful grasp of the point if the teacher talks through with them Picasso's *Guernica*, which is his depiction of the aerial bombing of a Basque village during the Spanish Civil War in the 1930s. The painting may serve as a code, in Freire's sense, the discussion of which allows students to bring into focus aspects of war and its toll, as well as to place themselves imaginatively in the situation, and thereby better appreciate the lived horrors of such an event. There are countless examples in all the arts of this sort of possibility, and the pedagogical value of them is limited only by a teacher's imagination.

The importance of art is, of course, not limited to its cognitive possibilities, which, as important as they are, do not exhaust the meaning and value of art and the aesthetic. Because the aesthetic is one of the pervasive dimensions of experience, and because art is one of the ways that people engage the world and thereby enrich its meaning, it should be clear to all educators, and to all people in a position to determine educational policy, that the centrality of art in the curriculum is necessary for a sound education. There are ways that painting, music, literature, and all the arts capture and exhibit aspects of the world and of our experience that are not available through any other medium. No education worthy of the name can isolate people from such an extensive component of their lives and their natures. To deny children an education in the arts is to do them a violence that has no justification. That the aesthetic is a pervasive dimension of experience leaves no doubt about that.

The centrality of power in experience has similarly profound implications for education. The enrichment of experience, which we have offered as a principle relevant to the goals of education, is constituted in part by what we have called one's mastery over one's own experience. This mastery, which is in principle an aspect of every individual's experiential potential, is the general exercise of the power that defines the political dimension of experience. Education is related to power in a most fundamental way, such that no conception of education that removes power from its heart can be adequate. This point should enable us to see why Freire's objections to the banking method of education are important. If in the name of education we treat our students as passive receptacles rather than as agents of their own meaning and experience, then we are undermining much of what constitutes their humanity. Again, we have come, though by a somewhat different route, to Freire's concern with humanization.

The centrality of power in experience, and its significance for education, also brings us necessarily to the problem of disempowerment. Dewey, Freire, and McDermott have all pointed to it, but Freire gives it the most sustained and explicit attention. And because we have posited the political as one of the three dimensions of experience, with power as its corollary, we are compelled to acknowledge that the denial to anyone of the power to master her own experience is a denial of her humanity. If education contributes to this situation, then education has not only abrogated its responsibility to enrich experience but also been warped into its opposite and actively distorts experience and undermines the human condition. Unfortunately, a good deal of contemporary social, political, and economic affairs is guilty on both counts. For many millions of people, their economic conditions, by driving them into and keeping them in poverty, rob them both of the material necessities of a prosperous and fulfilled life and of the control over their own circumstances that they need to create a better life, to imbue their lives with meaning, and to direct their experience toward richer and more fulfilled circumstances. Frequently, however, instead of being brought to bear to mitigate such conditions, schools and education are used to enforce them. Every time that we limit the curriculum to whatever we think children and students need to gain and keep employment in a certain job, we undermine their capacity to master and direct their own experience; every time we deny children exposure to and instruction in aspects of human experience, such as the arts or occasions for applied learning, we rip aspects of their own experience from their lives; and whenever we use education to enforce unacceptable and oppressive conditions in which people currently live by cutting short the understanding and empowerment they need to improve those conditions, we undercut what their own humanity provides them. It is the responsibility of educators at all levels to pursue policies and practices to ensure that education meets rather than subverts its responsibility to enrich experience.

We will be able to explore these topics in more detail in the following chapter, which is concerned with social and political theory, and its implications for educational philosophy.

CHAPTER 7

Education in Context

Society and the State

We begin with a point that ought to be fairly obvious by now. If people are what they are (and have the characteristics that they have) as a consequence of their relations with their surroundings, then human beings are by nature social creatures. The old idea that a society is simply an abstract concept and little more than a collection of individuals is, as we said in the previous chapter, no longer tenable. There are many different ways of saying this, but the basic point is that our inquiry into the state and society does not begin with individuals who then form societies, but rather with individuals who, by virtue of their natural condition, are social all the way down, we may say.[1]

If this is the case (and we will proceed here as if a compelling argument has already been made that it is the case), then a number of traditional ways of thinking about individuals and their relation to one another do not work. With respect to our economic life, traditional neoclassical economics assumes, as has already been mentioned, that there are discrete individuals who pursue in the marketplace their independently determined self-interest. The result of this self-interested activity by a large number of people, a process governed by the so-called laws of the marketplace, is the economic life of a society. But if individuals are from the beginning social beings (which means in part that their traits, including their interests and their understanding of their interests, are determined not independently but in relation with other people and other constitutive factors), then the neoclassical assumptions are misguided, as is, presumably, any economic theory based on them.

The same may be said about some traditional political theory. The modernist idea of the social contract, even granting that it was an idea not about the historical origins of the state but about how to determine the state's proper nature, also assumed discrete individuals as its point of departure. In this view, pre-political individuals, who inhabit a theoretical, nonsocial, and nonpolitical "state of nature," enter into an agreement with one another, from which the state emerges. But if the idea of a pre-social and pre-political person is a contradiction in terms, as our conception of experience would imply, then the idea of a social contract as an explanatory device makes little sense, as would more developed conceptions of the state that rest on it.

We may as well point out, though it has been said in previous chapters and will be discussed briefly at the end of this one, that prevailing conceptions of the relations among states have much the same problem. The traditional approach to international relations has assumed that states develop their interests independently of one another, in this respect mirroring the traditional conception of the individual, and then engage with one another in an effort to meet their interests. Sometimes this process engenders allies, and sometimes it results in conflict, but the assumption is that states are independent, sovereign entities, each with its self-determined interests to pursue. But if all things are relationally constituted, as we have argued they are, then this conception of the state cannot be right, in which case neither is the traditional understanding of their relations with one another. If states are constituted by their relations, then their traits (and to some degree their interests) are not independently determined. The picture we typically have of international relations no longer makes sense.

If our general ontology and theory of experience render such traditional conceptions as these obsolete, then it is incumbent on us to offer conceptual alternatives. This responsibility is all the more pressing because many of the principles we seek to develop as guides in handling the problems of education will be determined in part by our conception of the state and society. In other words, we need general ideas about the state and society in order to articulate sensible educational principles, and those ideas of the state and society have to be consistent with our other philosophical positions. Moreover, we should add, the entire conceptual edifice has to intersect with our experience in meaningful ways. This has been the whole point of a systematic philosophy of education. To think about education and educational principles adequately, we need to do so in relation to broader philosophical conceptions, and those broader conceptions are required to be coherent, plausible, and useful. Since we have articulated such conceptions with respect to nature, knowledge, and experience, we need to turn now to society and the state. Once reliable philosophical conceptions of society and the state are developed, it will be possible to draw from them educational principles that will help to guide educators as we address education's many and serious problems.

It was a bit foolhardy to think that we could do justice to the complexity of problems associated with nature and knowledge in a few pages with-

out distorting them, though one hopes that we managed to do so with
as little distortion as possible. We face the same problem here. The topics
of the general nature of the state and society have a broad reach and are
immensely complex. Treating them too quickly risks a superficiality that
could easily lead to ideas that do not advance our understanding. This is
obviously a danger against which we will have to guard. The difficulty of
doing so becomes apparent when we consider the range of topics, themes,
and ideas that arise when we look philosophically at the state and society.
Among the more important of them, and this is a partial list, are empowerment, autonomy, democracy, freedom, rights, justice, equality, ethics, law,
civil liberties, economic classes, common interests and conflicting interests,
among others. We will consider some of these points below.

The dimensions of the challenge we have set ourselves is even clearer
when we are reminded of some of the educational issues that are before us.
As was proposed in chapter 5, we are faced with such concerns as whether
education is a social or private good, or both, and the many questions
related to finances, censorship, social responsibility, pedagogical methods,
testing, equality in and of education, education and vocations, tracking,
schools as social institutions, education in relation to state or dominant
class interests, education and social justice, and the relation of schooling
and education, among others. In the end, the discussion of these and other
questions of educational principles must be folded into the account of the
general traits of the state and society, such that the end result is a set of educational principles that are applicable and useful in the social and political
contexts in which we find ourselves.

SOCIETY AND SOCIAL RELATIONS

The point of departure, then, is the relationality of the person, and what
amounts to the same point, the relationality of society and societies. Human
beings are by nature social beings. There are two points to make by way of
clarification. First, it is important to understand that when we talk about the
person as a social being, we are not making a psychological point. It may
or may not be the case that individual people require relationships of some
kind and to some extent with other people. It would seem reasonable to
think that we do in some ways need social relationships, but we must leave
it to the psychologists and sociologists to make the case for that claim. The
point we are making about the sociality of the person is not psychological
or sociological but ontological. This is what makes Nel Noddings's idea of
care rather than inferential rationality as a ground of educational purpose
as compelling as it is. Our relations with those we value are determinative
not for psychological reasons, which is to say because we have this or that

feeling about them, but because the very nature of people is to be located in human relations that are constitutive of us in significant ways. Human beings are social in the sense that what makes us human in any distinctive sense are the relations in which we stand with all entities that are relevant to us, especially with other people and the more complex social structures that those relations engender. To be human is to be constituted not by material and biological relations alone but by social and cultural relations as well. Without them, we would be something other than what we are, and that is what it means to say that human beings are by nature social.

The second point of clarification is that the inherent sociality of the person does not present any sort of origin problem. It may seem as if we are faced with a "chicken and egg" problem when we say that people are social, in the sense that if societies are constituted by people, there would already have to be people to constitute them, but if people are constituted by societies, then there would already have to be societies to constitute people. There seems to be a "which came first" sort of problem. Fortunately, however, there is no such problem. For one thing, and at a superficial level, we have no need to ask or answer the question "which came first," largely because our issue is not a question about the origins of the human species. More significantly, though, the "which came first" question does not make any sense at a structural level, because at that level there is no "first." Both individuals and societies arise in the ongoing push and pull of their interaction, and this point is as true of individuals as of the species, and of individual societies as of society in general. If we were to imagine a timeline, at one end of which there were neither humans nor societies, and at the other end of which there are clearly both humans and societies, it would be clear that over the course of the processes that occurred from one point to the other, both humans and societies arose. However, it would be arbitrary to select any one point along the line and say that "here is where human being arose" or "here is where society arose." There may be other reasons to say that at this or that point there is something we want to call a society, but there will already be something at that point that we could equally well call human being. The same is true if we were to make the alternative claim. If we were to say at any point along the line that here there are humans, we would also be able to say that at the same point there is something we can reasonably call society. To think that one has to precede the other is to think mechanically, not relationally. But if, by our natures, human being and society are relational and not mechanical, then we need to begin to think relationally.

Equality

We have described the relationality of human beings as the process of experience. Experience, in turn, is characterized most generally in terms of knowledge, art, and power. We may say of any individual that she has more knowledge of a certain kind than another person, or more knowledge at one time than at another. We may similarly say that one person has more power than another, or of one kind or another, or at one time than at another. But as dimensions of experience, it would be meaningless to say, for example, that knowledge is more definitive of this person than that, or that this person's experience is determined by power more than another's. At the general level, the dimensions of experience do not admit of degrees. One may not be more or less pregnant, though one may experience pregnancy differently from another. The dimensions of experience are rather like pregnancy in this respect, in that one may have varying sorts of cognitive, aesthetic, and political experiences, but the dimensions of experience do not vary. Experience for all people is characterized by knowledge, art, and power in the same ways, and those ways may not be calibrated in degrees. This is the reason that a denial to anyone of the opportunity to exercise one's power over one's own life and its meaning is equivalent to a denial of that person's humanity. These considerations suggest a feature of any social arrangement that is conducive to human being and human development, and that is equality.

In a sense, this is a relational and secular way of saying what many Enlightenment thinkers also said, which was, in the words of the American Declaration of Independence, that "all men are created equal, and endowed by the creator with certain unalienable rights." We will leave the issue of rights to consider later, but on the notion of being inherently equal, they had a point, as long as it is clear that we are referring to all people, and not one gender or race or ethnicity or class. For us, equality follows not from an act of creation but from what it means to be human. There are several related issues that arise at this point, which are certainly worth considering, but are beyond the scope of this inquiry. For example, what (if anything) follows, we are entitled to ask, from natural equality among people for relations with other animals or, for that matter, with the rest of the biological world—indeed, with the planet as a whole? As important as this sort of question is, we can stipulate that there is nothing about the inherent equality among people that implies their superiority over other living things, or of people's short-term interests over the long-term health of the environment. With that said, we have to leave it to ethicists and others to work out how best we should understand inter-species relations and ethical responsibilities, and our obligations with respect to the environment generally.

Equality, then, is an inherent feature of human beings by virtue of the moral parity implicit in experience. Each of us is a center of experience no more or less than any other, and if any of us are entitled to social conditions that enable us to exercise to our full potential the dimensions of experience, then all of us are so entitled. The Declaration of Independence uses the adjective "unalienable" in reference to the rights that it claims follow from human equality, but we may apply the same adjective to equality itself. All people are, by virtue of the nature of experience, unalienably equal. Another way to say this is that no one can relinquish this equality for herself without sacrificing her own humanity; similarly, no one can deny equality to another without denying her humanity. Again, Freire had a point that may not be overlooked.

This is a much different way of understanding a person than, for example, Plato's. He thought that there are fundamentally different kinds of souls, you may recall from the Myth of the Metals, in which respect people are inherently unequal, and thereby suited for different social roles and different educations. Plato's idea, or some version of it, has been commonly held throughout human history, and, it appears, by virtually all peoples and societies. Aristotle agreed with his teacher Plato that some people are naturally free, and some are naturally slaves. Over the centuries, men believed themselves to be superior to women, Christians superior to non-Christians, Muslims superior to non-Muslims, Europeans superior to everyone else, aristocrats superior to everyone else, or one race, nation, or ethnicity superior to another. Inequality has been the default position through human history, even by those who, like the founders of the American republic, proclaimed their commitment to equality. The point here is not to reveal hypocrisy, though there is no shortage of it on offer. The point to be emphasized, rather, is that any attempt to assume or to justify inequality, on any grounds, is intellectually impossible once we grant that there is a moral parity at the general level of experience, and therefore a moral equality among all people and peoples. And the fact that inequality has been the most common condition throughout society is not evidence that it must be. Slavery also prevailed in most societies for most of human history. It has now been overcome, for the most part, and so, too, can inequality be superseded.

It is possible to build gradually a fuller theory of society by spinning out the implications of this inherent equality. Once we acknowledge that all people are inherently morally equal, and that to deny that equality in practice is to deny a person's humanity, it is implied that, however they are organized, justifiable social conditions must make it possible for people's equality to be exercised in practice. Moral equality, if granted in theory but ignored in practice, is at best an intellectual confusion and at worst an ideologically driven fraud. This in turn has implications for a number of themes that are critical for an adequate social theory, including empowerment, autonomy, class, freedom, rights, and the relative importance of the individual and the community.

Power and Social Institutions

The power implicit in the human condition as a consequence of the nature of experience points to the necessity of empowerment in social relations. Our social relations are complex, and in many respects they are and probably have always been expressed through social institutions. Some social institutions are political, specifically state organs, legal structures, political parties, and military bodies, among others, and we will hold our discussion of the state until later. For now, we may focus on less overtly political institutions (for example, health-related institutions, cultural bodies, financial and economic organizations), the many kinds of groups that constitute civil society and, of course, educational institutions. All such institutions are intricately linked to the question of power and the capacity of individuals to exercise it.

As a general matter, we should recall, the exercise of power in individuals' lives amounts to the control people may—indeed, should—have over not only the conditions of our lives but also the determination of our own ends, the meaning we ascribe to our purposes, and the actions we take to accomplish them. The power inherent in experience is the ability to effect change in our environments, and therefore in our lives. When power in this sense is combined with the moral equality that is also implicit in experience, the result is that power in our lives means power over our own lives. It does not mean power over others' lives. Some of us, under certain circumstances, have such power over others' lives, but if we exercise it to undermine their control of their own experience, then we violate the moral equality that characterizes the human condition. As long as we take equality seriously, which, as we have seen, the nature of experience itself indicates that we should, then power has to mean, at least as a general matter, control of our own lives.

Because we are inherently social, such power, even as self-control, is in some respects expressed through social institutions. The first point to notice about this fact is that though we speak of the power of individuals to determine their own ends and meanings, this is never a process whereby individuals act entirely independently of one another. Our self-control is always conditioned and determined in relation to others. This is the reason that Rousseau's approach is, in the end, misguided. He saw, correctly enough, the ways that social relations and expectations can distort our nature and warp our capacities, but his response, which is to remove a child from (and to educate him outside of) social relations and structures, makes the wrong assumption about the nature of individuals. We are embedded in social relations as a result of being human. The distortion of our natures that badly formed social relations and institutions often

inflict on us can be avoided only acting to correct the relations and institutions, not by ignoring or avoiding them.

The second point to notice about the fact that the exercise of distinctly
human power occurs through social institutions is that such institutions
not only may undermine our individual capacity for self-control, as Rousseau saw clearly, but also are far too frequently established purposely to
enable one group of people to deny or undermine the power of the rest.
Instead of serving as the organizational vehicles through which people may
enrich their experience, social institutions far too often serve to impose
conditions that impoverish it.

Examples of such distortion through social institutions are not hard to
find. Religious institutions are a clear illustration. We may grant the possibility that religious institutions, and here we mean organized religions with
their complex traditions, literatures, and organizational structures, meet a
genuine need that countless people have for spiritual guidance and support.
It certainly appears that most people in the world at any given time would
attest to such a need, and we have no good reason to believe that the situation will change in the near future. Even those who do not feel such a need,
then, can recognize that many people do feel it, and that there is every good
reason for those who do to be able to organize their experience so that their
felt spiritual needs are met. This reasonable and defensible purpose is not
the problem to which we point in religious institutions. The problem is
that in the actions religious institutions undertake to meet people's spiritual
needs, they may easily, and frequently do, subvert people's entitlement to
control over their own experience and the details and trajectories of their
own lives. Traditional religious justifications of slavery and class oppression
are obvious examples. There is nothing about the spiritual dimensions of
people's lives that requires such subversion and subjection. On the contrary,
and this is the basic point and motivation of liberation theology, a spiritual
form of experience, like every other, is enhanced by the enrichment that is
possible through the exercise of power in the sense of self-control. Spirituality, to put the point in a less technical way, is best expressed within the
fullness of experience, not in its impoverishment.

Religious institutions can, and often do, fulfill these ends, but they
often do not. This is the reason Marx referred to religion as "the opiate
of the people." He did not mean that spirituality is somehow necessarily
inadequate, or at least he did not have to mean that. He meant, rather,
that the practice of religion, given how religious institutions tend to behave, subordinates rather than liberates people. This, unfortunately, is the
result of religious institutions that do not guide people in the enrichment
of experience through their spirituality, instead using their spiritual interests and concerns to deny their equality and suppress their power. When
people are told through their religious institution that their suffering is a

virtue, and that they should not struggle against it but can expect a reward in the afterlife, their experience is thereby impoverished and their power suppressed. In such a case, invariably, greater power, and usually wealth, is gathered in the hands of those who are not suffering in the same way, and who ignore people's equality and use the institution to deny other's power. In this way, religious institutions can, and frequently do, impoverish rather than enrich experience.

There are other kinds of social institutions that provide similar examples. Financial institutions come readily to mind. What we refer to in the contemporary world as an or the "economy" is an immensely complex set of activities and processes. It includes the production and distribution of goods and services, the infrastructure necessary for goods and services to be produced and distributed, the possibilities for employment on which most of us depend, and the consumption that most of us desire, among other aspects of contemporary life. It is small wonder that financial institutions are needed, given the central role of finance in the economy. Money has to be moved, stored, and, in a capitalist economy, put eventually to productive use. As in the case of religious institutions, we may assume (at least for the sake of argument) that financial institutions have a defensible role to play and that they can meet genuinely desirable ends. Banks, investment houses, insurance companies, equity funds, brokerage houses, commodities and equity markets, and similar institutions can and often do help people develop and maintain control over their lives and direct their experience. Consider, for example, companies that manage average people's retirement accounts, which in some countries, like the United States, are fairly common. By providing reliable, and reasonably safe, ways to prepare financially for life after one retires (at least in an economic and political environment in which that assurance is not provided by the state), such institutions genuinely contribute to people's well-being and to their direction of the course of their own lives.

Unfortunately, the same cannot be said about all financial institutions or all of the activities that any such institutions undertake. It is not uncommon for banks, insurance companies, private equity funds, and investment houses to devise ways, some of them complex and quite creative, to enrich and empower themselves to the serious detriment of others. Sometimes when they do this, they are violating laws or public regulations, in which case from time to time they are held to account. Often, however, their activity is fully legal and may even have the support of the state. In 2008, to offer an illustration that is widely familiar, there was a worldwide financial crisis brought about by certain dodgy forms of investment that were being practiced by a number of banks and investment houses. In the end, many people lost their homes and their livelihoods. For the most part, however, the bankers were not only not held to account for their actions but also rewarded by the state so that they and their institutions did not suffer from their own behavior. Unfortunately, no such support (or very little) was offered by the state for people whose homes and employment were gone because of the bankers' behavior. Equally unfortunate, similar events had happened before and presumably will happen again. They seem to be, if not endemic, then far too common within financial institutions. If that is the case, such institutions are examples of social bodies that undermine rather than enhance people's control of their own conditions and enrichment of their own experience. In this respect, they are no more defensible than are religious institutions that do much the same thing.

Such examples as these should be sufficient to sustain the point that social institutions far too often serve to undermine the exercise of the power that defines our lives and our experience. If in the exercise of our power we must engage one another through social institutions, and if those institutions act in ways that subvert rather than support us, then the conditions that we may expect, the conditions that are necessary for us to live human lives, are being denied rather than supported by our social circumstances. The consequence of this is to undermine the natural equality that is a trait of our experience. We have reason to conclude, then, that social institutions that disempower rather than empower us are failing to meet the expectations that, on the basis of the nature of our experience, we are entitled to expect. Whatever else such social institutions may do, and in principle they can do a great deal of good, to the extent that they undermine our equality and fail to empower us in the enrichment of our experience, they relinquish whatever moral and social legitimacy they may otherwise have.

It would be sensible to say a word about educational institutions at this point, since they are after all the social institutions of most direct concern for this study. What has already been said about the basic responsibility of other institutions refers to the educational ones as well. Educational institutions, which means schools and universities primarily, though there are related structures such as school boards to which the point would also apply, have a profound impact on the lives of the people who have a stake in them. This refers to students more than to any other stakeholder, but the impact on families, neighbors, teachers, and administrators is also significant. If we consider children and students alone, it is clear that schools and universities can and often do go a long way to determining the character and future trajectory of their lives. This determination can be, as we all know, for both better and worse. To the extent that educational institutions contribute to children's developing capacity to understand, engage, and direct their own experience, they are empowering children and students, and to that degree meeting their responsibility. If, however, they are constricting children and students' opportunities for growth and development, which can be done by offering only a narrow curriculum, or by distorting the understanding of material taught by disengaging it from their lives, or by funneling children and students into narrowly conceived future prospects, they are disempowering them and undermining the potential of their experience.

Perhaps the primary reason that educational institutions find themselves in a position to thwart rather than enable students is that those responsible for the institutions fail to understand the nature of the institutions, and their own consequent responsibilities. An educational institution, like anything else, is a relational entity. While the details differ considerably between primary and secondary schools, on the one hand, and universities and colleges, on the other, all of these institutions find themselves constituted by varying sets of relations. For example, all schools are importantly subject to economic factors in varying ways. They all have financial obligations that define their expenses in any given period. They are also subject to larger economic and financial forces that can determine the funding that is available to them. And in the case of universities, they can be important, sometimes necessary, economic drivers in their communities, especially if they are located in small communities that have a fairly low level of economic development. In this respect, it should be noted, schools are no different from other social institutions, in that all of them prevail within a set of constitutive economic relations.

One might be inclined to say, give the importance of economic factors, that schools and universities are to be properly understood as economic entities. Unfortunately, there are probably many people, especially among administrators and legislators, and perhaps even among many citizens, who understand them in this way. This is unfortunate because, despite the importance of economic relations among the constitutive traits of educational institutions, they are not primarily or fundamentally economic entities. One reason that it would be wrong to think of their economic relations as determining the character of educational institutions is that their economic relations are no more constitutive of educational institutions than are their political relations. Schools and universities are as much impacted by the political factors in which they are enmeshed as they are by the economic. By the term "political" here, we do not mean partisan politics, or not only partisan politics, but rather power at the social level, where those who wield the power have the legal responsibility to make decisions and judgments for the schools. This can most obviously include legislators who, even if they are not acting to achieve partisan ends, are responsible to weigh the needs and interests of schools, and at least public universities, against the needs and interests of other institutions for which they have oversight. Budgets must be set, general institutional directions established, and curriculum must be determined, and all these processes engage issues of social power, or what we mean here by politics and the political. This political aspect of educational institutions may be exercised at legislative levels, ministries of education, or in more local school boards. Wherever the necessary and inevitable social power resides and judgments are made, therein lie the political relations that contribute to the constitution of schools and universities. Educational institutions, then, are at least as much political entities as they are economic.

Just as all social institutions are constituted by their economic relations, so, too, are they constituted by their political relations. So far, then, we have said nothing about what is distinctive in educational institutions. What distinguishes educational institutions, and this applies to social institutions of any kind, is a third set of relations through which they are constituted. For health institutions, the third set of traits concerns their responsibility to see to the health of their patients, and often to broader, public health needs. These traits distinguish health institutions from others. Economic and financial institutions have economic stability and the fostering of financial opportunities, however they are defined, as their third relational and determining context. Religious institutions have as their third set of traits the support for the spiritual lives of their congregants, and cultural institutions have as their third set of traits maintenance and advancement of the cultural lives of a society and its people. It is, in all these cases, the third set of traits that gives an institution its distinctive features. For educational institutions, the third set of traits is the academic. The meaning of academic traits is no doubt different for a primary school than it is for a university, but both are distinguished from other social institutions by their academic character.

Educational institutions find themselves in a difficult situation if all of this is right. On the one hand, the economic and the political are among their constitutive traits, and to that extent can be expected—indeed, must— drive a good deal of what they do and how they do it. On the other hand, if economic and political traits are permitted to be the primary driving forces of an educational institution, then the traits that give it its distinctive character (in this case, academic traits) are submerged. In other words, as important and unavoidable as the economic and political are, they cannot be allowed to negate or undermine the academic character of educational institutions. This is the reason that those who think that schools and universities should be run like businesses are wrong. Businesses, for the most part, do not have academic purposes among their responsibilities, so to administer a school or university as if it were a business is to fail to understand its nature, and it is likely to lead to a failure of the institution to fulfill its purposes. Economic and business values, efficiency for example, are relevant for educational institutions, as they are for all others, but they cannot be permitted to override academic values. It is not efficient for a teacher to spend an inordinate amount of time with one student, to give one sort of example, and yet this may be precisely what the academic values of the institution and the academic responsibility of the teacher demand. Economic and political values have to be taken into account, but the default values have to be academic, to whatever extent is possible.

This is also the reason that it is improper to think of students as if they were customers, which happens far too often in universities. To think of students this way is to focus on the economic aspect of educational institutions and miss entirely the academic. Not all participants in a social institution are customers. Participants in a religious institution are not customers, they are congregants or parishioners, and participants in health institution are not customers, there are patients. In each case, the relation of the participant to the institution differs from the relation of a customer to a provider of goods or services. The same applies to education. The participants in an educational institution, and here we are focusing on only one set of participants, are not customers; they are students, and a student's relation to the institution differs considerably from a customer's relation to a provider of goods or services. A customer of a retail store, for example, does not need to meet any special criteria to enter and engage the store's services. She also has no responsibilities to the store once she enters, other than to behave civilly and to pay with legal currency or a valid credit card. She may decide to buy anything she wishes, or nothing at all. The store, for its part, has no responsibility to the customers other than to provide truthful information about its goods and services. It is not obligated to offer any specific goods on its shelf, and it is fully entitled to make its judgments about what to offer based on nothing other than financial and marketing considerations.

Schools and universities interact with their students in quite different ways. Schools, anyway public schools, are expected to allow anyone of the appropriate age and background to enter and participate, but universities typically have entrance requirements. Once a student is enrolled, the student has responsibilities to the institution, and the institution has responsibilities to the student, and both sets go well beyond simply behaving civilly and honestly. An educational institution decides what to offer its students based not on financial but on academic considerations. One cannot simply take history off the shelf if students seem not to be interested in it, for example. On the student's part, she cannot simply decide what to study and what not to study; rather, she must meet criteria established by the school or university in order to complete her studies and graduate or receive a degree. A student may not simply select a degree that she wants, pay for it, and leave the institution with the degree in hand. The institution has a responsibility to decide what she needs in her capacity as a student and the subsequent responsibility to provide it. Credits and degrees—indeed, knowledge and understanding—are not the functional equivalents of vacuum cleaners or toaster ovens.

A student is not a customer, and schools and universities are not primarily economic entities. They are, though, economic entities, and political entities as well, and no amount of wishful thinking by teachers and professors about being somehow separate from society can make it so. In the end, however, they are most distinctively academic entities, and those responsible for making decisions for an educational institution, whether with respect to finances or curriculum or personnel, have a responsibility to guide the institution in the pursuit of its academic ends. Those ends, as we have said, are to contribute to children and students' developing capacity to control their lives such that they are able to determine their own ends and guide their lives through enriched experience. There are certainly times when pursuing those ends while balancing economic and political factors can present difficult challenges, but that is the nature of school and university administration. As difficult as that process can sometimes be, if those responsible for leading and guiding educational institutions fail to understand it and fail to pursue education's proper ends (for example, by allowing economic or political values to submerge the academic), then they are abrogating their responsibility and damaging the institutions, the societies they serve, and everyone with a stake in a healthy educational environment. In the end, the empowerment of individuals that is the responsibility of social institutions requires that those institutions and their prominent values be correctly understood.

It should be clear through all of these examples that an adequate understanding of society requires that we come to terms with social institutions. As important as they are, however, many of the features that characterize a society prevail outside of institutions. Such central features of social relations as individual autonomy, economic classes, rights, freedom, and the relation of the individual and the community, all have their impact outside the purview of social institutions, and we need to consider them independently. These features of individual and social life are all intertwined in various ways, so talking about each of them independently is always a bit dangerous. To mitigate the danger, we will make an effort to clarify the relations among them at the appropriate points.

Autonomy, the Individual, and Class

The centrality of power in experience implies the importance of autonomy. At the same time, the social character of individuals suggests that the autonomy of individuals cannot be properly understood on individual terms alone. This is something that Dewey and Freire both seemed to appreciate. When Dewey emphasized the importance of self-control and self-direction, and when Freire highlighted the necessity of praxis, neither of them meant that individuals can or should be expected to act independently of others. Self-direction and praxis are both ways of pointing to the importance of autonomy, but they are understood as action in relation to others. Autonomy in a relationally understood context has to mean self-control informed by understanding, and the relevant understanding is a grasp of the conditions and circumstances in which one acts and exercises one's autonomy. One of the necessary features of the conditions and circumstances in which one acts is the autonomy and moral equality of others. Because the autonomy of others is always as significant as one's own, to act autonomously is always to act with regard to the autonomy of others. It often does not work this way in practice, in that too often we act in disregard of the other's equality and autonomy, but our analysis indicates that we are acting inappropriately when we do so.

Autonomy is important as an individual and social matter for two reasons. The first is that without it we are subject to the design and ends of others, and thus unable to exercise the self-control necessary for our own development. The second reason autonomy is important is that it is necessary in order to be able to assign responsibility for our and others' actions. If we are not able to act autonomously, then we cannot be responsible for our actions. But if we are not responsible for our actions, then several critical features of social life are impossible. Without individual autonomy, law, for example, is meaningless because no one can be accountable for observing or violating it. The same would apply to any sort of ethical responsibilities we may reasonably be expected to have. For such reasons as these, society cannot prevail without individual autonomy, but it is an autonomy that must be understood relationally. A healthy society requires autonomy exercised in concert with the features, to the extent that they are known and understood, of the contexts in which we act and of the other autonomous beings who constitute those contexts.

Even when we act in cognizance of the autonomy of others, the process will not always proceed smoothly; in fact, it quite often does not proceed smoothly. Our efforts to direct the course of our lives do not occur in the abstract, but in lived social contexts. In those social contexts, we encounter various sorts of possibilities and obstacles, and they may differ widely for many of us. The reason for these differences is that the social contexts do not provide balanced possibilities for all of us. We are, from the beginning, acting in a social context in which, for example, some people have greater wealth than others, or more coercive power than others, or more property than others. The fact that there is more or less of such goods as wealth, power, and property does not in itself have to be a problem. My neighbor may have more money in the bank than I without that presenting any problem at all for me or for her. The inequality of wealth, power, and property becomes a problem when it interferes with the ability of some to exercise the autonomy that is the entitlement of each of us.

This is the problem posed for individuals and societies by the existence of economic classes. Marx and others had argued that the ideal society is a classless society, by which they meant, generally, a society in which whatever disparities there may be in the distribution of wealth and property do not enable any person or group of people to prevent the pursuit by others of the ends to which they aspire. We may leave aside the question of whether such a society is possible, largely because there is no way to determine the answer to that question. On the face of it, there does not seem to be anything about individuals or societies that would render a classless society in this sense impossible, but we may leave it as an open possibility, and one can determine in other contexts whether it is possible or desirable. It is clear, however, that no society of any size with which we are familiar meets this description now. Contemporary societies, both developed and developing, are characterized by class differences that enable one class to dominate the others. Even in those societies in which there is little private ownership of capital, there appears to be what might be called a "political class" that wields inordinate power. It is also clear that in many respects, the class divisions in contemporary societies, the vast bulk of which are determined by disparities in the distribution of wealth and property, are indefensible in light of the analysis of experience, power, and autonomy that we have developed.

It is important to be clear about the meaning of this claim, because its implications for social relations, and for education, will differ with different meanings. We have made the case that the proper role of social institutions is to facilitate the exercise of the power implicit in experience for individuals to design and pursue their own ends. For their part, the proper role of educational institutions, or at least one of the most fundamental of them, is to help people develop the knowledge and abilities to grow and live as autonomous individuals. Differences of wealth and power are indefensible insofar as they impede these ends. This does not mean that everyone should have the same amount of anything or that everyone should be treated the same in all respects. What it means, rather, is that if disparities of wealth and power are justifiable, it can only be up to the point at which they impede the possibility of individuals to pursue, independently or together with others, their lives as they think best.

As a matter of social policy, then, there is no need to insist that everyone be treated identically in all respects. We all have different capabilities (for example, musical or athletic talents are distributed unevenly across any large population), and those differing capabilities engender different possibilities, which in turn can rightly be expected to justify differing opportunities. Indeed, there are a great many differences among us, and the point of emphasizing autonomy and the free exercise of one's capacities is precisely to acknowledge that the opportunity to act on those differences, to actualize the possibilities they create, is an important feature of being human. The point is not to emphasize sameness. It is, rather, to insist that no one set of individuals is entitled to pursue their possibilities by preventing another set of individuals from pursuing theirs.

We will return in due course to the educational implications of this approach to class differences. It should be clear even now, though, that it is incumbent on educational institutions, and educational practices, to undermine detrimental class disparities. Dewey advocated doing this by constructing environments within the schools that did not reproduce the class distinctions that are prevalent in the society beyond the school. He thought that in this way, children could learn to navigate their experience without class privilege or class oppression. Freire took a more revolutionary approach in his argument for education as a process that liberates and humanizes. Whether either approach can generate policies that can be effective in contemporary schools is up to educational practitioners to determine. Whatever the determination, though, it is clear that the dehumanizing consequences of class-based disparities of wealth and power are unacceptable for a healthy and just society, and for education understood as a process of empowerment.

Freedom and Justice

A discussion of autonomy leads smoothly to the idea of freedom, in that the first implies the second. Autonomy can be lived only if the conditions are there to do so, and those conditions are what we mean by freedom. This point is important to come to terms with, if for no other reason than that freedom is a value that is often, and powerfully, invoked in social circumstances to endorse one's ideas or practices, in that they promote freedom, or to reject others', on the grounds that they impede it. For our purposes, we need to understand the implications of freedom as a social and individual value because it has not been unusual in educational circles to invoke freedom as a primary goal of education. For example, one of the most important books on the philosophy of education in recent decades has been Maxine Greene's *The Dialectic of Freedom*, in which she explores the idea of freedom as an ideal end of the educational process.

This is not the place to examine the history of the idea of freedom, but it is important to understand that its meaning has changed over the years and that its meaning is often a point of contention, as Greene is at pains to point out. We saw in the previous chapter that many of the ideas and values that are prevalent in contemporary societies have their origins in the individualism and atomism that characterized the Baroque and Enlightenment periods. We looked briefly at its implications for physics, economics, music, the state, and international relations, and it was equally determinant of basic concepts like freedom. The Baroque concept of freedom means an individual untethered by social, legal, and political constraints. The problem is that no one does or even can live like this, which suggests that there is something wrong with the way we have understood the concept itself.

Greene makes the point that much of philosophical study has assumed that reason, knowledge, and understanding are matters of individual activity, and these have been taken to be the goals of education. But, she goes on to say, a great deal of feminist literature in epistemology and related fields has shifted the focus from an abstract conception of individuated rationality to the commonly lived experience of what she calls "mutuality and responsiveness to others' wants and concerns." We do not exist or live in isolation or independently of one another, but rather, to put the point in the conceptual categories we have been using, in mutually constitutive relations with one another. The implication for education, as Greene points out, is that we ought not try to pursue an ideal rationality of isolated individuality, but rather what she calls "connected teaching," as an example of which she proposes Nel Noddings's education rooted in caring.[2]

This is consonant with our discussion of autonomy and education for autonomous individuals. But if autonomy implies the necessity of freedom, and if autonomy embraces relationality, then so must freedom and our understanding of it. Freedom is not, as is often assumed, an independence from influence of and responsibility to others, but it is rather the social conditions that allow individual autonomy to flourish. It is, for example, the legal structures that we call traffic laws that enable us to drive from one place to another. The law promotes freedom, just as the rules of a game enable it to be played. Freedom is that social circumstance that enables our individual flourishing in relation with others.

Freedom in this sense is another way of referring to social justice. Recall that our autonomy has to be consistent with the autonomy of others, because we are all morally equal. In that case, it is never sufficient to accept conditions that we believe to be conducive to our interests if they are simultaneously impediments to the autonomous development of others. This would be the definition of social injustice. Justice, by contrast, is reflected in social structures and relations that provide the conditions necessary for all of us to achieve the autonomy, which is to say the enrichment of experience and the freedom, to which we are entitled by our inherent equality. In this sense, autonomy and freedom are ideal outcomes of education as they are simultaneously characteristics of a just society.

It is, however, often not easy to determine what those conditions are, or which practices and policies are most consistent with the ideals of autonomy, freedom, and justice, and reasonable people can disagree. It is a goal of education, one among others, to help children and students develop into the adults who possess the habits of mind necessary to work through these disagreements without undermining the ends of freedom and justice in the process. It is also the responsibility of those who educate to engage such disputes and resolve the problems while keeping in mind the most defensible social and educational principles.

Rights

One of the more common ways in which the differences between what is and is not legitimate in social relations has been articulated is in terms of the concept of rights. The French Revolution spoke of the "Rights of Man," the American Declaration of Independence of the "unalienable rights" with which we are endowed by our creator, and the United Nations' Universal Declaration of Human Rights speaks of the "inalienable rights" of all people as the foundation of freedom, justice, and peace. The idea of rights continues to be a powerful feature in our understanding of social realities and ideals. There are, in fact, at least two ways of thinking about rights. One of them—to which the French and American revolutions, as well as the United Nations, appealed—is what are typically called "natural rights." These are rights or entitlements that we presumably possess simply by virtue of being human. This is the reason they are "unalienable." The intellectual advantage of conceiving of rights as natural in this sense is that governments and other social institutions would be obligated to respect them. Others (John Stuart Mill, for example) have found the idea of rights that derive from nature to be intellectually dubious, and some have instead spoken of "social" rights. The idea in this case is that rights are the sorts of entitlements that we as citizens of a society possess because as a society we have decided to posit them.

One important difference between natural and social rights is that natural rights do not change, whereas social rights may differ from one society to the next and from one time to the next. One common feature of both kinds of rights is that though it is relatively easy to posit the existence of rights, it is much more difficult to determine which rights there are. The Declaration of Independence declared the unalienable rights to be "life, liberty, and the pursuit of happiness." About a dozen years later when the US Constitution was drafted, however, the rights claimed in the process of its ratification are, following an earlier formulation of John Locke, life, liberty, and property.[3] During the ensuing process to ratify and implement the Constitution, more radical members of the revolutionary coalition thought that the document itself was too weak with respect to the rights that citizens should be able to claim. This was the reason that the first ten amendments to the Constitution were added, the so-called Bill of Rights, which listed, among others, rights that citizens may claim to the freedom of worship, speech, assembly, the press, and the possession of firearms. Rather later, largely under the influence of socialist thinkers and activists, it has been argued that a proper list should include what are often called substantive rights, which are rights to such necessities as food and shelter and to such social goods as employment, health care, and education. Arguments about rights of all of these kinds continue around the world to this day.

Aside from the problem of which rights should be said to exist, there is also the question of the role the concept of rights should be expected to play in social life and policy. The modern idea of rights arose as part of the same process that gave rise to the modern forms of the state. We will deal more directly with the state in the next section, but to understand why the conception of rights was as central as it was to the revolutionary leaders of the eighteenth century, we need to see that for them, the purpose of the state was to ensure that natural rights were protected. Without belaboring the point, we can get a sense of what a nation and its government believe to be of greatest social importance by seeing which rights it believes to be central. When the US Constitution, then, asserts through its amendments that the state must defend the right to property, rather than, say, a right to employment or housing, it provides legal support for those who possess productive property, rather than for those who do not. All have a right to life and liberty, but only those who possess property can claim a right to it and to the wealth and power it conveys. The best that the others, which typically is the majority, can claim is that they should be able to try to gain property. The legal force, though, is on the side of those who possess property and endeavor to keep it because it is only they who can invoke a right.

This sort of thing indicates the problem that thinking in terms of rights has always presented. From the beginning, the concept of rights has been weaponized, and to such an extent that it has become less a feature of a strong and just society, and more part of the arsenal used to advance an individual or group's interests. The impact of the weaponization of rights can cut several different ways. Those who do not have access to health care, for example, may make the claim that policies should be established to provide them with health care on the grounds that health care is a right that they are being denied. As long as the concept of rights maintain some degree of moral import in social discourse, appealing to rights in this way can have some rhetorical value. In the end, though, its effectiveness will always depend on whether those with sufficient social power are prepared to acknowledge that health care is a right. Rights are a component of social struggles and are likely to remain so. They are also, one must acknowledge, a much stronger tool in the hands of those who wield power than of those who do not.

It is even common for rights to be used by the powerful to justify the exercise of their power over others. It is common to hear among some influential voices in government and the military a defense of the use of military force to prevent actions somewhere in the world that threaten to violate people's rights. This is the current conception, popular in Europe and the United States, and to some extent elsewhere, of humanitarian interventionism. The idea is that if people elsewhere in the world are suffering as a result of the violation of their rights (usually at the hands of their own government or leaders), then nations that have the power to do so are obliged to defend those people's rights, sometimes by economic sanction or boycott, but also by military means if necessary. The call to respond to a violation of people's rights has a strong moral pull. The problem with it is that it is rarely, if ever, used consistently, so that instead of being an argument for action that is morally obligatory, the appeal to rights is one more weapon used by governments to advance their own ends.

In recent years, to offer specific illustrations of the point, interventionist arguments of this kind were used among American leaders to justify bombing in Serbia in the 1990s, several years later in Libya, and much more recently in Syria. In each of these cases, there was no doubt dreadful suffering by many people. Civil wars in all three countries were having a terrible effect on innocent civilians, as such wars always do. One can easily imagine and understand a humanitarian impulse to help. The problem is that the impulse is suspiciously selective. There was no such impulse to intervene to defend the people of Guatemala in the 1980s when they were being murdered in numbers by their government, nor the people of Chile when they were being arrested, tortured, and murdered after a military coup in the 1970s, nor the possibly million Indonesians who were murdered by their government in the mid-1960s or, for that matter, the Palestinians who have been displaced and subjugated since the late 1940s. Along similar lines, it is impossible to imagine that the French government would have accepted intervention in its war against the Algerians on the grounds that Algerians' rights were being violated, or that the Americans would have accepted humanitarian intervention against their forces on the grounds that the US war in Southeast Asia was violating the rights of the millions of people who suffered under its military onslaught.

The obvious question is, why are rights appealed to in some cases and not others? The obvious answer is that in those cases in which interventionists appeal to rights to justify their military actions, their own military and political interests, and quite possibly the interests of the dominant class are being advanced by the intervention. In those cases in which they do not intervene to protect anyone's rights, it has been judged not to be in the economic, political, and military interests of the more powerful nations and classes to prevent the violation of rights. In fact, they have frequently supported the actions that violated rights, or were the violators themselves. The appeal to rights to justify military actions is, it appears, not only inconsistently applied but also largely cynical when it is applied.

Making this point does not minimize the suffering of victims of aggression, even or especially when directed by a government against its own people. It does, however, call into question the adequacy of the concept of rights in our understanding of social realities. If we are not able to agree on whether rights are natural or social, on what rights there are, and on how to appeal to them without hypocrisy, then it is not unreasonable to think that we would be better served to forgo the concept altogether, and consider other ways to capture what, at its best, the idea of rights is intended to mean.

To this point in our analysis, we have made the case that the equality implicit in the character of experience, and the expectation that each of us is equally entitled to pursue and exercise the power necessary to craft our own ends and the course of our lives, may do the job that the notion of rights has traditionally done, and without the layer of hypocrisy and duplicity we too often find associated with an appeal to rights. This would leave undetermined how, in our interactions with other people, in our engagements with social institutions, and through the social and political policies that affect us, such an entitlement can best be respected. In some respects, the answer is clearer than in others. We have made the case, for example, that disparities in the distribution of wealth and power are indefensible once they impede one's ability to control her own experience, as they generally do in the case of the poor, the dispossessed, and working people generally. We do not need to debate what is or is not a right in order to reach this conclusion. We can make a similar argument with respect to education. When education is so organized and conducted that it is a process whereby children and students are helped to develop the knowledge, understanding, and capacities they need to direct their experience and control their lives, then education is doing what it should. When it fails to effect these ends, it is abrogating its responsibility. These are conclusions we may reach based on our understanding of experience and what follows from it, and we do not need to be distracted by the question whether or to what extent education is a right.

Individual and Community

We may draw this admittedly sketchy discussion of society and social relations to a close by considering the relation of the individual and the community. There has been a good deal of thinking about where the priority should lie in understanding society and social life, with the individual or with the community. It is impossible to do the debate justice here, so we will not even try. The reason to bring it up, rather, is to suggest that the distinction between the individual and the community as it is traditionally drawn is inadequate. But we may look first at the traditional uses of the terms.

It has been pointed out several times that the modern concept of the individual is as something that possesses its character independently not only of social relations generally but even of her own community. Those of us who live in societies that embody the influence of this conception of the individual tend to presume, seemingly automatically, that the characteristics of our lives are for us to determine on our own. One of the most obvious examples may be the case of religious affiliation. Most of us are born into a religious community and typically receive instruction in its tenets and induction into its traditions and institutions. We also tend to think, though, that one's religious affiliation is a personal and individual matter, to be determined by the individual when she reaches a level of maturity at which she is able to decide the matter for herself. Consequently, many of us have a much different religious identity as adults than we had as children. Many people abandon organized religion, or even religious belief altogether. Many others change their religious affiliation, sometimes as a matter of personal conviction, sometimes to marry the person they love, or sometimes as a way of entering more fully into a new cultural identity. The presumption in all of this is that religion is something an individual adopts as a matter of personal choice.

A more traditionally communitarian picture is quite different. There are communities in the world today, prominent and influential ones, in which to endorse the idea that one decides one's religion is to have it backward. One enters a religious community at birth, and one is raised in, and formed by, its practices and its intellectual and moral commitments. In this kind of case, one's religion is somewhat like one's family, in that both provide the context in terms of which one's character and life are formed. Given an understanding like this, it makes no more sense to think of religion as something that one can change or give up than to think that one can change or give up one's family. One can walk away from one's family, and in this sort of communitarian environment one could, presumably, walk away from one's religion, though it would be extremely difficult. But even in abandonment, one's family does not cease to be one's family, and in a religiously communitarian society, one's religion does not cease to be one's religion. In such a view, community commitment is not a matter of personal choice. The secular West's embrace of freedom of religion is incomprehensible in a society in which the relation of the individual and the community is differently conceived. It is not that one is not permitted to change one's religion as much as it is that the idea of changing one's religion is incoherent.

There are many similar examples we may give of the differences between an individually oriented and a community-oriented understanding of society. We seem to be forced into making a determination about which is the more important, the individual or the community. On the one hand, if we value the community over the individual, it can appear that individual autonomy and self-determination are impeded. On the other hand, if we value the individual over the community, then we are failing to appreciate the degree to which community and social relations constitute the individual. Our analysis, through its relationality, has emphasized the importance of the society and community in the formation of an individual's nature; through its emphasis on autonomy, however, our analysis has highlighted the importance of individual self-determination. We seem to have backed ourselves into a conceptual corner.

This is, however, more an apparent than a genuine problem. There is a problem between emphasizing the individual and emphasizing the community only if the individual and the community are understood entirely independently of one another. The criticisms of the liberalism that prioritizes the individual are critical precisely of the tendency of traditional liberalism to conceive of the individual along the atomistic, modernist lines that we have described. In that conception, the individual is determined independently of the community and social relations, as a result of which community values can appear to be an imposition on a person's individuality and autonomy. Thus, communitarians tend to think that the liberals have the wrong idea about the nature of the individual, and the liberals tend to think that communitarians do not sufficiently value individual autonomy.

The problem seems to be that those who favor the discrete, independent individual do not accept the idea that social relations constitute individuals, and those who give priority to the community do not recognize the moral importance of individual autonomy. Our analysis, however, offers a way to cut across this debate and thus resolve the conceptual problem. We have argued extensively that individuals are constituted in part by their social relations, which is to say by virtue of their inclusion in the communities of which they are a part. There is every good reason to accept that view, and no good reason to discard it. At the same time, we have argued that the nature of experience is such that the moral equality among individuals imposes on social structures, both institutional and informal, an obligation to enable individuals to exercise the power available to them in the construction of their experience as autonomous human beings. There is nothing contradictory, or even conceptually problematic, about this understanding of individual autonomy and this conception of the constitutive nature of social relations. In fact, relationality implies autonomy. A general theory of constitutive relations implies the sociality of individuals, and experience understood on the assumption of the constitutive relations of the individual and the community implies the moral equality and autonomy of individuals.

This understanding will not, we should realize, provide automatic answers to any specific problems that may come up in relation to individuals and community. We can see this if we consider again the example of religion. We have no formula that will answer the question whether an individual should regard religion as something she may adopt or abandon, as one might a coat, or whether it is constitutive of an individual and therefore cannot simply be hung in the closet and forgotten. In practice, both are possible. Western, secular societies offer individuals the opportunity to abandon religion as an ongoing feature of their lives, even as one may recognize the formative and constitutive role religion may have played in one's life. In fact, such an opportunity is the sort of thing that is highly valued among at least many individuals in secular societies. At the same time, there are also societies in which such an action with respect to one's religion is simply not possible, and probably not even entertained by most members of the society. Such a situation, however, is not an abandonment of an individual's autonomy; rather, it defines the applicability of one's autonomy differently than it is defined in a secular society. We do not think that in a secular society our autonomy is constrained because it would be incoherent to change family in the way that one may change a religion. Autonomy is simply not understood that way. Along similar lines, in a more traditional society with respect to religion, autonomy is not understood as encompassing a choice of religions. In a secular society, one can stop communicating with one's family, but it remains one's family; in a religious society, one may stop practicing one's religion, but it remains one's religion. In both cases, constitutive relations and autonomy are acknowledged, but they are applied differently, and there is nothing in our theory of the individual or society that rules out the possibility of either scenario.

The details of how the individual and the community interact will always be sorted out in practice, and there are in principle many different ways that can happen. The same is true in the exercise of power and in the structure of social institutions. As we have said, our theory of society and social relations offers not formulas but principles, and the most important value those principles must respect is the moral equality of individuals, and everything concerning autonomy and the exercise of power that is implied by our moral equality.

Whatever we may say about education, educational principles, and educational policy will have to be consistent with the centrality of moral equality and respect for it in practice. If we implement educational policies that undermine or ignore people's moral equality and impede their autonomy and control of their experience, we will have abrogated our responsibility as educators. In practice, it is often impossible to respect such principles entirely. For example, we can (and often do) encounter cases in which the principle implies that we do both "a" and "b," but our financial situation forces us to choose between them. Every administrator is familiar with this sort of problem. Again, there is no formula available to solve it. Our responsibility in such a case is to consider the options as carefully as possible and to make a decision that we have reason to believe best fulfills our obligation, even as we grant that neither choice fulfills it as well as we might like.

Much more can be said about educational principles in relation to social theory of this kind, but it will be better to hold that discussion until we have a chance to look at specifically political experience.

POLITICAL RELATIONS AND THE STATE

Our theories of constitutive relations and of experience have compelled us to rethink the nature of the individual and of society, and the same applies to the nature of the state and political relations. In whichever ways we understand political relations and the state, they can be expected to be consistent with the constitutive relationality of all things, and with the approaches to equality, autonomy, and power that define our sense of the individual and of individual experience.

The State

In the case of the state, the fairly obvious entrée is through the centrality of power in experience. We have in chapter 6 referred to this centrality as the political dimension of experience, and that description is a generalization in its usage of the term "political." We want now to bring the term back to its more standard meaning and talk about the political in the sense of the exercise of state and generally public institutional power. Our interest at this point is to examine some of the details of our relations with one another in the context of political relations in this sense and, by extension, in and through the state. The state, as we mean it here, is the central social structure through which political relations are defined and, in the end, exercised. One may and often should draw distinctions between the state and government, and even between state and nation. These are important distinctions, but for our purposes, we can use the concept and term "state" to range over all of them, unless otherwise specified.

As we did with respect to both the individual and society, we may begin by clarifying the differences between traditional approaches to the state and ours. The initial theoretical underpinning of the modern state, we should recall, was articulated through the concept of the social contract. The idea, to offer a quick reminder, was that individuals find that our goals and interests cannot be met without some degree of more centralized and overarching authority, and so we agree with one another to create such an authority and give it power of certain kinds over us. The authority we create in this way is the state, and the agreement by which we create it is the social contract. Several serious questions arise immediately, which concern the purposes of the state and the extent of its legitimate authority. These turn out to be immensely difficult questions, and they have been (and continue to be) debated until the present day. Though the questions are not resolved, in the process of the evolution of the modern state, certain ideas have come to be generally accepted. It is for the most part agreed that the role and purview of the state is to protect individuals' rights, with the caveat of course that there are various ways of conceiving what those rights are and who has them.

Given the details of our theories of constitutive relations and of experience, these modernist theoretical conceptions of the rise and nature of the state are no longer acceptable. First, the very idea of the social contract is flawed from the beginning because it assumes nonsocial individuals who then enter into political relations. But, as was pointed our earlier, if individuals are constituted by our relations, and if among those relations are our social and political contexts, then the very idea of a nonsocial condition from which we create the polity is impossible even as a theoretical construct. It explains nothing because it begins with an untenable assumption. The modernist conception of the role of the state has the same problem. Leaving aside for the moment the fact that we prefer to get along without appealing to rights at all (a point defended earlier in this chapter), the modernist conception of rights as they contribute to an understanding of the state is in fact not helpful. The traditional idea is that the state exists to protect rights that individuals have independently of political and social relations. We have these rights, presumably, before we create the state, and in fact we create the state as a mechanism to protect them. But on a relational conception of human beings, the idea of the possession of rights independently of social and political relations is incoherent. The modernist conception of the individuals in a state of nature who create through a social contract a state and endow it with the authority to protect natural rights does not survive in a relational theory. We are in need of an alternative way of thinking about political relations and the state.

Interests

A potentially fruitful place to begin is with the fact that all of us, regardless of our ideas about ourselves, about one another, about society, and about politics, have interests. These interests can be mundane and involve our daily activities; they may address the goals we have for ourselves and our families; they may concern our neighborhood and its institutions, from schools to stop signs and traffic lights to public parks to the role of the police; they certainly have to do with our jobs and careers, and with whichever factors affect our financial situation; they may also concern larger scale matters, when, for example, they are engaged with national policy and even international affairs. We all have interests of these and other sorts, and we have them regardless of our ideas about individuals, or societies, or nations, and regardless of whether we agree with others about any specific ideas. When we talk about people's interests, we are not talking about their ideas about things, or a consensus of opinion about anything, but rather of what they aspire to with respect to some specific state of affairs. Political relations flow from these interests.

Dewey, you may recall from the discussion in chapter 3, had grounded his conception of democracy in the interests that people have, and that is the clue to the importance of interests for political theory generally. The point Dewey made was that in any community, members of the community have certain interests in common. These interests go some way toward defining the community, and the fact that people share them identifies them as members of that community. Members of a bowling league have a set of interests in common. By virtue of being members of the league, they do not share all their interests, because each is also a member of other sets of people with other interests. But as members of the bowling league they share—for the most part, anyway—the interests that are relevant to the league and its functioning. Similar observations may be made about countless other communities, from the neighborhoods people live in to the schools their children attend to the places they work to the states of which they are citizens. Dewey's point is not that they share all interests or that they have reached some consensus on political or any other ideas. It is simply the fairly obvious and mundane point that members of a community have some interests in common. His second observation is that members of successful communities tend to be open to interests they may have in common with members of other communities beyond their own. We not only acknowledge at least some common interests with members of other communities but even pursue them. These two features of our social lives—that we share some interests with members of the communities of which we are a part and that we pursue common interests with those beyond our communities—are, Dewey says, the foundation of his understanding of democracy.

We will return to the topic of democracy below. For now, let us dwell on the fact that we have interests and their possible political implications. Dewey introduced the idea of common interests, and he is surely right, not only that we have such common interests but also that they help to define the communities of which we are a part and the meaning of our membership in those communities. We do have to add, though, that society does not simply consist of sets of overlapping, shared interests. Our lives consist of not only shared interests but also conflicting interests. If Dewey had a point in highlighting the fact of common interests, Marx also had a point in highlighting the significance of conflicting interests, especially between economic classes, and at least in societies in which there is private ownership of capital.

As Freire and many others have made clear in their analyses of social relations, there are extensive conflicts (Marx called them contradictions) between the interests of those who own or control large amounts of wealth and capital, on the one hand, and most of the rest of us, on the other. At the simplest and most obvious level, it is in the interests of the wealthy to maximize their profit, which is after all the point of investment, and one of the ways to do that is to keep expenses, including salaries and benefits for their workers, as low as possible. At the same time, it is in the interests of those who work for a wage to earn as much as they can for their labor. Hence, a conflict of interests. Marx thought that the conflict of interests between economic classes is what drives social change. Sooner or later, people who feel themselves to be treated unfairly or unjustly will push back, occasionally with force. Marx had made the correct observation, and it is as true today as it was in his day, that improvements in people's lives come only after people who are oppressed by the power of the dominant class push back, either through a demand for reform or through revolution.

We must be careful not to exaggerate these points. Both Marx and Dewey understood that there are common and conflicting interests in society. Dewey understood the tensions caused by the wide disparities in the distribution of wealth, and their detrimental consequences for people, which is the reason that he wanted classrooms to be environments that do not simply reproduce them. For his part, Marx (and Freire) also realized that there are common interests in any society, which is what makes class solidarity possible. Dewey, though, may have underestimated the insidious effects of class conflicts, and Marx may have failed to understand the range of common interests, but we do not need to repeat their mistakes.

If we wish to understand political relations, and actually the same may be said for social relations generally, it is useful to focus on individual and community interests. The modernist political tradition had in fact begun here, when in social contract theory it was said that people are drawn to the creation of the state as a way of protecting and advancing their interests. By the eighteenth century, though, the focus in political theory had shifted to rights as both the foundation and the goal of political relations and the state. By positing the right to property, John Locke early in the eighteenth century, and the drafters of the US Constitution near the end of the century, elevated one set of interests, the interests of those with property, over other sets of interests by sanctifying one of them as a right, which the state must protect. However, there is nothing about the interests in property of those who own it that is more important than the interests in the material and other conditions of a good life of those who do not own property. If all have an equal claim to the conditions necessary for an enriched experience and the autonomy, freedom, and power necessary to achieve it, then interests of the majority in the necessary conditions for a fruitful life have to be at least as important and valuable as an interest in property. Talking about rights in this case simply serves to obscure the proper balance of interests, whether shared or conflicting.

This does not mean that every person or group of people is equally entitled to the conditions required to advance her or their interests. In the end, it is those interests that are consistent with moral equality and autonomy that warrant social and political support. What those are in any particular instance could vary from case to case. What does follow from this theoretical focus on interests is that when political and policy decisions have to be made, those with the responsibility to make the decision have an obligation not to consider their own personal or class interests, nor any alleged rights to which one or more parties may lay claim, but to look to the interests that are served by a given policy, and to policies and decisions that can best meet the legitimate interests of those involved. And legitimate interests, one needs to keep in mind, are those that derive from and are conducive to the equality that is implicit in experience and the autonomy required to exercise it in the course of one's own experience.

This means, among other things, that interests must be understood in the longer run. Interests, in other words, are not the same as desires. I may desire to drive across town more quickly than I can now, but that does not mean that it is in my, or anyone else's, interest that I be able to do so. If my driving across town more quickly requires that the town eliminate the traffic signals along the way, and if by eliminating the traffic signals the town creates a serious danger to public health and welfare, then my desire is inconsistent not only with my interests but also with those of the rest of the residents of the town. Those who exercise political authority may be expected to consider carefully genuine interests, and long- as well as short-term interests, rather than the desires for this or that end by any one or a number of individuals.

This is a general political principle that would apply to educators and educational administrators as much as to anyone else with social or political power. If, for example, a group of business owners were to say to a State Education Department, or to a Ministry of Education (or to a local school board, for that matter), that they need the schools to prepare people only with the skills necessary to be efficient employees and to perform certain tasks that the businesses identify, we would want our educational officials to ask serious questions about whose interests would be served by such schooling. We would also want them to ask whether the interests of the business owners might be inconsistent with the long-term interests of the children and students who would attend such schools. We would hope, also, that if such inconsistent interests were identified, the authorities would ask themselves whether there is any good reason to give the business owners' interests precedence over those of the children and families in the community. It is not impossible that authorities might comply in some respects with even such an outlandish request as organizing school solely to meet business' needs, but they would be justified in doing so only if the alternatives are reasonably judged to be genuinely worse for the interests of those who would be detrimentally affected. In this respect, we are following Dewey in holding that education and the schools have to be careful not simply to reproduce the inimical class distinctions that characterize the broader society.

Democracy

Dewey had argued that a focus on common interests serves as the foundation for a democratic society and polity. He thought this because in his opinion, a society predicated on the respect for one another's interests is the healthiest possible, and that a state based on the same principles is the most just. There is something attractive about Dewey's advocacy of democracy, especially for those of us who have spent our lives in societies that meet some of the criteria of a democracy, or for those who have lived in oppressive conditions and aspire to a more democratic life. Most of us would not choose a different social or political arrangement, though we might choose to live in places that do not claim to be democratic for other, more personal, reasons.

There is, however, something suspicious about the sanctification of democracy that one finds in Dewey and in other political theorists from the world's secular democracies. What is suspicious in the case of democracy is roughly what is suspicious about rights. It is not that what we recognize when we talk about rights (for example, life or liberty) is unimportant, and it is not that what we point to in the case of democracy (for example, social and political self-determination and some modicum of political freedom) is not important. They are all important. The problem lies in the fact that talk about rights and about democracy is not an adequate way to underscore their importance. Nor is such talk an adequate way to speak to the significant needs of people generally. Why, we may ask ourselves, are such social goods as freedom and self-determination important for us? The most reasonable answer we can give is that they are important for us because they best meet the demand of equality implied by the nature of experience, and they best allow for the autonomy and the exercise of power we need to advance and enrich our experience and our lives. These are the underlying goods, and we endorse freedom and self-determination because we have reason to believe that they are the social arrangements best suited to achieve those goods.

This claim may be true in modern, liberal democracies, though we should keep in mind that we give some of these concepts a general meaning when in practice their meaning is selectively applied. We talk, understandably, about the importance of liberty or freedom, but that can mean many different things, from the liberty to use my wealth as I please to the freedom from hunger and homelessness. When we advocate for the rights of liberty, it is not clear that we all mean the same thing. The commitment to liberty and self-determination is vaguer than we may think. But even if we grant that freedom and self-determination are valuable ways for societies to embody equality and autonomy, there is nothing necessarily true about it. There is the distinct possibility that other kinds of societies—for example, one, such as a religious community of the kind we discussed earlier, in which liberty is understood to apply differently than it is in the secular West—can meet the population's legitimate interests at least as well as we believe more democratic arrangements do in our case. To claim otherwise is to say that only people who live in societies fundamentally like those in the secular, liberal West can live fully human lives. Such a claim would be false on the face of it, since a great many people can and do live fulfilled lives in other circumstances, and it represents a degree of arrogance that speaks in no one's favor.

It is far more reasonable to acknowledge that the social and political requirements for a fully human life, which are defined by the equality implicit in experience, can be achieved in a variety of political circumstances. If that is the case, then it is not appropriate for those of us who are most comfortable in democracies to claim that under any circumstances, a democracy is the most appropriate form of social and political organization. To acknowledge this fact is not to collapse into an indefensible relativism, because the criteria for evaluation have been shifted from talk about rights and democracy to the recognition of legitimate interests and the equality implicit in experience.

One of the other advantages of letting go of an insistence of the supremacy of democracy is that such an insistence has become, like the distortion of the idea of rights, a weapon in the hands of those powerful enough to wield it. US foreign policy, to offer just one set of examples, has used democracy in this way since Woodrow Wilson urged during the First World War that the world be made "safe for democracy." To this day, the US government, and many of its people, regard democracy as so important, whatever is actually meant by the term in any given case, that its imposition is used as a justification for invasions of other countries and the overthrow of their governments. Sometimes those governments are genuinely oppressive and have little justification of their own beyond sheer power. But as in the case of the weaponization of rights, the same US government may overthrow democratically elected leaders abroad, or lend support to their overthrow, and demand to put in place decidedly nondemocratic, though friendly, governments. There is, it appears, no more consistency in the appeal to democracy than there is in the appeal to rights. We are better off without either of them as weapons of the state. Fortunately, we do not need either, because our understanding of experience and interests allows us to justify political relations, structures, and policies without them.

International Relations

This last point indicates one more feature of political relations and the state that should be mentioned before we move on directly to educational implications, and that is the issue of the relations among states. The same general philosophical commitment to relationality, and the conception of experience it implies, that has rendered obsolete the traditional ideas of the individual and society also requires a reconsideration of how we understand the state. If individuals and societies are constituted by their relations, then so is the state, and that shift in conception has important implications, not least with respect to international relations. The traditional way of understanding the state is as an atomistic entity, independent and sovereign, with its traits determined independently of other states. In this view, the state identifies its interests without regard to its relations with other states. It is this conception of the state that is no longer viable.

First, if all entities are constituted relationally, then so are states or nations. Every state exists in various sets of relations with other states, and those relations contribute to its nature, just as the contexts and sets of relations in which individual people find themselves contribute to our natures. States may be sovereign, in the sense that they define the parameters within which a state's legal structures and systems apply, but they are not independent of one another. The details differ from context to context, of course, but because states also prevail within relational contexts, in some respects or others, what nation A does impacts nation B. This impact is constitutive, not simply accidental to the nature of both states. The degree of relevance of a given action will differ from case to case, but the constitutive nature of one state's action on another is a feature of what it is to be a relational entity. The various alliances and agreements into which states enter are intentional expressions of an underlying ontological fact about them.

Second, if the state possesses its traits by virtue of its relational contexts and elements, this rule applies to interests as much as to any other trait. Some have questioned whether the state really has any interests of its own or whether it serves to underwrite the interests of some of its elements. Marxists, for example, have argued that the state has always been an organ of a society's ruling class, such that its structures and components function to serve the interests of that class. This is why, for example, the state in a capitalist society, through the law, defends the interest of the owners of capital to be able to hire and fire employees more or less at will, but it does not, unless it is compelled to by popular action, support working people's interests to have jobs. An owner is entitled to hire or fire a worker, but a worker is not entitled to have a job, only to look for one. This is the sort of thing that is meant when it is claimed that the state represents class interests, and that state interests generally are always the interests of the dominant, ruling class.

There seems to be no question that the state is more likely to defend ruling class interests than those of others in a society. A brief look at labor history makes that clear. But this is not—indeed, cannot be—the whole story of the interests of a state. A state is a more complex entity than simply the administrative arm of a ruling class, if for no other reason than that there are far more relations into which a state enters that are relevant to its nature and its traits. Interests arise in a web of constitutive relations, just as do other traits of the state. It may wish to protect property, but it may also have public health pressures that it must address, and the two may not be compatible in any given case. An example of such an interest would be in the US Supreme Court's argument in support of abortion access, when it argued that the state has an interest in the health of a pregnant woman and, eventually, in the health of a fetus. There are also environmental pressures on the state with which it must contend, and which it must balance with property and other interests. There are interests it has by virtue of its relations with other states, not all of which are tied directly to the interests of capital. The state's interests are many and varied and interact in complex ways. Understanding a state's interests requires that one engage the complexity of the state's constitutive relations.

Third, if states are related constitutively to other states, among other things, then the traditional conception of international relations has to be altered. The international environment is not a "state of nature" populated by independent entities engaging with one another to meet their respective interests. It is already an ecosystem, one in which the nature and interests of any one element, which is to say any one state, is of necessity constitutively related to the others. Some of those relations are more relevant than others, but all are constitutive. The state can no more withdraw itself from that environment than a plant can withdraw from the pond in which it is planted. In such a conception as this, states must realize that their actions occur in a complex and multileveled context. By entering into an agreement (or, for that matter, by withdrawing from an agreement), a state is not simply more or less advancing its interests; rather, it is acting in ways that, through its complex relations, will have many, often unintended, effects on other states and on itself.

Fourth, insofar as a state is a social institution, its responsibilities are to be construed in ways similar to those of other social institutions. In all of its actions, internal or external, the interests and welfare of the state's citizens are at stake. The state is likely never able to meet the interests of all its citizens, not to mention those of citizens of other states, if only because some of those interests are incompatible or even contradictory with one another. The state faces the same kind of challenges in this respect as do other institutions, and its responsibilities are comparable. The state's responsibility is to see to it that in its domestic and foreign policy, the equally legitimate interests of all people in their own autonomy and the conditions they need to exercise their power appropriately are met to the greatest extent possible.

This is an ideal that can probably never be fulfilled thoroughly, and unfortunately there has probably never been a state that has even come very close, but it is the standard that would apply to the state understood as a constitutively related entity. Perhaps the standard cannot be met, but even serious and sustained efforts to meet it would present a picture quite different from the one that current practice presents. Domestic policies, from tax structures to policing, among many others, would have to be undertaken with the interests of all in mind, to the extent possible. Internationally, relations with other states that are efforts to best them, in either economic or military competition, are fairly common in contemporary foreign affairs, but they are unlikely to meet this standard. There may be an argument for the state to maintain a military, but there will be at most relatively few legitimate arguments to support going to war. In short, much of what currently passes for domestic and foreign policy would not meet the standard we have proposed.[4]

All the considerations that have been raised with respect to social and political theory, institutions, and practice have implications for educational principles. We may now turn to them directly.

EDUCATIONAL PRINCIPLES

We have said that education is the process whereby children and students learn systematically to exercise their autonomy and power in order to control and enrich their experience through the course of their lives. This general conception is suggested by the view we have taken of experience, and it can be ramified more thoroughly given the current chapter's analysis of social and political relations. In the process, the problems and challenges facing education that were considered in chapter 5 may be addressed again here, and more thoroughly.

Because it is an issue that has a bearing on educational policy and financing, especially in the United States, the question whether education is a private or a social good has to be resolved. The answer is, one would think, blazingly obvious, and that is that education is both a private and a social good. It is a private good in that the value of education is properly described as enabling individuals to develop the abilities to direct their experience. Individuals are a beneficiary of education, a claim that ought not be controversial. Individuals, however, constitute societies, and the character of individuals is highly relevant to the character of the societies that they constitute. If individuals are educated in such a way that they acquire the knowledge and insight necessary to control their experience, then the society they constitute will take on comparable and consistent traits. Such a society will be far more likely than it would be otherwise to support, rather than hinder or impede, people's lives and their enrichment. Conversely, the society will be served by a well-educated populace, especially a society in which there is some measure of popular control of government, to the extent that people can think clearly about the problems the society faces. In these respects, education serves social as well individuals' purposes and is thereby a social good.

This point is widely enough accepted with respect to primary and secondary education, which is one of the reasons that continued funding for public schools is unquestioned, even if frequently insufficient. In the United States, however, it is still not commonly extended to higher education. There is, though, no good reason to reject the point in relation to universities and colleges. Education at that level, though it differs in any number of ways from the primary and secondary levels, is both a private and a social good for the same reasons that primary and secondary education is. Individuals are clearly advantaged by study at universities and colleges, and a society with a substantial number of well-educated people can be expected to achieve more and better than one without such people. Not only does higher education prepare the professionals that strong societies need, but it also, if done well, provides its students with a stronger foundation than they might otherwise have in the knowledge and sensibilities that are valuable as societies confront their challenges and enable their development. This is not to say that well-educated people are in any sense superior to those with less formal education, but merely that the systematic development of one's potential that education affords is more likely to be effective than if one's development is undertaken without it. What this may imply for policies related to funding, for example, is not something that can be decided in advance of any specific case. It does, however, offer a prima facie rationale for public support and funding of education at all levels.

The argument was made earlier in this chapter that in considering education as an institution, it is necessary to appreciate the fact that it is constituted as much by its economic and social relations as it is by academic ones. Another way of saying this is that none of these factors can be regarded as extrinsic to the nature of education. Nevertheless, education is distinguished from other social institutions by the fact that, unlike the others, it has as the academic a third set of constitutive relations. If education is to meet its own purposes and goals, the fact that it is distinctively academic cannot be overlooked by anyone who is involved in educational planning, funding, and administration, as well as by anyone in the classroom. Such abstract principles as this are not in the forefront of teachers' minds in the middle of the push and pull of everyday life in a school, but they should never be too far away. It is understandings such as this that in the end drive and justify what educators do.

Nevertheless, at any level, including the tertiary, education cannot be disentangled from the economic and social factors, including the political, of the society in which it functions. No position on any educational issue could rest on a claim that education should not have to deal with this or that economic or sociopolitical factor because its purpose is purely academic. The reason such a claim is vacuous is that no institution is "purely" anything. This points to the question of the social responsibility of education. In one sense, as education meets its academic goals, it is also fulfilling an important responsibility and function. A healthy society needs well-educated people, regardless of whether they complete or even attend university. A society constituted by people who understand their world in some of its complexity, and who have developed the habits of mind and action required to engage their individual and community challenges successfully, is likely to be a strong and healthy society. In this respect, education at all levels meets a social responsibility by being conducted properly.

There are also more specific ways in which it is reasonable to consider education to have a social responsibility. One of them concerns the range of ideas and information to which students are exposed, which is basically the problem of censorship. A second is the problem that Dewey had raised in the early twentieth century, which is whether and how the process of education can expect the support of the state without allowing the frequent narrowness of state interests to distort its own purposes. We may consider each in turn.

Plato was right about many things. One of them is the importance of education properly conducted to a strong and just society. This is the reason, the reader may recall, that he referred to education as "the one great thing." He was also right about the importance of equal education for boys and girls. But he was dead wrong in his advocacy of censorship. Plato thought that if we want people to think and act in certain ways, we should expose them only to the information and experiences that will support such thought and action. Anything that does not support the desired ideas and behavior will be kept out of the city, as he put it. Such a view, however, is not consistent with the general educational principles that we have endorsed. If education is to enable students to enrich their experience, it follows that students need to develop the ability, to the extent that each is able, to understand and evaluate whatever they may encounter in experience, and whatever they may creatively devise. This capacity can only be developed if children and students are exposed to the full range of human thinking and behavior. Such a process can happen only gradually, as children develop the necessary intellectual and emotional maturity to engage sensitive material. The general principle, though, is that censorship is inimical to this process because it necessarily impedes students' development.

As this is being written, there is a growing tendency for some educators, and students as well, to think that ideas that we have reason to believe are unacceptable, such as racist or sexist ideas, and the people who may hold them or even wish to discuss them, should be "kept out of the city," so to speak. Like much else in education, this can be a complex and difficult issue to deal with in any particular situation, especially in that it can involve understandable concerns and sensitivities of students and others. For such reasons, it is impossible to provide a simple guide for educators to follow when confronted with attempts to censor material or people. Educational administrators and others may reasonably insist that students and members of an educational community, which is to say a school or university, are entitled to a defense of their membership in that community in the face of challenges to it. This does not mean, however, that students are entitled to avoid anything with which they might disagree, or which may make them uneasy. Education, on the contrary, must be able to help students understand and address such ideas and material. The default position, therefore, should be clear, and that is that an educational institution has a responsibility to expose students to the range of ideas and behavior that human beings have devised, even ideas and behavior that students and their teachers may be convinced is mistaken or even immoral. Educators do not hide from mistakes and immorality, nor should we try to hide them from our students. Rather, we have a social responsibility to engage and correct them and to enable our students to do the same.

The second issue concerning education's social responsibility involves the role of the state and state interests in education. This can be a serious problem for educators, because as we have seen in an earlier consideration of the question, there are occasions in which the state chooses to manipulate the educational process (for example, through curriculum or the content of textbooks) to influence what children and students learn, and therefore what they are likely to take with them for the rest of their lives. This can be especially common, and pernicious, in the study of history and the social sciences generally. As this book is being written, for example, authorities in many US states are determining by law how issues of race in American society may or may not be addressed in schools and even in universities. It should be noted that this is not a new problem, and it is not peculiar to any particular country. Even long before there were organized schools, or modern nations, in Europe the Church made every effort to ensure that where education was being offered, it underscored Church doctrine and Church interests. Something similar was true in other world traditions—for example, in Islamic societies, and in even older cultures, such as China, education was organized to meet state interests as they were understood at the time. In Europe, as the modern state evolved and matured, it eventually took education under its wing as a branch of state service. This process was well underway by the late nineteenth century in Europe and European-inflected societies elsewhere in the world. It remains generally the case today.

The problem for educational principle is that we again face something of a conundrum. We have said that as a social institution, it is impossible for education to pretend or even aspire to independence from social and political factors. Education is, we must acknowledge, a political process in fundamental ways, as it is economic and academic. At the same time, the purposes of education are to enhance students' understanding and capacities such that they are able to deal intelligently and skillfully with the problems that arise in their experience. To meet this goal, it would appear, any sort of manipulation of educational factors by state authorities to mislead children and students is unacceptable. The challenge, then, is to understand how education may be a political institution and yet meet its general pedagogical responsibility.

The resolution of this apparent problem has to be that the social and political responsibility of education is best met in the process of achieving its basic academic goals. People are not formed into strong citizens by being presented with distorted information, a warped historical analysis, for example, any more than they are by having information withheld from them through censorship, either formally required or by tacit agreement. Both processes make understanding impossible, and without understanding, people cannot live lives of social and political responsibility. Any individuals in positions of political authority who think that state interests are being met by distorting the educational process are deeply mistaken about both education and state interests. A healthy society would not want such people in positions of authority, and a strong education will help a citizenry realize if and when such people find themselves in positions of authority. In the end, genuine social and political interests, including state interests, are best met by a well-educated populace, and to be well educated here means to be educated according to the principles we have been articulating. Precisely how to ensure that such a situation prevails is, as with many other issues, not something for which a formula is available. What is available to all educational stakeholders are the principles of a sound education, and an understanding of the nature of the political and social relations, and of experience, that is consistent with it.

There is an important feature of education at which the issues of the social role of education, the relation of education's private and social goods, and the question of curriculum all converge, and this is the issue of vocational education. The general goal of education that we have pursued throughout part II of this volume—for it to empower a person, with whatever knowledge and skills are necessary, to exercise control over the conditions of one's life in the interests of ever richer experience—does not roll off the tongue and can have an abstract and obscure sound to it. In fact, though, there is nothing abstract about it, or at least not in intention. You may note that certain words and phrases commonly used to describe the value of education, such as knowledge for its own sake, or continuing our intellectual tradition, or enjoying the life of the mind, are entirely absent from our discussion. This has been intentional, because such aspirations as these evaluate education as if its purpose is entirely conceptual or intellectual. This, however, cannot be right, if only because nothing is entirely conceptual. Based on the theory of experience, we may be able to speak of mind and the life of the mind, but it is always understood as constitutively related to the broader contexts that characterize our experience. Mind is always mind in social, historical, biological, and other contexts, so that the life of the mind has no meaning other than in experience. There is no such thing as knowledge for its own sake; the value of knowledge is always in what it does. Again, Freire and Noddings are both right to emphasize the constitutive relations to one another of knowledge and action.

Education, then, has to be tied in some explicit ways to what we do, or aspire to do. This is the reason that Dewey built vocation into his conception of education. It is more common to encounter a defense of vocational education in terms of tracking and the subjugation of educational goals to the wishes of local employers. It is often held that some children and students are not able to handle, never mind benefit from, academic subjects, so it is only fair to provide for them a course of study that is focused on explicitly identifiable future employment options. This, it is said, will be most beneficial for them, and it will meet the needs of employers and the economy generally. This, typically, is vocational education.

There are many things wrong with this understanding of the relation between education and the broader economic and social worlds. Fundamentally, there are two problems with this approach. First, it subjugates the academic values of education to the economic, and we have argued that though economic values are constitutive of education, they cannot be permitted to obscure the academic. Second, this approach to the relation between education and its social contexts ignores the fundamental equality in human experience, which is a way of referring to what Freire called the humanizing function of education. This is not to say that all children and students are the same with respect to their abilities and to the subjects and topics that interest them. It is to say, though, that all children and students have an equal claim to the conditions of their development that will allow for their growth and control over their own experience. To orient children and students to a narrowly employment-centered training, rather than to an education that can enrich their levels of development more generally and more completely, is to deny their implicit equality.

If the traditional approaches to vocational education are indefensible, but the academic ends of education ought not to be divorced from the lived social conditions in which people find themselves, then another approach is required. This other approach is what we mean by saying that a sound education must be vocational. If knowledge is not something that can be divorced from action, then the educational process must encompass the integration of inquiry and action. There are many ways this can be done, and, yet again, there is no formula to determine how best to accomplish it in any specific case. Clearly, it implies at least that the relation of teacher and student be structured in and through experiential situations, which in turn means that passively constructed classrooms and an emphasis on testing are not adequate pedagogical methods. This is not to say that students do not sometimes need to receive information from their teachers or that students should never be tested. It is to say, rather, that neither of these methods can serve as paradigmatic pedagogical approaches.

In addition to experiential pedagogy in the classroom, other activities—many of them already common in schools and universities—may prove useful. In primary and secondary schools, it is almost certainly valuable to integrate experiences in the economic and social world into classroom instruction. Field trips, time in offices and factories, exposure to the arena of social services, all have pedagogical value. At the university level, as we have indicated earlier, internships are useful, much in the way that we require student teaching experiences in teacher education programs. Service learning has become a significant feature of education in some places, as activity in the community becomes integrated into the course curriculum for university students. Experience abroad serves similar ends. This situation is now fairly common in Europe, as the Bologna process has integrated higher education across Europe and beyond to all signatory countries. Students elsewhere in the world, including and perhaps especially in the United States, remain, however, debilitatingly provincial in their understanding of other places and peoples. This is not a good situation, not only for the students individually but also for the health of their societies, economies, and polities. In short, anything that builds the local, national, and international contexts, as well as the social, economic, and political worlds, into children and students' education will enrich the experience immeasurably. In fact, such integration is not simply a pleasant possibility but also a necessity, given the ends and basic traits of education as we have developed them.

The only point that remains to be made is that having tied, as we have, education to the basic nature of experience, it has to be made explicit that education cannot be construed as if it were equivalent to schooling. We are centers of experience for as long as we live, and the value of systematic efforts to enhance the enrichment of our experience is always germane to the quality of our lives. Experience itself can be and typically is educative, but outside of schools and universities, it is left to us, individually and collectively, to understand how to benefit from that basic fact of our lives. There are some institutions that help us to do that—adult and continuing education programs, for example—all of which are worthwhile. But even beyond such programs, the educational capacity of experience in general is unconstrained. That capacity will express itself differently for each of us, if only because we each have our own interests and abilities. If we know what to look for and how to benefit from whatever we judge to be appropriate for us, our lives will be continually enriched.

Conclusion

These chapters have been an attempt to accomplish four goals. One of them is to introduce you to some of the highlights in the history of philosophical thinking about education. A second goal has been to clarify the kinds of questions and issues that a systematic philosophy of education addresses, and how answers to them are related to more general philosophical ideas. The third goal has been to develop and justify a general philosophical understanding of nature, knowledge and human experience, society, and the state, and the fourth has been to clarify the educational principles that flow from or are most consistent with those ideas.

The reader who has worked her way through the first four chapters should have a passing familiarity with four of the most insightful and influential philosophical treatments of education in the Western intellectual tradition. This exposure to the history of educational thinking does not by itself answer any specific questions about education, nor does it supply irrefutable principles to guide our thinking about education. What it does offer, though, is a firmer grounding in the methods and issues in thinking philosophically about education.

There are various ways to describe the value of studying the history of something, whether it is social or political history or the history of ideas. It is impossible to understand anything without some understanding of its history. There are several reasons for this, the most important of which—for me, at any rate—is that the meaning of anything is lost without a sense of how it came to be what it is. One might think about a musical note, say a B natural, to repeat an illustration that we used earlier. A B natural tone, sounded in isolation from other notes, has some aural and physical traits, but outside of any context it has little to no meaning. Think now of the same B natural after even a simple harmonic progression in the key of C leading back to the dominant note or chord. In such a musical phrase, our B natural, when sounded as the penultimate note in the passage, is rich with tension, a tension that most of us can feel and want to be resolved. Where does this tension come from? It comes from the whole phrase that led to the B natural. Without its history of and in the phrase, the note is barren; with its history, it is pregnant and meaningful.

The history of anything is constitutive of its meaning and import. If we are not familiar with its history (at least to some extent), then its meaning and import are closed to us, and it is impossible to understand anything that is considered largely in the dark. This may be what Cicero meant when he said that "To be ignorant of what happened before you were born, is to remain a child forever."[1] Our own intellectual growth and maturity require that we understand something of how we came to be who we are and to think what we think, and, more broadly, how the dominant ideas in our society came to be dominant. This is a tall order, and none of us is likely to accomplish it in full. The more we understand of the history of something, however (and, in our case, it is the history of educational thinking), the more available to us are the possible ways of thinking about our own circumstances and conditions.

A study of the history of philosophical thinking also gives us a vocabulary and a set of ideas to work with. A painter needs not just a blank surface and paint but also a specific color palette with which to work. When we are thinking about ideas, we need a language, and we also need a point of departure to help us think. When we see how others have approached education, and in our case we have looked at some of the best and brightest, we understand how they have addressed the relevant questions. This in turn gives us a point of departure for our own thinking. This is very much as it should be, because we never approach any topic in a vacuum, and if we think that we are beginning "from scratch," then we are sorely mistaken.

Once we enter the stream that moves educational thinking along, we begin to sort out some of the issues and problems. Plato and many others have helped us to understand that we need to consider carefully what the purpose or purposes of education are. Once we have a working sense of what education ought to try to accomplish, it becomes possible to think more carefully about other features of the educational enterprise, specifically pedagogical methods, content, and the various people who are the beneficiaries of education. The ways we answer the questions associated with those themes are guided by what we want to accomplish, which is to say by the educational goals that have been endorsed.

Another contribution that the study of Plato, Rousseau, Dewey, and Freire provides is that their analyses exemplify the claim that educational ideas are necessarily integrated with broader philosophical concepts. The point should be clear by now that without examining educational issues in the context of thinking about nature, knowledge, a conception of the person, and ideas about society and the state, which taken together we have here called a systematic philosophy of education, it is impossible to arrive at a coherent and justifiable set of ideas. Educational philosophy is not a closed set of issues and problems. It is integrally related to many of the other issues and questions that constitute philosophy generally, just as the educational process is integrally related to the broader features of the society and the lived contexts in which it occurs.

Another relevant point that should be clear by now is that philosophers disagree with one another about many topics, big and small. Studying the history of philosophical ideas is not like studying the history of science, where one can see fairly readily the development and increasing sophistication of the understanding of material entities and processes, even if that development sometimes happens in fits and starts. There is a great deal of value in studying the history of science, but one typically does not go to it in order to learn how to do science now, or to do it better. In the case of the history of philosophy, by contrast, we can learn from our predecessors even while disagreeing with them, and we can even adapt ideas that they had to our own cases. We can appropriate the history of philosophy in ways that are much less likely in or available to the sciences. We may put them to work for us even as we disagree with them, just as they disagreed with one another. Rousseau's thinking was done explicitly with Plato in mind, and *Emile* was written as a response to the *Republic*. Dewey responds directly to Plato and Rousseau, and to others, as he appropriates their traditions to make them his own. The same is true of Freire. In these chapters we have attempted to do much the same.

There is an implicit danger in this, however, and it is the temptation to let our forebears do the thinking for us. Our philosophical models are impressive, and one may be to some extent awed by them. Their considerable talents give us a great deal to think about, and they may even serve in some ways as intellectual guides. But they do not answer our questions or resolve our problems. We must do that ourselves.

There are several reasons for this. First, as we have just said, they disagree with one another, and so even if we were inclined simply to appropriate ideas for ourselves, we cannot appropriate all of them. Some critical judgments and conceptual discriminations would have to be made. The more important reason that they cannot do our thinking for us is that our circumstances are different from theirs. With respect to time and place, we in the West at this point in history have more in common with Dewey and Freire than we do with Plato and Rousseau, so it would be easier to adopt some of their ideas because they are likely to be more directly applicable for us. As close as they are, though, they are still not thinking and writing in our conditions and circumstances. In one sense, this does not matter too much, because we are in search of educational principles that are not themselves stuck in, which is to say applicable only in, a specific time and place. This openness is what makes it possible to benefit from the inquiries and analyses that our forebears have left us. In another sense, though, even if there are ideas from our intellectual history that we may adopt here and now, a careful analysis on our part is necessary to determine what they might be and how best to put them to work in our circumstances. Our philosophical ideas generally, and our educational principles, do not come ready-made for our use. We are obliged to sort it out for ourselves, as will also be true for the generations after us.

Though they have not done the thinking for us, our predecessors have pointed out various ways we may approach the issues ourselves, and taking up the philosophical consideration of general and educational themes has been the third goal of this study. The argument has been made that though the atomistic and mechanistic approaches to nature, knowledge, human being, society, and the state served the European world for hundreds of years (if unevenly with respect to virtues and vices), there are several good reasons for us now to think that they are no longer sustainable. In philosophy, physics, and biology, as we have seen, developments took place and discoveries were made in the nineteenth and twentieth centuries that rendered the old way of thinking obsolete. We have taken these facts of the matter and generalized them into an alternative way of thinking about nature, and everything else. In this respect, the general ontological conception that has been presented here borrows heavily from Dewey and others.

The entities of nature, and here the term "nature" refers to everything that exists in any way at all, are relational in the sense that they are constituted by their relations. This means that everything is what it is by virtue of the relations among its parts and components, as well as of its relations within the many broader contexts in which it prevails. A tree, for example, has leaves and roots and branches and other component parts, the relations among which contribute to the nature of the tree. But the tree also is rooted in soil of a certain chemical consistency, and it lives within an atmosphere with a specific set of characteristics, and these contexts also contribute to its nature. Furthermore, that it is old and has stood on the family land for generations, and that it provides shade for the family picnic table, or a location for the nest of local birds, are among its constitutive traits no less than its parts and its physical environment. This idea of what at the most general level makes anything what it is is then generalized to apply to all things and all kinds of things. Everything is relational.

When this general idea is applied to the nature of human beings, we derive a specific understanding of experience. People, like anything else, are relationally constituted, and the ongoing constitutive give and take between an individual and her many environments is her experience. In this sense, experience is not the passive intake of sensory data, which has been the traditional way of thinking about it; rather, it is both the passive undergoing and the active undertaking that characterize a person's life. Because experience is passive as well as active, we both receive and contribute to the process, and it is in these ways that our lives unfold. At the most general level, we can see that experience has three dimensions. In that we have the ability to engage our environment and creatively act, and at a fundamental level a power to craft our lives, there is a political dimension; that the actions we undertake can succeed in the sense that we confront and resolve problems such that we direct the trajectory of our lives indicates the achievement of knowledge and that there is therefore a cognitive dimension in experience; that our experience hangs together in a general harmony, notwithstanding whatever dissonances occur along the way and that require resolution, indicates the aesthetic dimension of experience. All of the constituents of experience, such as language and emotions, as well as the various forms that experience takes (for example, religious experience, social experience, musical experience, athletic experience, or any of its many other forms), partake in one way or another of the political, cognitive, and aesthetic dimensions that characterize experience generally.

One of the implications of this conception of the person is that there is an equality built into the nature of experience itself. All of us are enmeshed in a situation, which is to say in experience, in which we act to craft, to the extent possible, the character and meaning of our lives. There is nothing in that situation from which one can infer that one person or set of persons is more entitled than another to the opportunity to exercise the power that lies at the heart of experience. This is the basis of a natural equality, and it is the point from which flows a set of social and political principles. If equality is a basic trait of experience, then the expectation of an equal opportunity to realize that equality in practice implies an equally fundamental autonomy of individual persons. Autonomous persons, however, are as much relationally constituted as is everything else, and consequently the autonomy implied by experience has to be understood as action within social relations. Furthermore, because one person's claim to autonomy is no greater than anyone else's, one's exercise of the power that autonomy enables is always undertaken within social relations, and its meaning is always conditioned by its impact on other's lives.

Our moral equality, we may say, implies a social ethics, the details of which may wait for another occasion for articulation. For our purposes, the fact that autonomy is socially circumscribed means that the institutions and practices that constitute our social life have to be understood in inherently relational terms. Human beings are not pre-social "atoms in a void," but rather social beings who live in contexts that are necessarily socially constituted. This places on us an intellectual responsibility to understand social activity and social institutions in relational contexts. Our economic, political, spiritual, familial, and educational lives, to mention some of the more important and prevalent aspects of social experience, are not isolated areas of our lives, but are integrally, and in some cases intimately, related. The details of those relations cannot be determined in the abstract, but it can be determined that to understand them usefully requires understanding them in relation.

This general point applies equally to our political lives and institutions. Political values, such as freedom or liberty, cannot be sensibly interpreted or understood without realizing that it is always a relational condition. Freedom is not the abstract independence of each of us from one another but the opportunity to act autonomously in relations with one another. This has implications, some of which we have seen, for political organization (for example, an understanding of democracy) and for political concepts that we employ in our analyses of situations (for example, the concepts of justice and rights). It also has implications for how we understand the state in general, in both its domestic and its international activities. With respect to the former, we find it necessary to reconsider what counts as interests and goals on the state's part; with respect to the latter, it becomes necessary to think differently than we have about the relations of states to one another. The state, too, is constituted relationally, and among those relations are its interactions with other states. If states' engagements with one another are among the relations that constitute them, then the very nature of the practices and institutions of international affairs has to be reconsidered.

All of this has explicit implications for the general principles in terms of which we understand education and guide its activities. Given the relational understanding of experience, the general goal of education has to be consistent with the centrality of equality and autonomy that is implicit in experience. Education, then, whatever else we should say about it, in the end aspires to enable students to direct their experience to achieve a rich and meaningful life. The equality implicit in experience means that this end applies equally to all people, a principle that places responsibilities on those who control educational policy. There is no justification, in light of our philosophical anthropology and social theory, for allowing one set of individuals to have greater access to educational opportunities than another. Class, family income, race, and ethnicity do not justify inequality in educational opportunity, nor do any other traits of an individual or group of individuals.

This principle has its own implications for how we may approach curriculum. It can no longer be acceptable to think that some people should be educated narrowly to fit into some slot in the society, while others are educated differently in order that they may have greater authority in their work and in their societies. In this respect, we disagree profoundly with Plato. If all people have an equal claim on the exercise of their inherent power to craft their own experience and lives, and if education's goal is to enable that effort, then all children and students are entitled to an education through which they are exposed to the highest human achievements in all fields, and to the skills and capacities they need to control and direct their experience. If we educate some to be leaders and other to be followers, we have already failed education's primary responsibility.

We need, though, to be careful to think relationally. Just as an emphasis on autonomy does not obviate the fact that we act in relation to one another, which means that autonomy is always simultaneously social, so an emphasis on educational quality does not mean that we divorce education from its lived contexts. Thinking and doing, as both Dewey and Freire might have said (and as is echoed by Noddings), are two sides of the same coin, because neither is adequately undertaken without the other. In this sense, education, at its best and most aspirational, is vocational. Children and students are most effectively enabled to control and direct their experience when they study and learn in experiential contexts. Those responsible for curriculum and policy (and, most important, for teaching) must determine how best in practice to meet such expectations; the details will of necessity differ from case to case, and from one educational level to another. Whatever the details in practice are in any given case, the old Aristotelian distinction between leisure and labor, and differing educations for each, or the old imperialist assumption that some must be educated to run the empire while most people are trained to do the work and to do what they are told, are not in any form acceptable. They defy the nature of experience itself.

The relationality of nature, of experience, and therefore of education, has other implications as well. We must realize, for one thing, that the far too common assumption that some disciplines or fields of study are "practical," while others are not, has to be abandoned. Experience is embedded in the full complexity of its environments and the full richness of life. Maxine Greene makes this point in her emphasis on the importance of art in education.[2] Nothing about that is unimportant or frivolous, and all of it is, in its own way, practical. The last thing that we would want to be teaching children is that, for example, accounting matters but music does not, or that physics matters but physical education does not, or the other way around. Approaching education in those ways not only ignores obvious features of experience but also distorts them. Our goal as educators is to enable students to control and direct their experience, not to constrict it.

Relationality also implies that in the approach we take to the material we teach, we are careful to understand for ourselves and to highlight for our students the interaction with one another of the fields we teach. The world, and therefore experience, is not divided neatly among disciplines, and none of them can be understood, and therefore should not be studied, in abstraction from all the others. Some are more relevant than others in any given case, but it is always preferable to focus on interdisciplinary and multidisciplinary approaches to any topic. As in other cases, how this can best be accomplished has to be decided by those in authority at specific times and places. The principle, however, is generally applicable and should be expected to guide decisions about curriculum and pedagogical methods as thoroughly and consistently as possible.

With respect to pedagogical methods, there is and should be a great deal of flexibility for teachers to determine how best to meet their and their students' needs. Some general principles are clear, though, and the most basic of them is that students must be expected to be active in their own education. At all levels, this is a guided process, one in which teachers are expected to be in control. Saying that students should be active in their education does not mean that children and students should do whatever they want or study whatever they want. It does mean (and this principle follows from the nature of experience itself) that children and students should not be regarded as receptacles. Education is not a process of filling students with information. It is a process whereby they learn to control their experience, and, as a general principle, the best way for them to learn to control their experience is through controlling their experience. As educators, we of course need to organize that process for them and to guide them through it. One would hope that the knowledge and skills necessary to aid students in this regard would be the primary focus of teacher education programs. If it is not, then our general sense of the goals of education would suggest that those responsible for teacher education programs would be advised to reconsider their approach to the education of teachers.

In general, human beings are social creatures, and education is a social process. Its advantages accrue to individuals as well as society, which means that it is both an individual and a social good. This means, though, that understanding educational principle is an immensely complicated matter, as is the determination and implementation of educational policy. Educational institutions are not simply academic. Though they are distinctively academic, they are also economic and political institutions, and they have no option but to function in economic and political environments, even as they meet their academic ends. This fact can present difficult challenges for those who have responsibility for educational policy. That fact, however, is all the more reason to be clear and confident about the educational principles to which one appeals and the justifications for doing so.

We began early in the book by noting that Plato referred to education as "the one great thing," and everything about this study has underscored his point. Human beings are resilient creatures, and even if we suffer from inadequate education, we can often adjust and claw our way back. But that fact is never a justification for educators, and those who make decisions concerning funding and other educational policies, to fail to meet our own responsibilities. To us falls the charge to organize and implement the systematic process whereby children and students develop the capacity to understand and command their own lives. That is a great challenge, and a great responsibility, but when we achieve it, or even come close to achieving it, we make as important a contribution to our children and our communities as anyone might hope.

Biographical Sketches

PLATO

As with many classical figures, Plato's precise dates are uncertain, but he is generally believed to have been born around 428 BCE and to have died in 348 or 347. He was born into a prominent Athenian family, and his upbringing took place through the length of the Peloponnesian War waged by Athens and Sparta. Athens was defeated in 403 BCE, which marked the end of its still-famous period of democracy. The political turmoil that followed Athens's defeat surely had an effect on Plato's thinking, political and otherwise.

As would have been common for an Athenian of aristocratic birth, Plato received a good education in the topics common at the time—grammar, music, and gymnastics—and he was an accomplished wrestler. He received some of his education from Socrates, a well-known Athenian teacher. Socrates developed a reputation as something of a nonconformist and a public nuisance. He was inclined to examine people's opinions on various matters of individual and social import, the frequent result of which was that people—often prominent people—were forced to acknowledge that they were not able adequately to support their own views or that their ideas were hopelessly confused. For his troubles, Socrates was arrested, tried, convicted, sentenced to death, and executed by the Athenian citizens in 399 BCE.

Plato was deeply shaken by Socrates's execution, and it no doubt had an impact on his distrust of prevailing political systems and social structures. Plato, in fact, wrote about the trial and death of Socrates in some of his works. Regardless of his death, however, Socrates greatly influenced Plato's thinking, so much so that Plato typically used the character of Socrates to represent many of his own ideas in his dialogues, which was the form in which Plato wrote. Socrates figures so prominently, in fact, that it is a matter of controversy in some cases whether an idea was Socrates's or Plato's. The likely explanation is that the general ethical and methodological aspects of Plato's works owe a great deal to Socrates, while the rich metaphysical, epistemological, sociopolitical, and psychological ideas were Plato's own.

Plato founded a school known as the Academy, which continued in existence until 84 BCE, when it was closed by the Roman general Lucius Sulla. The Academy was renowned through that part of the world as a seat of learning, and a number of prominent scholars spent time there. The most well known of them was Aristotle, who himself spent some time in Macedonia as the tutor of the young man who came to be known as Alexander the Great.

Plato traveled a fair amount during his life, spending time in Italy, Sicily, Egypt, and elsewhere. There seems to be no doubt that he was influenced by many of the streams of thought that were prominent at the time, both in Greece and abroad. Much of his work has a somewhat mystical character and resembles ideas then available in Egypt and farther east through Persia to India. The influence Plato had on posterity is even clearer. Through Aristotle and Alexander, Greek ways of understanding the world (including Plato's) were spread as far east as what is now Afghanistan and northern India, and they penetrated well into Egypt. Plato's thinking also had a strong impact on the early theology of Christianity through the Neo-Platonists Plotinus and Porphyry and the early church father Augustine. Some of Plato's writings were translated into Latin during the Roman period, even by prominent thinkers in their own right such as Cicero. They were also maintained in the original language in the Byzantine world and in Arabic translation in Islamic areas, where they were taken up in the tenth and eleventh centuries by no less than Al-Farabi and Ibn Sina, among others.

JEAN-JACQUES ROUSSEAU

Rousseau was born in Geneva in 1712. At that time, Geneva was effectively an independent republican city governed by Calvinist elders. Rousseau was born into a Calvinist family, and his father (a watchmaker by trade) was a citizen of the republic. His mother died only days after his birth, and Rousseau was raised and educated by his father. At the age of sixteen, he left the city and came under the influence of a French Catholic noblewoman. He shortly thereafter converted to Catholicism. For a time, he worked in Turin as a servant, and then he briefly studied for the priesthood. Because of his conversion to Catholicism, Rousseau was no longer eligible for citizenship in Geneva.

In 1731, he returned to France, where he managed a house in Chambery, and in 1740 he moved to Lyon. In 1745, Rousseau met and eventually married Thérèse Levasseur, a laundry maid with whom he had five children. It should be noted—especially considering Rousseau's prominence as a philosopher of education—that he abandoned all five children, placing them in a foundling hospital within days of their birth. At the time, such an action did not imply anything good for the children's future—or even whether they would have a future. What it implies about Rousseau is an open question.

In 1750, Rousseau wrote his first influential work, *Discourse on the Sciences and Arts*, for a competition sponsored by the Academy of Dijon. He won first prize, and his reputation was thereby established. It was in this work that Rousseau first developed his thoughts on the innate goodness of human nature and the threat posed to it by aspects of social life. His other primary interest in these years was music, and Rousseau became an accomplished composer. His most well-known work was an opera called *Le Devin du Village*, which he wrote in 1753 and which remained in the popular repertoire until well into the nineteenth century.

In 1754, Rousseau converted back to Calvinism and was consequently granted citizenship in Geneva. The next seven or eight years were the most intellectually productive of his life. In 1755, he published his *Discourse on the Origins of Inequality*, in which he developed the themes of social and moral development. His most productive year, however, was 1761, in which three major works appeared: *The Social Contract*, the novel *Julie, ou La Nouvelle Héloïse*, and *Emile*. In the latter work, Rousseau applies to education the ideas that are explicated and defended in all the other works, including his conceptions of nature, human nature, moral development, knowledge and learning, religion, and social and political theory. Unfortunately for Rousseau, the heterodox ideas about religion that he expressed in these works, especially in *Emile*, did not meet with the approval of the Geneva Calvinists, or of the Catholics in France, and he was forced to flee the continent. By 1766, in order to avoid arrest, Rousseau fled to Great Britain, at the invitation of the Scottish philosopher David Hume.

Rousseau's later years were characterized in part by a developing mental instability but at the same time by the writing of his *Confessions* and other works. He was able to return to France in 1767, where, among other interests, he continued to work in music, corresponding with the influential operatic composer Christophe Gluck. Rousseau died in 1778, and in 1794, during the early years of the French Revolution, his remains were moved and installed in the Panthéon in Paris.

JOHN DEWEY

John Dewey was a native Vermonter, whose life span ranged from before the American Civil War into the atomic age. He was born in Burlington in

1859, to a family of shopkeepers, and died in New York City in 1952, arguably the most celebrated public intellectual in America. Along the way, he was a student at the University of Vermont, received a PhD in philosophy from Johns Hopkins University, and served on the faculty at the University of Michigan, the University of Chicago, and (for the bulk of his career) Columbia University in New York City, in all three cases in the Department of Philosophy. While at the University of Chicago, Dewey created the first Laboratory School in the country, and at Columbia University he was an influential figure at Teachers College. In philosophy, he was the most well-known representative of the pragmatist point of view, and he was a leading figure in the school of American (or Columbia) naturalism through the first half of the twentieth century. He was easily the most influential figure in educational philosophy through that same period, associated with some misgivings on his part with the movement called progressive education, and he remains the single most important American philosopher of education to this day.

In addition to his influence in the United States, Dewey was a celebrated philosopher and educator around the world. He was invited to lecture at length in Japan and China in 1919. His impact in China in those years was especially strong, in that he had a colleague and former student, Hu Shih, who was influential in academic and governmental circles there. In 1924, the Ministry of Education of the young Turkish Republic invited him to spend time there and to make recommendations on the development of the Turkish school system, which at the time was being reinvented as it emerged from its Ottoman background. In 1928, Dewey visited the Soviet Union, as part of a larger delegation that was studying Soviet educational experiments. As in China, Dewey's work was known to Soviet educators, and there were one or two influential figures who were trying to apply his ideas. In 1934, he delivered several talks in South Africa, and in the 1930s he led a group to Mexico to preside over a hearing that examined the charges Josef Stalin had leveled against Leon Trotsky, who was in Mexico at the time.

In addition to his impact on philosophical and educational matters, Dewey was throughout his life a prominent social activist. During his years in Chicago, he worked closely with Jane Addams and her Hull House settlement, and he was a frequent participant in issues of progressive social import in New York. By the late 1920s, and especially during the years of the Great Depression in the 1930s, Dewey wrote in support of union activity, workers' rights, and other progressive issues.

Throughout his long life, Dewey championed equality of access to education, experiential education, and education for democracy. In philosophy, his many works in metaphysics, epistemology, logic, ethics, and aesthetics are still being closely studied and remain influential on contemporary philosophers in the United States and abroad.

PAULO FREIRE

Paulo Freire was born in 1921 in Recife, Brazil, and died in 1997, in São Paulo. Recife is the capital city of the Brazilian state of Pernambuco. Though his own family lived in middle-class conditions, Freire was directly familiar with conditions of deep poverty from an early age, largely because the Great Depression hit Pernambuco and Recife quite hard. He completed studies in law at the University of Recife, and during his university years he also studied philosophy, primarily phenomenology, and the psychology of language.

Freire began his working life not in law, which in fact he never practiced, but rather in the Department of Education and Culture in Pernambuco, where he took the position of director in 1946. His experiences for more than a decade in educational efforts with the poor in Pernambuco were the source of the theories that would ultimately be developed in *Pedagogy of the Oppressed*. In 1961, Freire joined the University of Recife as director of the Department of Cultural Extension, where he was able to put his pedagogical ideas about literacy education to work more systematically.

In 1964, the Brazilian military mounted a successful coup, which initiated a period of political and intellectual repression. Freire's pedagogical theories were regarded by military leaders as subversive, and he was promptly arrested, imprisoned for seventy days, and then exiled. He did not return to Brazil until 1979. In exile, Freire went first to Bolivia, but he quickly moved to Chile. For five years in Chile, Freire worked for the Christian Democratic Agrarian Reform Movement and for the United Nations Food and Agriculture Organization.

In 1968, *Pedagogy of the Oppressed* was first published, in Portuguese, though it was banned in Brazil until 1974. Its international success was such that Freire was invited in 1969 to take a visiting professorship at Harvard. He spent one year in Cambridge, after which he moved to Geneva, where he took a position with the World Council of Churches. In 1980, Freire moved back to Brazil and undertook political work with the Workers' Party, and for several years he supervised the party's literacy programs around the country. The party won the mayoral race in São Paulo in 1988, after which Freire was appointed the city's minister of education.

After the translation of *Pedagogy of the Oppressed* into Spanish and English in 1970, Freire's international reputation quickly grew, and he was in demand in many parts of the world as an educational advisor and consultant. His work was especially valued in the former Portuguese colonies in Africa, especially Guinea-Bissau and Mozambique, where he served as an advisor on educational reform. Academic interest in Freire's ideas grew as well, and he was invited by universities in many countries around the world to lecture and participate in conferences on critical education. His experience in literacy education also played important roles in the literacy campaigns in the early years of both the Cuban and Nicaraguan revolutions, in the early 1960s and early 1980s, respectively.

Freire's ideas are in some sense markers for the political climate of a place and time. While his writings continue to inspire countless educators around the world, he can still attract the ire of powerful political forces. In 2010, for example, the Arizona State Legislature passed a bill that allowed the state's superintendent of public instruction to restrict cultural studies programs, which in Tucson High School had been using *Pedagogy of the Oppressed*. After the passage of the bill, the Tucson United School District confiscated all copies of the book that were available to Mexican studies programs. For reasons such as this, and many more, Freire continues to be read in Tucson and throughout the world.

Notes

INTRODUCTION

1. Nel Noddings, *Philosophy of Education* (Boulder, CO: Westview, 1995), 1. A newer edition appeared in 2015. We will have occasion to turn again to Noddings in a later chapter, in reference to her innovative and influential work on care and pedagogy.

2. There are other books available that do this well. For example, I refer the reader to Amélie Oksenberg Rorty, *Philosophers on Education* (New York and London: Routledge, 1998), and to Steven M. Cahn, *Philosophy of Education: The Essential Texts* (New York and London: Routledge, 2009).

3. The most extensive, and controversial, of such studies has been Martin Bernal's three-volume *Black Athena: The Afroasiatic Roots of Classical Civilization* (New Brunswick, NJ: Rutgers University Press, Vol. 1, 1987; Vol. 2, 1991; and Vol. 3, 2006).

4. For a broader and enlightening sense of the breadth and depth of the American intellectual environment from the late nineteenth century through the twentieth, which is for the most part Dewey's time, see Erin McKenna and Scott Pratt, eds., *American Philosophy: From Wounded Knee to the Present* (London: Bloomsbury, 2015).

5. Kohli's article is in Wendy Kohli, ed., *Critical Conversations in Philosophy of Education* (New York: Routledge, 1995), 103–115. See also Maxine Greene, *The Dialectic of Freedom* (New York: Teachers College Press, 1988). Another useful source in this regard is Randall Curren, *Philosophy of Education: An Anthology* (Oxford: Blackwell, 2006).

CHAPTER 1. REALITY, THE GOOD, AND THE STATE: PLATO'S *REPUBLIC*

1. The English translation that is being used and cited in this chapter is by G. M. A. Grube, revised by C. D. C. Reeve (Indianapolis/Cambridge: Hackett, 1992). There is a pagination system typically used in editions of the *Republic* that identifies the text at any given point with pages in an original Greek version. This is helpful because it means that one can track down a reference even if using a different

translation from the one cited. All page references to the text use this system. For example, you may see a quotation followed by page references in parentheses that will look like this: (467a-b). In nearly any translation of the text, such pagination is provided, usually in the margins.

CHAPTER 2. NATURE AND THE INDIVIDUAL: ROUSSEAU'S *EMILE*

1. References are to *Emile, or On Education*, translated by Allan Bloom (New York: Basic Books, 1979). Page numbers for quotations and other references to *Emile* will be indicated in the text within parentheses immediately following the reference.

2. See René Descartes, *Meditations on First Philosophy*, translation by Donald A. Cress (Indianapolis: Hackett, 1979). Descartes's famous "cogito, sum" ("I think, I am") occurs near the beginning of the Second Meditation.

3. See Cadwallader Colden, *The Principles of Action in Matter* (1751), excerpted in Scott L. Pratt and John Ryder, eds., *The Philosophical Writings of Cadwallader Colden* (Amherst, NY: Humanity Books, 2002).

4. The reader should make of this interpretation whatever she will. There are as many interpretations of the general will as there are people who have thought about it. That it is an obscure concept is well expressed by Amélie Oksenberg Rorty: "Rousseau's conception of the relation between the General Will and private interest remains obscure. That obscurity is marked by the fact that almost no two commentators agree about how best to interpret it." See "Rousseau's Educational Experiments," in Amélie Oksenberg Rorty, ed., *Philosophers on Education* (New York and London: Routledge, 1998), 238–54.

5. Margaret Thatcher's comment was made in *Women's Own*, October 31, 1987. For a sense of Carl Schmitt's concerns with liberalism, see his *The Crisis of Parliamentary Democracy*, translated by Ellen Kennedy (Cambridge MA: MIT Press, 1988).

6. See Josiah Royce, *The Problem of Christianity* (Chicago: University of Chicago Press, 1968).

CHAPTER 3. EXPERIENCE AND DEMOCRACY: DEWEY'S *DEMOCRACY AND EDUCATION*

1. Dewey's writings span close to seventy years, and in that time he wrote a great deal. The definitive edition of his collected works is published by Southern Illinois University Press, divided into three sets of *Early*, *Middle*, and *Later Works*. *The School and Society* was first published in 1899 and is now in print in *The Middle Works*, Volume 1, 1976. *The Child and the Curriculum* first appeared in 1903 and is published in *The Middle Works*, Volume 2, 1976. The edition of *Democracy and Education* (1916) to which we will refer is *The Later Works*, Volume 9, 1985. Specific references in the text will be given, in parentheses following the reference, as DE followed by the relevant page number. For *Experience and Education*, which first appeared in 1938, we refer to *The Later Works*, Volume 13, 2008, and references are designated EE and page number.

2. In the late 1920s, Dewey was part of a delegation that visited the Soviet Union and made a study of educational experiments that were underway there. Dewey was very much impressed by what he saw, including the fact that in some of the schools set up for orphans and wayward children, the children themselves had extensive authority to make and enforce the school's rules. What he saw there was in many ways like the institution presented ten years later in the classic American film *Boys Town*. For a detailed discussion of the Soviet experiments, and Dewey's reactions to them, see Lyubov Bugaeva, "'The Road to Life': Educating the New Soviet Man," *The Art and Science of Making the New Man in Early 20th-Century Russia*, edited by Yvonne Howell and Nikolai Krementsov (London: Bloomsbury, 2021). For Dewey's extended commentary, see "Impressions of Soviet Russia" in *The Later Works*, Volume 3, 1984.

CHAPTER 4. DOMINATION AND LIBERATION: FREIRE'S *PEDAGOGY OF THE OPPRESSED*

1. The edition of *Pedagogy of the Oppressed* from which citations are drawn is the 1993 English edition published by Continuum (New York) in 1993. This is the same text as the original English translation from 1970, also published by Continuum, but the language has been revised by Freire to eliminate the traditional, sexist terminology of the original. References to the 1993 revision will be given in the text as PO and the page number. The other books mentioned are all published by Continuum: *Education for Critical Consciousness* (1981); *Learning to Question: A Pedagogy of Liberation*, with Antonio Faundez (1992); and *Pedagogy of Hope* (1994).

2. See Martin Heidegger, *Being and Time* (New York: Harper Perennial Modern Classics, 2008); Jean-Paul Sartre, *Being and Nothingness* (New York: Routledge, 2018).

3. See Albert Memmi, *The Colonizer and the Colonized* (Boston: Beacon Press, 1991); Frantz Fanon, *Wretched of the Earth* (New York: Grove Press, 2008).

4. Gustavo Gutierrez, *A Theology of Liberation* (Maryknoll, NY: Orbis Books, 1988).

CHAPTER 5. EDUCATION AND ITS PROBLEMS

1. See, for example, a study that was completed not long after the end of the war: William L. Griffen and John Marciano, *Teaching the Vietnam War* (Montclair, NJ: Allanheld, Osmun & Co., 1979). A second edition appeared as *Lessons of the Vietnam War* (Totowa, NJ: Rowman and Allanheld, 1984). Marciano published another book that made the same general point, but with a broader focus than just the war in Vietnam: *Civic Illiteracy and Education* (New York: Peter Lang, 1997).

2. Howard Zinn, *A People's History of the United States* (New York: Harper & Row, 1980).

3. In the spirit of full disclosure, the reader may want to know that I was instrumental in the creation in the early 2000s, and in collaboration with several other colleagues, of what came to be called the COIL Center at the State University of New York. The acronym stands for Collaborative Online International Learning,

and the idea was to foster the development of team-taught courses with a faculty member from a SUNY campus and one from a university abroad, to be taught entirely online and asynchronously, and which would enroll students from both universities. This is a case in which the technology enables an opportunity that would not be there otherwise.

CHAPTER 6. EDUCATION IN CONTEXT: NATURE, KNOWLEDGE, AND EXPERIENCE

1. Hegel's argument is abstract and difficult to follow. The reader brave enough to try will find it in G. W. F. Hegel, *Logic* (Oxford: Oxford University Press, 1975).

2. Much of this account of a viable metaphysical position is articulated in much more detail in John Ryder, *The Things in Heaven and Earth* (New York: Fordham University Press, 2013). That analysis, and this one, draws heavily on the pioneering ideas of Justus Buchler, especially his *Metaphysics of Natural Complexes* (New York: Columbia University Press, 1966).

3. On intersectionality, see Kathleen Wallace, "Intersectionality and Fragmentation," *Pragmatism Today* 11, no. 2 (2020): 65–78. The more fully developed relational theory of the person is in her book *The Network Self: Relation, Process, and Personal Identity* (New York: Routledge, 2019).

4. The conception of experience discussed here is developed and defended in far greater detail in John Ryder, *Knowledge, Art, and Power: An Outline of a Theory of Experience* (Amsterdam: Brill, 2020).

5. See Timothy Fuller, ed., *The Voice of Liberal Learning, Michael Oakeshott on Education* (New Haven, CT: Yale University Press, 1989), 70.

6. For an overview of McDermott's educational thought, see John Ryder, "The Necessity of a Cultural Pedagogy," in James Campbell and Richard E. Hart, eds., *Experience as Philosophy, On the Work of John J. McDermott* (New York: Fordham University Press, 2006), 211–36. The citation can be found in John J. McDermott, "From Cynicism to Amelioration: Strategies for a Cultural Pedagogy," in his *The Culture of Experience: Philosophical Essays in the American Grain* (New York: New York University Press, 1976), 118–49. The passage cited is on 134–35.

7. See, among other works, Nel Noddings, *Care: A Relational Approach to Ethics and Moral Education* (Berkeley: University of California Press, 2013); *The Challenge to Care in Schools* (New York: Teachers College Press, 2005); and *Philosophy of Education* (New York: Routledge, 2018; first edition; Boulder, CO: Westview Press, 1995).

8. Noddings makes one of the more succinct statements of this point in her *Philosophy of Education* (1995), on pages 186–196.

9. There are other recent and contemporary philosophers who have made valuable contributions to our understanding of educational issues. In part because of its focus on Richard Rorty and Martha Nussbaum, I would direct the reader to Nicholas C. Burbules, Brian Warnick, Timothy McDonough, and Scott Johnson, "Education," in Armen Marsoobian and John Ryder, eds., *The Blackwell Guide to American Philosophy* (Oxford: Blackwell, 2004), chapter 22.

CHAPTER 7. EDUCATION IN CONTEXT: SOCIETY AND THE STATE

1. I have explored some of the ideas about society and the state that are developed in this chapter in other publications. See especially *The Things in Heaven and Earth*, part III in particular, and *Knowledge, Art, and Power*, especially chapter 5.

2. Maxine Greene, *The Dialectic of Freedom*. See page 120 for the reference. The most recent edition appeared in 2018.

3. The body of the US Constitution does not mention property rights, though they are described in the Fifth and the much later Fourteenth Amendments. That the drafters of the Constitution had property rights in mind, though, is clear from the arguments they made in favor of its ratification in *The Federalist Papers*. One may consult, for example, the well-known *Federalist 10*, in which James Madison speaks to the importance of the right of property and argues that the proposed Constitution will be able to defend that right better than the alternative possibilities. He makes a similar argument in his *Notes of Debates in the Federal Convention of 1787* (Athens: Ohio University Press, 1976), for example, on page 194.

4. For a recent sustained argument that grounds nonviolence in a pragmatism related to ours, see Andrew Fitz-Gibbon, *Pragmatic Nonviolence: Working toward a Better World* (Amsterdam: Brill, 2021).

CONCLUSION

1. "Nescire autem quid antequam natus sis acciderit, id est semper esse puerum." M. Cicero, *Orator* XXXIV.120.

2. See Maxine Greene, *The Dialectic of Freedom* (New York: Teachers College Press, 1988), especially chapter 5.

Index

aesthetic dimension of experience, 187–88; pervasiveness of, 191–92, 201
agriculture, for Rousseau, 58–59, 74
Algeria, 223
Aquinas, Thomas, 7
Aristotle, 67, 92, 171, 208, 256
astronomy, importance for Rousseau, 58
Augustine, 7
autonomy, 205, 216–19, 220, 227, 249
Avicenna. *See* Ibn Sina

Bacon, Francis, 100
Beauvoir, Simone de, 121
Belgium, colonial history of, 117
Brazil: and Freire's background, 113–14; literacy teaching in, 111–12, 125; military dictatorship in, 6
Buddhism, 72

Casablanca, 105
Cato, 61
censorship, 12, 47; of Freire in United States, 149; and goals of education, 149, 238–40; in Plato, 25–26, 44–45, 238–39
Center for Collaborative Online International Learning (COIL), 263n3

children: development of self-control in, 98; moral development of, 24, 52–53; raised in common, 29, 43; for Rousseau, 56, 58, 60
Chile, 223, 259
Cicero, 181, 246, 256
class divisions: and conflicting interests, 230–31; as inimical to democracy, 94–95, 107, 109; as mechanisms of oppression, 117–18; in relation to labor and leisure, 98–99; as threat to autonomy, 218–19
Colden, Cadwallader, 63
Columbia University, 79; Teachers College at, 83
common interests: and definition of democracy, 94–95; Dewey on, 70, 102–3, 230; in pragmatic naturalism, 205, 229–33, 250
community: and common interests, 230; and conflicting interests, 230–31; and individual, 224–28
Confucius, 7, 166
Constantine (emperor), 165
Constitution of the United States, 221–22, 231; and Bill of Rights, 221
content of education (curriculum), 12, 160–65; and arts, 161–62, 201; control over, 13; for Dewey, 100, 104–6; and Freire on "cognizable

Smith, Adam, 70, 121, 172

social contract, concept of, 66, 67–68, 121, 228–29, 231; modern roots in slave societies, 7

social institutions, 209–16; cultural, 214; educational, 212–16, 238–39; financial, 211–12, 214; religious, 210–11, 214

socialism, for Freire, 137

social justice: as goal of education, 149–51, 165–66; and intersectionality, 185–86; for pragmatic naturalism, 205, 220–21; in relation to reason, freedom, and education, 8

social responsibility of education, 239–41

social theory, 15, 172, 205–28

Socrates, 22–23, 30, 31–32, 61

state, 228–29; interests of for education, 151–52, 240–241; and international relations, 235–37, 250; as relational, 235–37

Supreme Court of the United States, 236

Syria, 223

teaching, 13, 43, 46, 75, 153, 251; online, 167; as political, 111; and teacher education, 83, 252

testing, 13, 153–55

Thatcher, Margaret, 70

theater, 179, 180

tracking: in contemporary education, 47, 155–60; in Plato, 39, 43

Tucson, Arizona, 149, 260

United Arab Emirates, funding of higher education in, 148

United Kingdom: colonial history of, 117; funding of higher education in, 148

United States of America: funding of higher education in, 148–49; and Latin America, 114, 117; role of state in education in, 163–65; and weaponization of democracy, 234–35; and weaponization of rights, 223–24

upbringing, and education, 38, 50

Vietnam War, 164, 223

Virgil, 181

vocational education, 242–43, 251. *See also* Dewey, John

Wagner, Richard, 172

Wallace, Kathleen, 185–86

wealth, need to avoid excess of, 28–29

Wilson, Woodrow, 234

Zinn, Howard, 164

About the Author

John Ryder holds a PhD in philosophy from Stony Brook University and has been a full professor of philosophy in several universities in the United States and abroad. He has also served as a senior administrator in the United States and elsewhere—dean of arts and sciences at SUNY Cortland; director of SUNY's Office of International Programs and of the SUNY–Moscow State University Center on Russia and the United States; rector of Khazar University in Azerbaijan; provost of the American University of Ras al Khaimah in the UAE; and provost of the American University of Malta.

Ryder's scholarship includes over one hundred publications that focus on the history of American philosophy, metaphysics and epistemology, social and political theory, aesthetics, and the philosophy of education. He is the editor of *American Philosophic Naturalism in the 20th Century* and coeditor of *The Blackwell Guide to American Philosophy*, *The Philosophical Writings of Cadwallader Colden*, and others. He is the author of *Interpreting America: Russian and Soviet Studies of the History of American Thought*, *The Things in Heaven and Earth: An Essay in Pragmatic Naturalism*, and *Knowledge, Art, and Power: An Outline of a Theory of Experience*, as well as many articles and book chapters. His work has been translated into several languages, including French, German, Polish, Slovak, Romanian, and Russian.

Ryder cofounded the Central European Pragmatist Forum and for ten years served as the president of the Alliance of Universities for Democracy. He is currently retired and splits his time between homes in Tucson, Arizona, and St. Petersburg, Russia.